Confirmation

Anchor Books

NEW YORK · LONDON · TORONTO · SYDNEY · AUCKLAND

Confirmation

The Spiritual Wisdom That Has Shaped Our Lives

Edited by

KHEPHRA BURNS AND SUSAN L. TAYLOR

AN ANCHOR BOOK

PUBLISHED BY DOUBLEDAY

a division of Bantam Doubleday Dell Publishing Group, Inc.

1540 Broadway, New York, New York 10036

ANCHOR BOOKS, DOUBLEDAY, and the portrayal of an anchor are trademarks of Doubleday,

a division of Bantam Doubleday Dell Publishing Group, Inc.

Library of Congress Cataloging-in-Publication Data:

Burns, Khephra.

Confirmation : the spiritual wisdom that has shaped our lives / Khephra Burns and

Susan L. Taylor. — 1st Anchor Books ed.

p.   cm.

Includes bibliographical references.

1. Spiritual life.   2. Afro-Americans—Religion.   3. Burns, Khephra.   4. Taylor, Susan L.

I. Taylor, Susan L.   II. Title.

BL624.B89   1997

291.44—dc21   96-52005

CIP

Book Design by Julie Duquet

ISBN 0-385-47869-0

Printed in the United States of America

First Anchor Books Edition: September 1997

10   9   8   7   6   5   4   3   2   1

To the teachers,
the wise ones
and guiding lights,
to incarnate angels
who forgot themselves
and perhaps never knew us
or, knowing, never knew
how they changed our lives.
To them we dedicate these truths.

Acknowledgments

We want to express our love and appreciation to our family and friends, old and new, especially Rosalyn Ilunga, Darryl and Andriette Bozeman, Michael Burns, Michael Butler, Lena Sherrod, Horace Mansfield, Mari Evans, Haki Madhubuti, Reverend Aaron Zerah, and Rich Sheinin, all of whom have led us to many diverse sources of inspiration and the wisdom of their own favorite writers; to our agents, Marie Brown—who brought us this exciting project—and Faith Hampton Childs, for their support; to our editor, Roger Scholl, whose respect and sensitivity make him among the best in the business; to Jayna Brown for her fine research; to Linda Tarrant-Reid for her perseverance in tracking down publishers and securing permission to use much of the material in this book; and to Debra Parker and Susannah Vance for their administrative assistance throughout the project.

Contents

CONCEPTUALITY

I am a wisp of energy
flung from the core of the Universe
housed
in a temple
of flesh and bones and blood

in the temple
because it is there
that I make my home
Free
of the temple
not bound
by the temple
but housed

no distances
I am everywhere
energy and will of the universe expressed
realizing my oneness my
indivisibility/ I

I am
the One Force
I . . .

— MARI EVANS

Our Shared Journey

Ours is a shared journey, a marriage of hearts and minds on a voyage of discovery. And while we've been blessed to travel to many wondrous places throughout the world, we are far more blessed to have been transported and transformed by the wisdom we have discovered—in times of need and in quieter moments of reflection—from a font of myriad sources: the sacred texts of the diverse cultures of the world, the epiphanies of the poets, and revelations of mystics, ministers, seers, and scientists from throughout the ages. This wisdom has been a spiritual beacon in guiding us on our life path.

It's a blessing we've been longing to share with others. And it's a joy for us to share that blessing through this, our first book together. *Confirmation* gathers in one volume a broad selection of the inspirational writings that have moved us most deeply and helped to shape our inner lives over the past two decades. These writings—some of which we collected long before we married or even knew each other—have pointed the way for us and defined the path of our spiritual development. They have encouraged us to look at life with fresh eyes, to live life more fully, and to honor our visions and dreams. They contain the wisdom we ourselves turn to for the clarity, comfort, and assurance we all need for the journey. Like maps, or markers carved into the rocks, they reveal the well-worn paths of those knowing ones who came before us and those whose words of wisdom light a way over rocky terrain and through stormy climes to the tranquil place where we come to know God's presence in us.

We've taken the proverbs, poems, prayers, and longer narrative passages from chapters and verses we've underlined in our many books, torn from periodicals, copied into our journals and onto scraps of paper to be tacked above our desks as daily reminders. The year spent working together and revisiting the wisdom that has illuminated our lives has been a richly rewarding experience.

Over the years, during my many travels, people who've heard me speak or have read my books or monthly editorial, "In the Spirit" in *Essence*, have often asked how I manage to remain happy and hopeful. Invariably, people who meet Khephra are struck by his easy way of being. And because in my talks and writings I often speak about his openheartedness and how much I love and appreciate him, some folks are curious about our relationship as well, especially about how we have succeeded in making it work.

The truth is both of us at times are assailed by fears and uncertainties that cause us to lose our way. But as we grow in our awareness of God's boundless grace, the distance between our missteps and stumbles also grows. Our relationship works, primarily, because we share a philosophy, faith, and outlook that prompt us to seek God in all and wholeness within ourselves. The inspirational words of wisdom included in *Confirmation* reflect the truths we need most to remember, but too often forget. Surrendering to these truths and continuing to grow in wisdom is part of our ongoing challenge. Just as sharing these words of wisdom with each other has strengthened us and given us greater joy, we have found that bringing them together to share with you has amplified and increased that joy.

In reading through the many inspirational passages in *Confirmation*, you may find, as we often did, that they have a déjà vu feel about them. Rather than learning something new, you may feel as if you've only been reminded of truths you already knew, but had somehow forgotten or lost sight of in the fray. Such truths are more of a confirmation than a revelation. When it comes, this confirmation is always a matter worth witnessing. Whether we are sitting alone reading or gathered in congregation, we have to say, *Amen, um-hm, I hear you, word!* —something to acknowledge that the truth was told. It affords us an opportunity to rejoice in our connectedness, in our recognition that deep down we are all one in the Oneness of God.

This communion of souls is the very goal and purpose of our churches, mosques, temples, and halls. It is the Body of Christ of Christianity, the *minyan* of Judaism, the *sangha* of Buddhism, the *satsang* of Hinduism, and the *hajj* of Islam. All of these forms of communion hint that we are a part of something larger, something that loves and embraces us all without regard to our religious, linguistic, and cultural differences.

That something—God, the Universe, One Mind, the Ultimate Ground of Being—has ninety-nine names, as the Prophet Muhammad reminded us. And one of those names must surely be Relationship. As children of God, or manifestations of the One, we are all related to all that is — not just to one another, but to the earth and stars and the whole of creation. That ultimate relationship, God, is the source and ultimate aspiration of all our relationships. More than anything, we long for the union that is God. Even our most determined attempts at being an individual — at standing out among the crowd — have no other purpose than attracting the attention, admiration, and love of those who we want to surround and enfold us. Each connection we make with another human being is a starting point, an opportunity to love and learn, to grow in wisdom, and, with practice, expand the sphere of our love from that one relationship to many relationships to the One, all-inclusive, all-encompassing Relationship that is God.

Our challenge is not to look for love, but to be it. Love knows its own and it will find you. Ultimately, the person you're seeking is *you*. Find yourself and you will find a source of love sufficient to fulfill your desires, attract your greatest good fortune, and create abundant happiness in your life.

It was on an Easter Sunday more than a decade ago that I first saw something of my true self in Susan—something of the person I aspire to be. She has an openness and generosity of spirit that seems the perfect antidote to the creeping cynicism of our age that at times threatens to smother hope and joy in me. And her sincere belief in a world of possibilities had a world-transforming magic all its own. As we walked along Broadway, then east to Central Park, sharing observations on life and the nature of love, I knew instinctively that I was with my sister or even some more intimate relation I hadn't identified until that moment—my soul mate.

It was one of those rare, graceful, grace-filled moments when, completely poised and unselfconscious, we move through life effortlessly, encountering no resistance, and everything we say and do seems to flow forth in harmony with the universe; when the dreams we have long pursued seem to want to rush forward to embrace us without our having to take another step in their direction. I felt at that moment that if I, a Black man, had tried to hail a cab, a dozen would have raced forward, cutting one another off, screeching to a stop, competing for the honor. Even New York City's cracked and crowded sidewalks, which generally conspire to cripple its citizens or cause them to clot up at the corners . . . even the sidewalks seemed to open like an aisle before us.

It was spring, and evidence of the truth of the resurrection was apparent all around us—in the bright midmorning sun, in the budding green of trees in Central Park, and the budding of new love, which holds the promise of transcending death. This Love—the Love that raises new life from bare ground and leafless vines each spring—shows us what caring can do. And it inspires in us a desire to give ourselves away completely, to invest ourselves so totally in others that we will live on in them even after we have gone, leaving little for the grave to claim. We sometimes call this delicious madness spring fever, but it's love; and it was this love that Susan seemed always to be giving—in her smile, in her attention to others, in her concern and kindness to everyone around her.

We had just come from Easter Sunday service where Unity minister Eric Butterworth had spoken on the symbolism and meaning of Christ's crucifixion. As we walked, discussing the sermon, we realized that we were on a common path and glimpsed the first signs of what we sensed would be a lifelong journey together. That path, we knew, was one of love, openness to change, and faith in the essential goodness of life.

I remember telling Khephra that magical Easter Sunday, only weeks after our first date, "I'm going to enjoy my life with you." We had known each other casually and professionally for years when in the early spring of 1986 our mutual friend Terrie Williams suggested Khephra call and ask me out. We went to a local jazz club to hear Wynton Marsalis put March madness into music, and afterward to dinner to talk and discover each other. I was utterly captivated by Khephra's love for life and enthusiasm for sharing it. Over dessert, he entertained me with tales of the romantic Afro-French writer Alexandre Dumas and the great Black Russian poet Alexander Pushkin, their duels and adventures and genius for living. Khephra's mind leapt from literature to language to mythology, science, and religion, making unexpected and fascinating connections. He spoke passionately about jazz as a reservoir of wisdom that transcends words. (Years later, while telling me of the love he'd felt from a piece of John Coltrane's music, his eyes would fill with tears.)

Khephra is hip *and* smart, down-to-earth and a dazzling galaxy of insight and information. During our first evening together, I remember thinking, *Here is an active participant, a seeker of truth who is embracing life from its many different and interconnected angles.* From our first date, I knew I wanted him to be my friend.

CONFIRMATION is an extension of our ongoing collaboration. It represents the timeless wisdom that has touched our lives on subjects ranging from truth and beauty to love and relationships, from death and dying to rebirth, forgiveness, and communion with the divine. What is the meaning of life? What is its purpose? What is my relationship to God? How do I love? How much should I give? Whom should I forgive and how often? These are some of the questions we have asked and sought answers to. The answers do not come easily, but they do come. And truth has a way of resonating deep within our soul. We read, for example, that we are human and divine, that God is One, that God is Love. When expressed in just the right way, such simple ideas can be more easily perceived and accepted, can fill us with light and awaken us to a reality we might have only glimpsed before. All at once, a door is opened and something inside us is liberated. A veil is lifted and truth reveals itself everywhere we turn. These proverbs and allegories and words of wisdom, we hope, will inspire you as well, illuminating, as they did for us, the truths we were born to discover.

For me, these writings represent confirmation of my own direct experience with that truth. Susan's path and mine converged from quite different beginnings. Mine was not a "coming to faith," as she so movingly describes in her first book, *In the Spirit,* but a dramatic awakening to reality, much as mystic Aleister Crowley describes happened to his friend Allan Bennett when he was a young man: a revelation that literally came from out of nowhere to change the course of my life. It didn't come as the result of an emotional or spiritual crisis. And the pursuit of spiritual enlightenment, at the time, was the farthest thing from my mind.

I had grown up Catholic: I went to Catholic schools; attended Mass every morning, Monday through Friday; studied the Bible and the lives of the saints; went to catechism classes and, later, altar boy practice on Saturdays and Mass again on Sundays. My exposure to God had been carefully mapped out by the Church. Even the theological underpinnings of the Church were handed to us. In high school we were schooled in the great philosophical systems, comparative religion, and Christian theology so that we would be intellectually equipped to defend the faith. I learned my lessons well, but whatever I was supposed to feel beyond a conditioned sense of guilt eluded me. I later played music at a praise-shouting Baptist church. Apart from the music, nothing moved me there either. God, for me, was an abstract idea that evoked a response somewhere between a baffled shrug and indifference. It was a response I kept to myself so as not to send missionaries into a feeding frenzy at the first sign of my "unsaved" soul.

As an undergraduate at the University of California in Santa Barbara, I found myself sitting one day with my girlfriend at the time, Sharon, and my cousin Scott, laughing so hard that my side ached. Scott was improvising a satirical riff on the all-too-human folly of pride and man's penchant for erecting ever-bigger, more phallic monuments to progress—from cathedral spires to Trident missiles—all of which promise a climax in annihilation. He was on a roll.

The laughter was liberating, like riding in a fast car with the top down. What happened next was much like an accident. Unable to see what was looming large just ahead of me, I collided head-on with a planet-sized . . . blank. Nothing.

As the last of our laughter drained away with a sigh, I found myself struck dumb and stranded somewhere, or nowhere, empty. Emptied of laughter, emptied of words, emptied of thought, emptied of identity. And with no "I" in sight, what had been me until that moment vanished into one monumental void. Not a void in the sense that it lacked anything. On the contrary, it was a void that encompassed all. Words cannot adequately describe the experience of transcendence, but it was as if a great silent gong had been struck at the center of my soul, announcing the end of the world, a Judgment Day without judgment.

For me, it was the end of one life and the beginning of another. That silence, which expanded outward in concentric circles, *was* my soul, reaching into the limitless reaches of the universe. Past and future collapsed into eternal now as the essential, irreducible part of me rushed outward beyond time and space to fill an unfillable infinite consciousness — God, the circle whose center is everywhere, whose circumference is boundless.

That experience was the turning point in my life that put me on a path of spiritual development. The truth, which all my years of religious training and all the sermons and preaching had failed to impart, had been revealed to me in one blinding flash, without a single word being uttered. Suddenly I was an initiate, though I had been initiated into this mystery of mysteries unwittingly, accidentally, without a guide and protected only by the grace that hovers over innocents and fools.

The ecstatic experience of transcendence was followed by a jumble of emotions: shock, awe, excitement, and serenity; even depression at the prospect of having to take up the burden of the body and, once again, assume the role of Khephra Burns when I knew in fact I was all things as one with God. And once you know that, you can never *not* know it again. You may lapse back into old patterns of thought and behavior, but ever after, you will always know what God is, who you are, and that both are one. Nothing can change that. In the twenty-six years since, that transcendent experience, that moment of awakening, has exerted a steady, relentless tug at my soul, drawing me along the path of spiritual development.

The first thing I wanted to do was to tell somebody. You *have* to tell somebody. You *want* to tell the whole world. But when I searched my thoughts for the right words, I quickly discovered they weren't there. So I embarked upon the search to find the words. I went back to half-remembered passages I had come across in literature and discovered that what had previously seemed impenetrable, now revealed its truth between the lines.

These writings, and others like them included in *Confirmation,* have led us to yet other sources of wisdom and to people over the years who have recommended related works. What we found are writings that reveal truth beneath the veil of words, like the answer to an enormous riddle. Sages and mystics insist that the ultimate reality can't be put into words. "If it could be talked about," said the fourth-century B.C. Taoist Chuang-tzu, "everybody would have told his brother."

The insights they offer are a never-ending source of inspiration and joy for us. There is Malidoma Somé's magical recounting of his experience of the Spirit of Love ("a love that surpassed any known classifications") during his initiation as a member of the Dagara people of Burkina Faso. There is Nasrudin, the wise fool of Sufi tales, who searched the world for the perfect wife and, having found her, discovered she wasn't the least interested in him. "Alas," he lamented. "She was, unfortunately, waiting for the perfect husband." It speaks volumes about our expectations of perfection in others when we are less than perfect ourselves.

One of the delights of the great body of wisdom from throughout the ages is the sense of humor the enlightened seem to share. In contrast to the dour seriousness organized religion sometimes implies, they insist that God has a sense of humor, too. Alan Watts, a onetime Episcopalian priest and chaplain at Northwestern University, ventured that, if the Lord veils his glory as too bright for mortal eyes, maybe he also veils his mirth as something too funny for us to withstand.

Susan and I share these insights with each other over dinner when taking some quiet time for ourselves, when she's working on an editorial for "In the Spirit" in *Essence*, and occasionally on long drives through the country. But any observation, any chance thought that comes to us throughout the day can cause us to recall some fragment of these inspirational writings. They come to us while moving through crowded airports, while cleaning out the closet, while reading, writing, and thinking about things that at first seem totally unrelated. But nothing is unrelated, and helping us to re-member that is part of the great value of this wisdom.

Helping us to grow in wisdom and self-assurance is the goal of all of the world's major religions, philosophies, and therapies, and the many books about spirit that I've collected over the years. They all point us in the same direction: inward—a difficult route for us to take consistently, given our focus on the outer world.

Intellectually, we know that silence and stillness are the doors to un-derstanding. They open the way to intuition and a deeper experience of our spiritual self. But the busier and more complex our lives become, the more difficult it is to create space for contemplation and reflection. Our ongoing challenge is to continuously devote to our spiritual development the time and commitment we easily give to less important but more apparent aspects of our lives.

For me, attempting to stay on a spiritual path hasn't numbed the ache of living. But I've come to understand that pain has a purpose: It encourages introspection and change. My challenge, still, is feeling beyond the pain, seeing beyond the difficulty, to the meaning of the experience and how these turning points usher in new beginnings. When I take time to listen, to commune with myself in silence, I hear. Now I try to heed the words so many wise souls have bequeathed to us, pointing the way toward enlightenment.

The sages, seers, and mystics have suggested various paths by which we might arrive at a realization of the Ultimate Reality we call God, but they can't tell us precisely how to get there. They are inclined to agree with Adrienne Rich, however, in recognizing that "the awakening of consciousness is not unlike crossing a frontier—one step and you are in another country." That "country" is native to us all, and the terrain described by the words of those who have traveled there before us will, hopefully, remind you of home, of an abode of abiding truth and peace and love.

Those whose counsel and wisdom we have collected in *Confirmation* have not let the inadequacy of language deter them in their attempts to communicate the inexpressible. In the image and likeness of our Creator, they have been amazingly creative themselves, describing the transcendent experience of our Oneness with God in a variety of inventive images. But all are metaphors, and any metaphor will do if it works for you. And what works—whatever awakens us to consciousness—is the sole concern of these wise teachers.

This fundamental truth—that we share in the divinity of God—echoes the teachings not only of Jesus of Nazareth, but the Hindu Upanishads, Sufi mystics Jalal al-Din Rumi and Amir 'Abd al-Kader, thirteenth-century Kabbalist Moses de León, Dame Julian of Norwich, and enlightened souls and saints down through the ages who tell us that we and the Father/Mother are one, that the servant is the Lord manifesting as the servant, that God is the Self you discover upon surrendering your self.

In organizing the selections into subjects, we found that they often overlapped one another: that innocence and grace are attributes of a kind of selflessness or self-forgetting, and that the transcendent experience of losing one's self is simultaneously an awakening to the Oneness of God; that love for all is therefore love of Self, that forgiveness of all is therefore acceptance of Self; and that fear is merely an inability to see that we are not separate from the things we fear, which, like us, are also of God and *are* us.

In *Confirmation* we have drawn from the sacred texts of the New Testament, the Torah and Zohar (the Book of "Splendor" or "Illumination"), the Koran, the Bhagavad Gita, the Upanishads, the Papyrus of Ani, and the Tao-te Ching; from Martin Luther King, Jr.; the Buddha, Siddhartha Gautama; the Russian sage G. I. Gurdjieff; Tenzin Gyatso, the XIVth Dalai Lama of Tibet; Christian theologian Howard Thurman; the African shaman Malidoma Somé; Squamish medicine man Chief Seattle; theosophists Annie Besant and Madame Blavatsky; from physicists, physicians, and biologists like Albert Einstein, Fritjof Capra, Amit Goswami, Deepak Chopra, and Lewis Thomas; from musicians and songwriters; from proverbs; from poets like Maya Angelou, Mari Evans, and many others.

Through the chorus of their voices, we hope that you, too, will hear what the enlightened in all cultures throughout the ages have understood—that beneath the various devices of paradox, parable, and *koan*, beneath the superficial differences of language and religious expression, the essential underlying message is the same: God is One.

KHEPHRA BURNS AND SUSAN L. TAYLOR, NOVEMBER 14, 1996

CHAPTER ONE

Challenge:
God's Invitation to Grow

Life is a challenge, and each of us has his own cross to bear, her own pain to endure and obstacles to overcome. What is not always understood is that every adversity undergone is necessary and important to our life work, our soul work. Challenge is one of the many ways that life seasons and, in time, reveals to us our deeper self, the self we know in God.

In meeting life's challenges and finding within them their deeper meaning in our life, we begin to see them and ourselves differently. They no longer are the curse of an unjust universe or an uncaring God, but just the exercise needed to garner strength for the next leg of our journey. Our self-limiting attitudes dissolve because the challenges won't allow us to deny our God-given potential. We already have everything we need—all the right tools—within us to live a full and meaningful life. Challenge calls upon us to use these gifts creatively. And it is in meeting our challenges that we expand our awareness of the creative power that is our divine inheritance. Without the challenges, without the difficulties, problems, and obstacles, life would have no purpose.

When adversity comes we must look deeply to see the lessons there that we need to learn. In every job lost there is an opportunity for self-reevaluation, for setting a new course, for optimism and the exercise of faith. In every relationship that ends in disappointment there is reason to reflect on what went wrong, to forgive and resolve to choose more wisely or love more deeply the next time around. Our health challenges may signal the need to change our lifestyle or diet, or may be yet another call to explore the depths of our spiritual resources. And the grief we feel when we've lost a loved one can be life-transforming; it has turned surviving parents into compassionate community activists.

Our challenges are essential to our spiritual growth and development, and we must trust that each comes to us fashioned to meet our need to grow and change. A thousand gurus and personal psychics couldn't guide your progress along the path as surely as the seemingly inscrutable challenges God sends our way. But we must be willing to face them, look at them and search them for their meaning in our life. Experience is still the best teacher, in part because we don't listen.

"You don't hear," Susan chides playfully, mimicking her grandmother's lilting West Indian accent, when the pressure of writing deadlines forces me to stay up around the clock. One of our challenges—Susan's and mine—is to create more balanced lives for ourselves; to get a life outside of work, take a stroll, see a movie once in a while. Friends have insisted as much for years, and we've agreed wholeheartedly, and nothing much has changed. But the look of concern on my doctor's face when she saw me after "The 1996 Essence Awards" got my attention. Susan often says that Spirit will first tap us on the shoulder. If that doesn't get our attention, we'll get slapped upside the head. And if we still fail to heed the call and make the changes life is encouraging us to make, we may find ourselves hurting, looking up from the floor and wondering what happened.

Life is a schoolroom, Susan reminds us. And the only way to learn the lessons we are here to learn is to accept, or better, embrace the challenges.

It used to be in our schools that if you skipped out, refused to participate in the learning process, you would be held back and would have to repeat the same grade over again. Something similar happens in life. When we don't learn a particular lesson, we are confronted with the same challenge again and again for as many times as it takes. Hindus and Buddhists believe that you are confronted with lessons you don't learn in this lifetime again in the next. In other words, you get held back; you repeat the same grade as many times as it takes for you to learn the lessons, and you don't graduate until you do.

In his book *Soul: An Archaeology,* Phil Cousineau observed that the West, with its emphasis on individual identity, has misinterpreted reincarnation as a desire for ever more incarnations. Like a twenty-year-old hoping and praying to repeat the third grade for the twelfth time, those who look forward to another go-around haven't figured out what their purpose is in this one.

It's a matter of being alert and paying attention. There is something to be learned from every situation, but we may miss it if we're not fully present, if we're looking out the window and not focused on the problem at hand and finding solutions for it. Moreover, as M. Scott Peck notes, if we're big enough or powerful enough, we're likely to bully our teachers to keep them from challenging us. What makes learning so hard is that our ego keeps getting in the way.

Challenge is what life is about. For our African ancestors, the challenge of daily survival and ensuring a strong sense of community was the substance of life. The rhythm of a workaday routine adhered to faithfully through the changing of the seasons, year in and year out, in time gave depth to the soul. It was the mastery of self in meeting the daily challenge that linked them, like a river through time, to their remotest ancestors. The strength they drew from this saw many of them through the holocaust of the Middle Passage and two and a half centuries of brutal slavery in the Americas. Our challenges pale by comparison.

The notion many of us have that the ideal life is one of long and uneventful leisure enjoyed in the lap of luxury is a late-twentieth-century aberration. If life had taken such a laid-back attitude, we never would have evolved beyond single-cell bacteria. We owe our hands with their all-important opposing thumbs, our upright stance, the fact that our eyes face forward and not off to the sides, our ability to think and speak, all to challenges met and accepted over the last ninety million years. We have no better idea of what the next million years holds for us than our primate ancestors had a million years ago. But the dinosaurs can certainly tell us a thing or two about the consequences of *not* meeting the challenge to adapt to change.

Unable to meet the challenges of our rapidly changing environment today, hundreds of species in the plant and animal kingdoms are going the way of the dinosaurs. Unable to meet the challenges of a changing economy, industries are drying up, jobs are disappearing, and families are coming apart under the stress. Unable to see past personal greed to the value of an equitable distribution of resources, the nation is slowly strangling itself. Unable to get over its racism, sexism, and other isms, the world is tearing itself apart. Today, we are challenged by the delivery of affordable health care, an effective, useful, and affordable education, by the lack of hope, the prevalence of drug abuse, the proliferation of violence, the need to accept one another despite our different colors, cultures, religious beliefs, class, and sexual orientation, by the frightening numbers of young Black people suffering and dying from AIDS who are crying out to be claimed and cared for. In every instance the challenge is ours, for as these go, so goes humankind. It comes down to us — each of us — and how we respond to the call to love that these crises represent.

It's easy to feel overwhelmed and to shut down or try to shut it all out. After all, we each have our own personal challenges. But all of these are also personal, because whatever affects any of us ultimately affects all of us. We're all connected. Realizing this and living its truth may be our greatest challenge.

There is no end
To what a living world
Will demand of you.

—OCTAVIA BUTLER, *Parable of the Sower*

No one is promised complete immunity from the discords of life while he is on earth living a human life. Problems must inevitably arise, but they can only be a blessing because it is through these problems that we rise higher in consciousness and through that rising, harmony is brought into our daily life.

—JOEL S. GOLDSMITH, *Practicing the Presence*

Do not believe that he who seeks to comfort you lives untroubled among the simple and quiet words that sometimes do you good. His life has much difficulty and sadness and remains far behind yours. Were it otherwise he would never have been able to find those words.

— RAINER MARIA RILKE, *Letters to a Young Poet*

To move from darkness into light we need to be willing to embrace the twilight within — the times of disillusionment with ourselves, the chaos and disorder — and sustain our inner exploration. We empower ourselves not only by discovering resources of joy, peace and wisdom within but also by cultivating the strength and dedication to move through our own distress and discontent. Our trust in ourselves is strengthened when we experientially understand that we have the inner resources to withstand being overpowered, whether the source of that domination is outside or within ourselves.

— CHRISTINA FELDMAN, *Woman Awake*

People have (with the help of conventions) oriented all their solutions toward the easy and toward the easiest side of the easy; but it is clear that we must hold to what is difficult; everything alive holds to it, everything in Nature grows and defends itself in its own way and is characteristically and spontaneously itself, seeks at all costs to be so and against all opposition. We know little, but that we must hold to what is difficult is a certainty that will not forsake us; it is good to be solitary, for solitude is difficult; that something is difficult must be a reason the more for us to do it.

— RAINER MARIA RILKE, *Letters to a Young Poet*

This is the "goal" of the soul path — to *feel existence;* not to overcome life's struggles and anxieties, but to know life first hand, to exist fully in context. Spiritual practice is sometimes described as walking in the footsteps of another: Jesus is the way, the truth, and the life; the bodhisattva's life models the way. But on the soul's odyssey, or in its labyrinth, the feeling is that no one has ever gone this way before. People in therapy often ask, "Do you know anyone else who's had this experience?" It would be a relief to know that the blind alleys of this soul path are familiar to others. "Do you think I'm on the right track?" someone else will ask.

But the only thing to do is to be where you are at this moment, sometimes looking about in the full light of consciousness, other times standing comfortably in the deep shadows of mystery and the unknown. . . .

It is probably not quite correct to speak of the soul's *path*. It is more a meandering and a wandering. The soul path is marked by neurotic tendencies as well as by high ideals, by ignorance as well as by knowledge, and by daily incarnated life as well as by high levels of consciousness. Therefore, when you call up a friend to talk about the latest mess that has come into your life, you are tending another turn in your polytropic path. The soul becomes greater and deeper through the living out of the messes and the gaps. . . . To the soul, this is the "negative way" of the mystics, an opening into divinity only made possible by giving up the pursuit of perfection. —THOMAS MOORE, *Care of the Soul*

The whole man is challenged and enters the fray with his total reality. Only then can he become whole and only then can God be born. —CARL GUSTAV JUNG, *Memories, Dreams, Reflections*

"It says that whenever people cross our paths, there is always a message for us. Chance encounters do not exist. But how we respond to these encounters determines whether we're able to receive the message. If we have a conversation with someone who crosses our path and we do not see a message pertaining to our current questions, it does not mean there was no message. It only means we missed it for some reason."

She thought for a moment, then continued. "Have you ever run into an old friend or acquaintance, talked for a minute and left, then run into him or her again the same day or the same week?"

"Yes, I have," I replied.

"And what do you usually say? Something like 'Well, fancy seeing you again,' and laugh and go on your way."

"Something like that."

"The Manuscript says that what we should do instead in that situation is to stop what we are doing, no matter what, and find out the message we have for that person, and that the person has for us. The Manuscript predicts that once humans grasp this reality, our interaction will slow down and become more purposeful and deliberate." —JAMES REDFIELD, *The Celestine Prophecy*

When you feel frustrated or upset by a person or a situation, remember that you are not reacting to the person or the situation, but to your feelings about the person or the situation. These are *your* feelings, and your feelings are not someone else's fault. When you recognize and understand this completely, you are ready to take responsibility for how you feel and to change it. And if you can accept things as they are, you are ready to take responsibility for your situation and for all the events you see as problems.

This leads us to the . . . *Law of Least Effort:* responsibility. What does responsibility mean? Responsibility means not blaming anyone or anything for your situation, including yourself. Having accepted this circumstance, this event, this problem, responsibility then means the *ability* to have a creative *response* to the situation *as it is now*. All problems contain the seeds of opportunity, and this awareness allows you to take the moment and transform it to a better situation or thing.

Once you do this, every so-called upsetting situation will become an opportunity for the creation of something new and beautiful, and every so-called tormentor or tyrant will become your teacher. Reality is an interpretation. And if you choose to interpret reality in this way, you will have many teachers around you, and many opportunities to evolve. —DEEPAK CHOPRA, *The Seven Spiritual Laws of Success*

It is not the conduct of others but our reaction to it that makes or mars our life experience.

—ERIC BUTTERWORTH

How can it possibly be that everything in life is a positive lesson? Nearly every day we hear of horrendous situations that cause us to ask, "Is there really a loving force in the world?" Countries are torn apart with civil strife and war, with families being divided by violence and death. Many people are fighting just to survive disasters such as floods, pollution of the environment, hurricanes, tornadoes, rampant fires, and earthquakes. Others are challenged with the loss of loved ones through life-threatening illnesses such as cancer and AIDS. How is it possible to find positive lessons in all these?

In and of themselves, these experiences are not positive. Yet out of our responses to them there can come many learning experiences that do, in the final analysis, prove to be beneficial. It is often at critical junctures in our lives, where we face what seem to be insurmountable challenges, that we also discover our greatest opportunities for growth. We rise above what we believed were our limitations, discovering that we are stronger, wiser, more compassionate, or more creative than we ever imagined we could be. . . .

To have the belief that every experience, without exception, is a positive lesson in our lives, from which we can learn and grow, itself generates our willingness to receive all of life's experiences. We can then create positive results from all that life offers us, accepting each lesson with gratitude even before we know what the benefits might be. While our willingness opens us up to the opportunity for growth, our gratitude opens us up to receiving it.

— GERALD G. JAMPOLSKY AND DIANE V. CIRINCIONE, *Love Is the Answer*

Adversity is a profound teacher. We should rejoice and give thanks when difficulties occur, not because of the suffering itself, but because of what will come of it, if we lean on God.

— JOAN WESTER ANDERSON, *Where Miracles Happen*

"Be not therefore anxious for the morrow. Sufficient unto the day is the evil thereof." The term "evil" signifies incompleteness, or that which needs perfecting, development and fulfillment now. The statement therefore means that we have sufficient to do to make the present moment full and complete, without giving any thought to what we are to be or do in the future. When the present moment is filled with the most perfect life that we can possibly realize, the seeming incompleteness of the present moment will simply become a perpetual growing process. Incompleteness will thus become a real step in growth; it will be like a growing bud, and will not be evil, only lesser good on the way to greater good. When the bud ceases to grow it decays, and becomes unwholesome, disagreeable. Likewise, when the buds in human life are checked in their growth they produce disagreeable conditions. And here is the cause of all the ills of the world. The remedy is to so live that all the power of life is centered upon the present moment. To give the whole of life to the present moment is to promote the growth of everything that exists in the life of the present moment. To live a full life now is to live more and more life now.

—CHRISTIAN D. LARSON, *The Pathway of the Roses*

To have the desire to quit in the face of despair is not a new story. As long as time, people have wanted to give up when something hindered their progress. But such adversity is sometimes the right time for people to become acquainted with themselves.

It has been written that a smooth sea does not make a skillful mariner. The storms of human life, like those of the seas, awaken us to sharpening our abilities and strengthening us to overcome these present storms to the point where we seldom have to face them again. Most of living is a lesson, and the sooner we learn to study and develop the sooner we are rid of the teacher.

But in the words of Jeremy Taylor, "It is impossible for that man to despair who remembers that his Helper is omnipotent." And it is impossible for people not to progress if they acknowledge their Helper in the most minute details of their lives.

Prepared for the worst? Forget it! Only worry prepares for the worst. If problems come to you, meet them with courage when they arrive. And worry has never produced courage. Faith produces courage, and keeps us from crossing all those unnecessary bridges. In fact, we cross bridges that have never been in existence, and have no strength except that which we give them by constant preparation for something that isn't good.

Promise yourself to cross no bridges this day except those you find immediately before you. And nine times out of ten they will lead only to happiness.   —JOYCE SEQUICHIE HIFLER, *Think on These Things*

Poppa taught me a lot about life, especially its hard times. I remembered one of his lessons one night when I was ready to quit a political campaign I was losing, and wrote about it in my diary:

Tired, feeling the many months of struggle, I went up to the den to make some notes. I was looking for a pencil, rummaging through papers in the back of my desk drawer, where things accumulate for years, when I turned up one of Poppa's old business cards, the ones we made up for him, that he was so proud of: *Andrea Cuomo, Italian-American Groceries—Fine Imported Products.* Poppa never had occasion to give anyone a calling card, but he loved having them.

I couldn't help wondering what Poppa would have said if I told him I was tired or—God forbid—discouraged. Then I thought about how he dealt with hard circumstances. A thousand pictures flashed through my mind, but one scene came sharply into view.

We had just moved to Holliswood, New York, from our apartment behind the store. We had our own house for the first time; it had some land around it, even trees. One, in particular, was a great blue spruce that must have been 40 feet tall.

Less than a week after we moved in, there was a terrible storm. We came home from the store that night to find the spruce pulled almost totally from the ground and flung forward, its mighty nose bent in the asphalt of the street. My brother Frankie and I could climb poles all day; we were great at fire escapes; we could scale fences with barbed wire—but we knew nothing about trees. When we saw our spruce, defeated, its cheek on the canvas, our hearts sank. But not Poppa's.

Maybe he was five feet six if his heels were not worn. Maybe he weighed 155 pounds if he had a good meal. Maybe he could see a block away if his glasses were clean. But he was stronger than Frankie and me and Marie and Mamma all together.

We stood in the street looking down at the tree. The rain was falling. Then he announced, "O.K., we gonna push 'im up!" "What are you talking about, Poppa? The roots are out of the ground!" "Shut up, we gonna push 'im up, he's gonna grow again." We didn't know what to say to him. You couldn't say no to him. So we followed him into the house and we got what rope there was and we tied the rope around the tip of the tree that lay in the asphalt, and he stood up by the house, with me pulling on the rope and Frankie in the street in the rain, helping to push up the great blue spruce. In no time at all, we had it standing up straight again!

With the rain still falling, Poppa dug away at the place where the roots were, making a muddy hole wider and wider as the tree sank lower and lower toward security. Then we shoveled mud over the roots and moved boulders to the base to keep the tree in place. Poppa drove stakes in the ground, tied rope from the trunk to the stakes, and maybe two hours later looked at the spruce, the crippled spruce made straight by ropes, and said, "Don't worry, he's gonna grow again. . . ."

I looked at the card and wanted to cry. If you were to drive past that house today, you would see the great, straight blue spruce, maybe 65 feet tall, pointing straight up to the heavens, pretending it never had its nose in the asphalt.

I put Poppa's card back in the drawer, closed it with a vengeance. I couldn't wait to get back into the campaign.
— MARIO CUOMO in *More Reflections on the Meaning of Life*

God offers to every mind its choice between truth and repose. Take which you please, you can never have both.
— RALPH WALDO EMERSON

WE ARE SPIRITUAL BEINGS GOING THROUGH A MATERIAL EXPERIENCE.

This was the precious awareness that enabled Luke to rise above evil attempting to seduce him into believing he was born of darkness, and not light. It was the ancient memory that gave him the strength to turn his back on a life that was not true to his heart's aspiration. And it is the very awareness that you and I need to remember — and practice — a thousand times a day, whenever we are assailed with questions, fears, or doubts about our self-worth or dignity. It is the affirmation that carries us past television commercials that tell us we need to brush with *Ultrabrite* to have sex appeal, or when we see newspaper headlines purposely fabricated to arouse emotions of fear or indignation, or when we watch an irate taxi driver shake his fist at us for driving at a reasonable speed. It is the truth that we must hold on to when it seems that the world has gone crazy and there is no God. We must constantly say "No!" to all that would offer to make us whole, for such a "No!" is a resounding "Yes!" to the truth that we are *already* whole, and could never be otherwise.

Why, then, have we not lived in constant abiding awareness of our wholeness? We simply had a case of spiritual absent-mindedness, Cosmic Amnesia. We used to know, we started out knowing, but somewhere along the way we forgot; we became distracted into thinking that we are less than Divine. We believed someone who threatened to keep us locked in a closet because he forgot the goodness of his own self. And the glorious conclusion of this whole melodrama is that even though we seemed to forget how to love ourselves, we still remain Skywalkers. Our forgetting, you see, could never change our identity. Our attack thoughts could never touch our invulnerability. Our heritage is eternally ensured.

—ALAN COHEN, *Rising in Love: The Journey Into Light*

Trials are but lessons that you failed to learn presented once again, so where you made a faulty choice before you now can make a better one, and thus escape all pain that what you chose before has brought to you. In every difficulty, all distress, and each perplexity Christ calls to you and gently says, "My brother, choose again." He would not leave one source of pain unhealed, nor any image left to veil the truth.

—FOUNDATION FOR INNER PEACE, *A Course in Miracles*

In order to rise
From its own ashes
A phoenix
First
Must
Burn.

—OCTAVIA BUTLER, *Parable of the Sower*

African tradition deals with life as an experience to be lived. In many respects, it is much like the Eastern philosophies in that we see ourselves as a part of a life force; we are joined, for instance, to the air, to the earth. We are part of the whole-life process. We live in accordance with, in a kind of correspondence with the rest of the world as a whole. And therefore living becomes an experience, rather than a problem, no matter how bad or how painful it may be. Change will rise endemically from the experience fully lived and responded to. . . .

It's not a turning away from pain, error, but seeing these things as part of living, and learning from them. This characteristic is particularly African, and it is transposed into the best of Afro-American literature. In addition, we have the legends of our struggle and survival in the New World.

—AUDRE LORDE, a dialogue with Claudia Tate, *Black Women Writers at Work*

Won't you celebrate with me
what i have shaped into
a kind of life? i had no model.
born in babylon
both nonwhite and woman
what did i see to be except myself?
i made it up
here on this bridge between
starshine and clay,
my one hand holding tight
my other hand; come celebrate
with me that everyday
something has tried to kill me
and has failed.

—LUCILLE CLIFTON

no more ugly days for me
the sun shines always
and the rain is sweet and cleansing
washing my gutters clean

cloudy days will be soft and hazy
not blue or lonely

problems will only be challenges

and sickness will just be
a signal to listen

Even My Pain's Gonna Be Pretty.

disappointment will be growth
because it will teach me
to choose more carefully

delays will be lessons in patience
because I know everything comes in time
on time
even when I'm late
I'll be
on time

there is no loss
if anything goes

I gave it away
and blessed
whoever
got it

Even My Pain's Gonna Be Pretty.

    closed doors are wrong paths
    jammed doors will be opened
    since I will learn the truth

    I'll not be tired
    only resting

    no mistakes
    only lessons
    and growth
    and change
    movement

Joy! Joy! Joy!
    Even My Pain's Gonna Be Pretty.

Glory! Glory! Glory!
    EVEN MY PAIN'S GONNA BE PRETTY.

—C. TILLERY BANKS

CHAPTER TWO

The Wisdom of Patience

I've missed much of the pleasure along my journey, simply because too often I wasn't "there." This was especially true as a young mother. When my daughter, Nequai, was a child, I was always anxious for her to move on to the next stage of development. When she was an infant, I was eager for her to walk, talk, and feed herself. Then I couldn't wait until she could dress herself and see herself off to school. When she was in grammar school, I was anxious for her to be in high school. Once she was in high school, I was focused on getting her off to college. Yet when she finally left home for college, I remember wishing she was a toddler again, because I'd missed it. I'd missed some of the most precious moments of her childhood and important markers in my own life.

So often, our bodies are in one place while our minds have rushed down the road. We routinely race through our days—in our cars, in our careers and conversations—moving faster than we should for safety's sake and often not seeing the accident or ulcer or aneurism in our path until too late. More often, in our haste to "get there," we miss out on a world of experience the journey itself has to offer. And most tragic of all are those who get to that final *there*—the end of their life—only to discover they missed it; that the entire experience went by so fast and they were so focused on destinations that their life was just a blur in their peripheral vision.

Patience is the proverbial ounce of prevention that's worth more than a pound of Maalox. We are a society addicted to speed. We want shortcuts, faster cars and fax machines, computers with turbo chargers and phones with speed dialing. We don't want to stand in line. We want instant everything. Ironically, our fear is that we may miss out, not get our share. And so we rush, make mistakes, take wrong turns, end up having to do things over, and often *do* miss out. This, of course, adds to our frustration, making us even less patient and those around us uncomfortable.

But the patient person—the one who is without anxiety—has a calming effect on others and helps them to feel less anxious. He knows that everything is unfolding according to plan, even though what unfolds may not fit with his plans. She knows that everything is in divine order, that whatever she is facing—whether joy, sorrow, pleasure, or pain—this, too, shall pass, and all her needs will be met in the fullness of time.

Life's secrets unfold over time, and many of the answers to the profound questions about life for which we are searching are found not at the end of the novel, concerto, or journey, but in the process of getting there. That process requires that we be fully present each moment, not missing it because we are anxiously looking ahead or behind.

Howard Thurman's prayer for a grander perspective on time is, in essence, the longing of all souls for a unity in which time ceases to exist, the unity of past and future in the eternal now and oneness of God. Some modern theologians have interpreted the Fall and our expulsion from the Garden of Paradise as a fall into time when we ate of the tree of the knowledge of duality—the knowledge of good and evil, past and future, male and female, God and humankind. This is why the poet W. H. Auden calls impatience the only cardinal sin. "Because of impatience," he wrote, "we were driven out of Paradise, because of impatience we cannot return." Adam and Eve just couldn't wait, and most of the time, neither can we. But if we were to adopt a just-wait-and-see attitude, we would probably gain a much larger perspective on most things, and a better perspective would in turn make us more patient.

People are as likely to try our patience as anything. But a little perspective is helpful here, too. I find it's much easier to be patient with others when I recall some of my own foolish behavior as a young man and wince at the thought that there were those, older and wiser, who were called on to exercise great patience in guiding me to maturity. Undoubtedly, they were individuals of great faith since, given my progress at times, there was no way to know whether they would see their efforts rewarded. But with the wisdom that a larger perspective provides, they saw the futility of casting blame simply to vent their anger and frustration. As Jon Kabat-Zinn points out, the throat we'd sometimes like to get our hands around turns out to be too big; ultimately, it's society's, or the world's. Ultimately, it's our own. What can we do but show compassion and patience?

Khephra's patience is a virtue I could have used a great deal of in my relationship with my mother. Babs wasn't easy. Throughout my teens and much of my life, ours was a test of wills. But observing how Khephra deals with his own father's willfulness helped me to be more accepting of Babs instead of determined to change her. Khephra's father, Rusty, is a former Tuskegee Airman with unfailing self-confidence and occasional gusts of bluster. When my mother would express her opinions with force in the way that Rusty often does, or say something I viewed as disparaging, it would irritate me, and without pausing for a moment to consider that Babs had always been a complainer and was just being herself, I'd be on her case, correcting her. Watching Khephra interact easily and patiently with his father has been instructive. Khephra is rarely fazed by other people's behavior. He lets folks be who they are. After having him in my life, my relationship with my mother grew calmer and ever more rewarding.

Patience is a virtue because it brings us into closer relationship with one another, with the peace of each moment lived in the eternal present, and with our divine Self. By practicing patience we strengthen our faith in our ultimate invulnerability. Knowing we are protected, secure, and abiding, we are patient.

Patience is an ever present alternative to the mind's endemic restlessness and impatience. Scratch the surface of impatience and what you will find lying beneath it, subtly or not so subtly, is anger. It's the strong energy of not wanting things to be the way they are and blaming someone (often yourself) or something for it. This doesn't mean you can't hurry when you have to. It is possible even to hurry patiently, mindfully, moving fast because you have chosen to.

From the perspective of patience, things happen because other things happen. Nothing is separate and isolated. There is no absolute, end-of-the-line, the-buck-stops-here root cause. If someone hits you with a stick, you don't get angry at the stick or at the arm that swung it; you get angry at the person attached to the arm. But if you look a little deeper, you can't find a satisfactory root cause or place for your anger even in the person, who literally doesn't know what he is doing and is therefore out of his mind at that moment. Where should the blame lie, or the punishment? Maybe we should be angry at the person's parents for the abuse they may have showered on a defenseless child. Or maybe at the world for its lack of compassion. But what is the world? Are you not a part of that world? Do not you yourself have angry impulses and under some conditions find yourself in touch with violent, even murderous impulses? . . .

In taking up meditation, we are cultivating the quality of patience every time we stop and sit and become aware of the flow of our own breathing. And this invitation to ourselves to be more open, more in touch, more patient with our moments naturally extends itself to other times in our lives as well. We know that things unfold according to their own nature. We can remember to let our lives unfold in the same way. We don't have to let our anxieties and our desire for certain results dominate the quality of the moment, even when things are painful. When we have to push, we push. When we have to pull, we pull. But we know when not to push too, and when not to pull.

Through it all, we attempt to bring balance to the present moment, understanding that in patience lies wisdom, knowing that what will come next will be determined in large measure by how we are now.

— JON KABAT-ZINN, *Wherever You Go, There You Are*

When it is said that one should be patient and withstand trouble, that doesn't mean that one should be defeated, should be overcome. The very purpose of engaging in the practice of patience is to become stronger in mind, stronger in heart. And also you want to remain calm. In that atmosphere of calm, you can use real human beings to learn wisdom. If you lose patience, if your brain founders by emotions, then you've lost the power to analyze. But if you are patient, from a basis of altruism, then you don't lose your strength of mind; you can even increase your strength of mind and then use your powers of analysis to figure out ways to overcome the negative force that is opposing you.

—THE DALAI LAMA, *Ocean of Wisdom*

Waiting is not mere empty hoping. It has the inner certainty of reaching the goal. Such certainty alone gives that light which leads to success. This leads to the perseverance that brings good fortune. . . .

—THE I CHING

Man is extremely impatient, but God is immensely patient and careful about His creation. Impatience destroys. Think of the warning you see on road signs, "Speed kills." Speeding is impatience. Human beings are impatient; they are always in a hurry. Hurrying is necessary sometimes. But mostly, hurrying kills. When you give medicine to someone who is critically ill, don't hurry. Even if the medicine must be given immediately, even if it is an emergency case, still you should not hurry. If you hurry, in your excitement, your hands might tremble while pouring water into the patient's mouth while giving him pills to swallow. You may miss and water might go into the nose. That can cause trouble. In your hurry, you may give too much or even the wrong medicine to the patient, and this could kill him. Be patient. Real life is love. When you love, you cannot hurry. You must be patient.

—SRI SRI MATA AMRITANANDAMAYI, *Awaken, Children!*

No one is given a gift that is better or greater than patience.   —THE PROPHET MUHAMMAD

Sometimes we get what we want right away. At other times, we wonder if our desires will ever be fulfilled.

We will be fulfilled in the best way possible and as quickly as possible. But some things take time. Sometimes, we have lessons to learn first, lessons that prepare us so we can accept the good we deserve. Things are being worked out in us, and in others. Blocks in us are being removed. A solid foundation is being laid. . . .

Wait. If the time is not right, the way is not clear, the answer or decision not consistent, wait.

We may feel a sense of urgency. We may want to resolve the issue by doing something—*anything* now, but that action is not in our best interest. . . .

We do not ever have to move too soon or move out of harmony. Waiting is an action—a positive, forceful action.

Often, waiting is a God-guided action, one with as much power as a decision, and more power than an urgent, ill-timed decision.

We do not have to pressure ourselves by insisting that we do or know something before it's time. When it is time, we will know. . . .

The answer will come. The power will come. The time will come. And it will be right.

—MELODY BEATTIE, *The Language of Letting Go*

Do you have the patience to wait
till your mud settles and the water is clear?
Can you remain unmoving
till the right action arises by itself?

—LAO-TZU, Tao-te Ching

There is here no measuring with time, no year matters, and ten years are nothing. Being an artist means, not reckoning and counting, but ripening like the tree which does not force its sap and stands confident in the storms of spring without the fear that after them may come no summer. It does come. But it comes only to the patient, who are there as though eternity lay before them, so unconcernedly still and wide. I learn it daily, learn it with pain to which I am grateful: *patience* is everything!

—RAINER MARIA RILKE, *Letters to a Young Poet*

Have patience with all things but first of all with yourself. —St. FRANCIS DE SALES

When we become lost in desire, we are put firmly into the framework of linear time. We become focused on getting what we do not yet have, or on keeping what we do have. We become oriented toward the future. To be caught in this concept of linear time brings us to what in Buddhist teachings is called *bhava,* or becoming, always falling into the next moment. It is as if before each breath ends, we are leaning forward to grasp at the next breath.

If we walked around all the time with our bodies leaning forward, can you imagine the kind of aching we would experience? Our backs, our necks, our legs would really hurt. In just that same way, our hearts really hurt because we are thrust forward all of the time, in wanting, in seeking, in leaning into things, in being dependent on particular things or people or even beliefs for our happiness. We have one impermanent experience, and, unable to be at peace as it passes, we reach out and grab for another. . . .

We have a moment of seeing, a moment of hearing, tasting, touching, smelling, thinking—just a moment, and then it is gone. . . . If we rely upon any one of these transiencies for a sense of permanent satisfaction, we lose the happiness of simply being. . . .

—SHARON SALZBERG, *Lovingkindness: The Revolutionary Art of Happiness*

I exist as I am, that is enough,
If no other in the world be aware I sit content,
And if each and all be aware I sit content.

One world is aware, and by far the largest to me, and that is myself,

And whether I come to my own today or in ten thousand or ten million years,

I can cheerfully take it now, or with equal cheerfulness, I can wait.　—WALT WHITMAN, *Leaves of Grass*

O GOD, I NEED THEE

I Need Thy Sense of Time

Always I have an underlying anxiety about things.

Sometimes I am in a hurry to achieve my ends

And am completely without patience. It is hard for me

To realize that some growth is slow,

That all processes are not swift. I cannot always discriminate

Between what takes time to develop and what can be rushed,

Because my sense of time is dulled.

I measure things in terms of happenings.

O to understand the meaning of perspective

That I may do all things with a profound sense of leisure—of time.　—HOWARD THURMAN

From cane reeds, sugar.

From a worm's cocoon, silk.

Be patient if you can, and from sour

grapes will come something sweet.

—JALAL AL-DIN RUMI

4 7

[The Dogon man] is patient . . . ; he knows how to hold back his words when it is necessary; he does not get angry and he avoids disputes by not responding to provocations. This rare quality requires much force of character; . . . the patient man is sometimes sad and must make an effort to forget the "bad words" to which he did not wish to respond. Such a man is highly valued in the village; he makes the people around him happy; "the patient man has peace," goes the proverb. . . . He is "refreshing" like water.

—G. CALAME-GRIAULE, *Ethnologie et Langage: La Parole Chez les Dogon*

When we feel we ought to be more patient with someone, we usually think in terms of restraining ourselves in some way. We tend to equate patience with holding back our annoyance at another person's way of thinking and doing things.

However, patience under any circumstance is not just a matter of self-restraint. It goes much deeper than that. In its fullest sense it is the direct outflow of other positive qualities we have acquired.

When we try to be kind and giving, rather than brittle and uncaring, we are far more likely to be patient. When we have a positive and accepting outlook, rather than an angry "chip-on-the-shoulder" disposition, patience more easily becomes part of our nature. We are apt to have the greatest degree of patience when we try to relate to others with that deepest level of understanding—empathy.

Patience flows more freely when we have faith and trust—not only in the abilities and inner resources of others, but in our own as well. In that regard, becoming more patient with ourselves first requires that we become more kind, understanding, and accepting of ourselves. This is our greatest challenge.

—ANONYMOUS, *A New Day: 365 Meditations for Personal and Spiritual Growth*

I have omnipotence at my command, and eternity at my disposal.   —ALEISTER CROWLEY

[B]egin to patiently rely on the gentle counsel that spirit provides.

The need to strive for answers will disappear. It will be replaced by a patient knowing that divine design will reveal what the next step along the path of your sacred quest will be.

I have found this kind of patience to be an enormous virtue and guide in my life. When I feel inclined to listen to my ego, I am able to call up the attitude of patience and say simply, "I am leaving it in your hands. My ego is pushing but it just doesn't feel right, so I will silently wait to see in what direction I am to go. Use me as you see fit." . . .

Great things have absolutely no fear of time—they are patient, largely because your higher spiritual self knows that time does not exist except in our minds. Infinity and eternity are concepts that deny the existence of time. Your higher self is a part of infinity and eternity and offers you patience.

—WAYNE W. DYER, *Your Sacred Self*

At the bottom of patience is Heaven.

—KANURI PROVERB

CHAPTER THREE

Grant Us Grace, Show Us the Way

There's something about certain people, about the way they move through the world, that suggests they have unlimited inner resources and universal carte blanche. They may not have a dime, and yet they go on their way as if money doesn't matter, as if everything they want or need is theirs for the asking. They seem to walk in harmony amid the dissonant bustle of the world, and their every gesture appears as natural as if Nature herself had choreographed it. It's not where they're going that fascinates us, but the way they are getting there, the way they do the things they do.

Grace. We easily recognize it and esteem those who exude it. We admire them for their regal ease, their surety of movement. But beneath the poise, the presence, and confident bearing there is the hint of something more. While we admire them, we also suspect the influence of divine favor surrounding and protecting them. That divine Presence is the source of their presence, and those who feel it walk with amazing grace through walls which, although invisible, stop most of us in our tracks.

What the graceful have that others don't is the ability to relax, to let go and go with the flow of life. They greet the world each day knowing that they are life itself, unfolding in its perfect pattern. The Taoists call this pattern of flowing and unfolding The Way. In the West we call it God's will. Whatever we call it, those who surrender to it find grace. In following The Way they become The Way. Like Jesus, they aren't searching for anything "out there" because they know the kingdom is within, that they are in God's care and that the universe is always there to support them. That assurance gives them the ease we call grace.

Children, in their innocence, show us the way. They can cry one minute and laugh the next, taking each moment for what it is—a unique experience to be engaged in fully. We marvel at their open minds and supple nature and refer to this precious time in their lives as "days of grace."

The truth is we fair better when we are absorbed in the doing of life than when we constantly try to calculate the odds for success. Mary McLeod Bethune worked miracles in this way. With $1.50 and supplies salvaged from a local dump, she founded a school for girls in 1904. Today it's the prestigious Bethune-Cookman College. Mrs. Bethune was not daunted by the alleged impossibility of her undertaking. She knew she would find a way. She simply moved forward, taking it one step at a time. Hers was a stately grace that allowed her to walk with humility among the poor and with pride and dignity among presidents. At a time when African Americans had virtually no access to the higher reaches of power in the United States, with her innate nobility, wisdom, and grace, Mrs. Bethune became an advisor to five U.S. presidents.

The sages tell us that this uncommon self-possession arises from a fearlessness of death and from taking no thought for oneself. Otherwise ordinary citizens we sometimes see on the news, who are praised as heros and heroines for some extraordinary act of kindness or bravery, seem to have this trait in common. In the moment of crisis they respond automatically and without regard to their personal safety. In fact, they often don't seem to be aware that there is any risk to themselves. Later, when they are asked by reporters what they were thinking about at that moment, the answer is often that they weren't thinking at all (at least, not about themselves). Whatever it was they did, they just did it. With all concern for self set aside, the grace that flows through the universe was allowed to move through them, guiding their steps in ways they could not have calculated. Jean Toomer, a writer from the Harlem Renaissance, made the point that being on guard against the unpredictability of life actually keeps us from experiencing life in all its wonder and variety. Our past experiences can jade us and even blind us to the uniqueness of new experiences. This seems to be especially the case in our personal relationships. Having been hurt or disappointed in the past, we are often reluctant to risk letting go in subsequent relationships. And that reluctance or inability to let go becomes the very thing that keeps us from developing deep, emotionally fulfilling relationships. We are afraid for ourselves, and that fear impedes our forward progress and keeps us out of the flow we call grace. Self-consciousness, which is only fear for oneself, is what keeps us off beat, wary of surrendering to the rhythm of life.

Perhaps more than anything else, music shows us what grace is. We don't appreciate good music cautiously. We don't listen to it fearful of where it might take us emotionally. Nor do we enjoy it by anticipating the end of the song or the silence that will follow. We give way to it, allowing it to move us as it moves through us. In this same way, we can live our lives gracefully.

Musicians understand this better than most of us. A good musician practices long hours for many years until the music and the instrument become part of her being. Then she forgets about the notes and technique and lets the music flow through her, using *her* as a finely tuned instrument. This is what dancers do, too. And athletes. It's not something you can do well by thinking about each and every note or movement. You have to become the music. It's when we let go and just allow ourselves to be in the flow that the magic happens.

It's at such moments, when some unexpected but timely blessing falls into our laps, that Susan will ask rhetorically, "Isn't that divine order?" That was exactly her response when we were discussing the idea of grace in the car one Saturday and Sam Cooke's classic "A Change Is Gonna Come" came over the radio. We sang along with the familiar first lines: "I was born by the river in a little tent, and just like the river, I've been running ever since." But for some reason, I've always heard those soulful lyrics slightly paraphrased: *I was borne by the river where the river went. . . .* My interpretation probably comes from mishearing the words as a kid, though in retrospect I count it as an instance of grace. I like my lyrics better because I think life is a river. It flows from its source and winds its way through varied terrain toward an ocean beyond its imagining. Standing apart, we can see that the river and the ocean are one body of water, ever in motion and constantly changing form; now ocean, now water vapor drawn up into the air by the heat of the sun, now a passing cloud, now rain or snowfall, now a spring, a river, an ocean again. But the river takes no thought of these changes, nor how long it will run or to what end it is destined. With majestic grace, it flows. And so the river is timeless.

This feeling of being loved and supported by the Universe in general and by certain recognizable spirits in particular is bliss.

— ALICE WALKER

Our true home is in the present moment. To live in the present moment is a miracle. The miracle is not to walk on water. The miracle is to walk on the green Earth in the present moment, to appreciate the peace and beauty that are available now.

— THÍCH NHẤT HANH, *Touching Peace*

THE COSMIC BEIST

To be is the word of the isness . . .
To create is to be
Because to be is to cause to be . . .
Thus speaks the Cosmic Beist.

— SUN RA, *The Immeasurable Equation*

There was a Master come unto the earth, born in the holy land of Indiana, raised in the mystical hills east of Fort Wayne. The Master learned of this world in the public schools of Indiana and as he grew in his trade as a mechanic of automobiles.

But the Master had learnings from other lands and other schools, from other lives that he had lived. He remembered these and, remembering, became wise and strong, so that others saw his strength and came to him for counsel.

The Master believed that he had power to help himself and all mankind, and as he believed, so it was for him, so that others saw his power and came to him to be healed of their troubles and their many diseases.

The Master believed that it is well for any man to think upon himself as a son of God, and as he believed so it was, and the shops and garages where he worked became crowded and jammed with those who sought his learning and his touch; and the streets outside with those who longed only that the shadow of his passing might fall upon them, and change their lives.

It came to pass, because of the crowds, that the several foremen and shop managers bid the Master leave his tools and go his way, for so tightly was he thronged that neither he nor other mechanics had room to work upon the automobiles.

So it was that he went into the countryside, and people following began to call him Messiah and worker of miracles, and as they believed, it was so.

If a storm passed as he spoke, not a raindrop touched a listener's head; the last of the multitude heard his words as clearly as the first, no matter lightning nor thunder in the sky about. And always he spoke in parables.

And he said unto them, "Within each of us lies the power of our consent to health and to sickness, to riches and to poverty, to freedom and to slavery. It is we who control these, and not another."

A mill-man spoke and said, "Easy words for you, Master, for you are guided as we are not, and need not toil as we toil. A man has to work for his living in this world."

The Master answered and said, "Once there lived a village of creatures along the bottom of a great crystal river. The current of the river swept silently over them all—young and old, rich and poor, good and evil—the current going its own way, knowing only its own crystal self.

"Each creature in its own manner clung tightly to the twigs and rocks of the river bottom, for clinging was their way of life, and resisting the current what each had learned from birth.

"But one creature said at last, 'I am tired of clinging. Though I cannot see it with my eyes, I trust that the current knows where it is going. I shall let go and let it take me where it will. Clinging, I shall die of boredom.'

"The other creatures laughed and said, 'Fool! Let go and that current you worship will throw you tumbled and smashed against the rocks, and you will die quicker than boredom!'

"But the one heeded them not, and taking a breath did let go, and at once he was tumbled and smashed by the current across the rocks. Yet in time, as the creature refused to cling again, the current lifted him free from the bottom, and he was bruised and hurt no more.

"And the creatures downstream, to whom he was a stranger, cried, 'See a miracle! A creature like ourselves, yet he flies! See the Messiah come to save us all!'

"And the one carried in the current said, 'I am no more Messiah than you. The river delights to lift us free, if only we dare let go. Our true work is this voyage, this adventure.'

"But they cried the more, 'Savior!', all the while clinging to the rocks, and when they looked again he was gone, and they were left alone making legends of a savior."

And it came to pass when he saw that the multitude thronged him the more day on day, tighter and closer and fiercer than ever they had; when he saw that they pressed him to heal them without rest and feed them always with his miracles, to learn for them and to live their lives, he went alone that day unto a hilltop apart, and there he prayed.

And he said in his heart, *Infinite Radiant Is, if it be thy will, let this cup pass from me. Let me lay aside this impossible task. I cannot live the life of one other soul, yet ten thousand cry to me for life. I'm sorry I allowed it all to happen. If it be thy will, let me go back to my engines and my tools and let me live as other men.*

And a voice spoke unto him on the hilltop, a voice neither male nor female, loud nor soft, a voice infinitely kind. And the voice said unto him, "Not my will but thine be done, for what is thy will is mine for thee. Go thy way as other men and be thou happy on earth."

And hearing, the Master was glad and gave thanks and came down from the hilltop humming a little mechanic's song. And when the throng pressed him with its woes, beseeching him to heal it and learn for it and feed it nonstop from his understanding, and to entertain it with his wonders, he smiled upon the multitude and said pleasantly unto them, "I quit."

For a moment, the multitude was stricken dumb with astonishment.

And he said unto them, "If a man told God that he wanted most of all to help the suffering world, no matter the price to himself, and God answered and told him what he must do, should the man do as he is told?"

"Of course, Master!" cried the many. "It should be pleasure for him to suffer the tortures of hell itself, should God ask it!"

"No matter what those tortures, nor how difficult the task?"

"Honor to be hanged, glory to be nailed to a tree and burned, if so be that God has asked," said they.

"And what would you do," the Master said unto the multitude, "if God spoke directly to your face and said, 'I command that you be happy in the world as long as you live.' What would you do then?"

And the multitude was silent, not a voice, not a sound was heard upon the hillsides across the valleys where they stood.

And the Master said unto the silence, "In the path of our happiness shall we find the learning for which we have chosen this lifetime. So it is that I have learned this day and choose to leave you now to walk your own path as you please."

And he went his way through the crowds and left them, and he returned to the everyday world of men and machines.
— RICHARD BACH, *Illusions: The Adventures of a Reluctant Messiah*

The state of grace is a condition in which all growth is effortless, a transparent, joyful acquiescence that is a ground requirement of all existence. Your own body grows naturally and easily from its time of birth, not expecting resistance but taking its miraculous unfolding for granted; using all of itself with great, gracious, creatively aggressive abandon.

You were born into a state of grace, therefore. It is impossible for you to leave it. You will die in a state of grace whether or not special words are spoken for you, or water or oil is poured upon your head. You share this blessing with the animals and all other living things. You cannot "fall out of" grace, nor can it be taken from you.

You can ignore it. You can hold beliefs that blind you to its existence. You will still be graced but unable to perceive your own uniqueness and integrity, and blind also to other attributes with which you are automatically gifted.
— JANE ROBERTS, *The Nature of Personal Reality* (Seth speaking through Jane Roberts)

The soul which is inwardly united to God, becomes, in the greatness of its joy, like a good-natured simple-hearted child, and now condemns no one, Greek, heathen, Jew, nor sinner, but looks at them all alike with sight that has been cleansed, [and] finds joy in the whole world.
— ST. MARK PODVIZHNIK in *The Way of a Pilgrim & the Pilgrim Continues on His Way*, translated by R. M. French

Verily I say unto you, Whosoever shall not receive the kingdom of God as a little child, he shall not enter therein.

— JESUS OF NAZARETH

He is enlightened who joins in this play knowing it as play, for man suffers only because he takes serious what the gods made for fun.

— ALAN WATTS

There is vitality, a life force, an energy, a quickening that is translated through you into action. And because there is only one you in all time, this expression is unique. And if you block it, it will never exist through any other medium . . . the world will not have it. It is not your business to determine how good it is, nor how valuable, nor how it compares with other expressions. It is your business to keep yours clearly and directly, to keep the channel open.

— MARTHA GRAHAM

I love jazz. And I really enjoy the challenge and the honesty of playing this music onstage.

When it all clicks, it's bliss. It really is. You're not worrying about whether your fingers are working right—you're not in control at all. It's as if you don't have anything to do with the music anymore. And that's when it's the best, because you're not thinking about anything. That's the goal, really—to be able to get that to happen consistently, to connect, to not have anything to do with it, every time. There's no ego in there, there's nothing in there but the music. You're not thinking *Are my heels too high?* or *What's this critic going to think?*—none of that. It's no concentration—and complete concentration—at the same time.

— GERI ALLEN, *Essence* magazine

When the deepest part of you becomes engaged in what you are doing, when your activities and actions become gratifying and purposeful, when what you do serves both yourself and others, when you do not tire within but seek the sweet satisfaction of your life and your work, you are doing what you were meant to be doing. The personality that is engaged in the work of its soul is buoyant. It is not burdened with negativity. It does not fear. It experiences purposefulness and meaning. It delights in its work and in others. It is fulfilled and fulfilling.

—GARY ZUKAV, *The Seat of the Soul*

Prince Wen Hui's cook
Was cutting up an ox.
Out went a hand,
Down went a shoulder,
He planted a foot,
He pressed with a knee,
The ox fell apart
With a whisper,
The bright cleaver murmured
Like a gentle wind.
Rhythm! Timing!
Like a sacred dance,
Like "The Mulberry Grove,"
Like ancient harmonies!

"Good work!" the Prince exclaimed,
"Your method is faultless!"
"Method?" said the cook
Laying aside his cleaver,
"What I follow is Tao
Beyond all methods!

"When I first began
To cut up oxen
I would see before me
The whole ox
All in one mass.
After three years
I no longer saw this mass.
I saw the distinctions.

"But now I see nothing
With the eye. My whole being
Apprehends.
My senses are idle. The spirit
Free to work without plan
Follows its own instinct
Guided by natural line,
By the secret opening, the hidden space,
My cleaver finds its own way.
I cut through no joint, chop no bone.

"There are spaces in the joints;
The blade is thin and keen:
When this thinness
Finds that space
There is all the room you need!
It goes like a breeze!
Hence I have this cleaver nineteen years
As if newly sharpened!

"True, there are sometimes
Tough joints. I feel them coming,
I slow down, I watch closely,
Hold back, barely move the blade,
And whump! the part falls away
Landing like a clod of earth.

"Then I withdraw the blade,
I stand still
And let the joy of the work
Sink in.
I clean the blade
And put it away."

Prince Wen Hui said,
"This is it! My cook has shown me
How I ought to live
My own life!"

— CHUANG-TZU, Chinese Taoist philosopher and teacher

Until one is committed,
there is hesitancy,
the chance to draw back,
always ineffectiveness

Concerning acts of initiative (and creation)
there is one elementary truth
the ignorance of which kills countless ideas

and splendid plans:

    that the moment one definitely commits oneself

    then Providence moves too.

All sorts of things occur to help one

that would never otherwise have occurred.

A whole stream of events issues from the decision,

raising in one's favor all manner

of unforseen incidents and meetings

and material assistance

which no one could have dreamt

would come one's way.

Whatever you can do,

or dream you can, begin it.

Boldness has genius, power, and magic in it.

Begin it now.

                                 —JOHANN WOLFGANG VON GOETHE

Most of us feel we must be mentally fortified in advance of experience. This is one of the reasons why we are buffers rather than experiencers.

                                 —JEAN TOOMER

The Fall was the acquisition of technique and self-awareness. It led men to mistrust their immediate impulses and to try to rely on conscious rationality. . . .

    Holiness is close to, but not quite the same as, a return to innocence and to the life of spontaneous impulse. A. K. Coomaraswamy called it "a perpetual uncalculated life in the present." For holiness is the life of spontaneity and self-abandonment *with humor*, which includes the wisdom of serpents as well as the gentleness of doves, because humor is nothing other than perfect self-awareness. It is the delighted recognition of one's own absurdity, and a loving cynicism with respect to one's own pretensions. A person who has learned to be fully self-aware can safely return to living by impulse. Humor is the transformation of anxiety into laughter: the same trembling, but with a different meaning. Holy humor is the discovery of the ultimate joke on oneself, and this is why Dante heard the song of the angels as the laughter of the universe.

—ALAN WATTS, *Beyond Theology*

I am especially glad of the divine gift of laughter; it has made the world human and lovable, despite all its pain and wrong.

—W. E. B. DU BOIS

Angels can fly because they take themselves lightly.

—G. K. CHESTERTON

He who laughs, lasts.

—MARY POOLE

THROW IT AWAY

I think about the life I live,
a figure made of clay,
and think about the things I lost;
the things I gave away,
and when I'm in a certain mood

I search the halls and look.
One night I found these magic words
in a magic book.

Throw it away. Throw it away.
Give your love, live your life,
each and every day,
and keep your hand wide open.
Let the sun shine through,
'cause you can never lose a thing
if it belongs to you.

There's a hand to rock the cradle
and a hand to help us stand,
with a gentle kind of motion
as it moves across the land,
and the hand's unclenched and open.
Gifts of life and love it brings,
so keep your hand wide open
if you're needing anything.

Throw it away. Throw it away.
Give your love, live your life
each and every day,
and keep your hand wide open.
Let the sun shine through,
'cause you can never lose a thing
if it belongs to you.

—ABBEY LINCOLN

God gives nothing to those who keep their arms crossed.

— BAMBARA PROVERB

By example and not by precept. By living, not by preaching. By doing, not by professing. By living the life, not by dogmatizing as to how it should be lived.

— RALPH WALDO TRINE, *In Tune with the Infinite*

INDEBTED TO A VAST HOST

He was a very ordinary-looking man walking along the sidewalk. It was at the close of day but darkness had not yet begun to spread its mantle everywhere. About three feet from the curbstone, a group of birds was pecking away at a small opening in the side of a pink paper bag. They were quarreling as they pecked because there must have been many suggestions being offered as to the best way to get to the crumbs that were hidden there. The man walked over to the spot; the birds took rapid flight, settling at a respectful distance in the grass, watching. With his foot he turned the bag over, examined it with some care, then reached down and emptied the bag and its contents of bread crumbs. When he had done this, he resumed his walk. As soon as he disappeared, the birds returned to find that a miracle had taken place. Instead of a bag full of hidden crumbs, only a glimpse of which they had seen, there was before them now a full abundance for satisfying their need. The man had gone on his way without even a backward glance. . . . We are all of us the birds and we are all of us the man. It is the way of life; it is one of the means by which God activates Himself in the texture of human life and human experience.

— HOWARD THURMAN, *Meditations of the Heart*

So live your life that the fear of death can never enter your heart. Trouble no one about his religion; respect others in their view, and demand that they respect yours. Love your life, perfect your life, beautify all things in your life. Seek to make your life long and its purpose in the service of your people.

. . . Always give a word or a sign of salute when meeting or passing a friend, even a stranger, when in a lonely place.

— TECUMSEH, Chief of the Shawnee

There are seven kinds of offering which can be practiced by even those who are not wealthy. The first is the physical offering. This is to offer service by one's labor. The highest type of this offering is to offer one's own life. . . . The second is the spiritual offering. This is to offer a compassionate heart to others. The third is the offering of eyes. This is to offer a warm glance to others, which will give them tranquillity. The fourth is the offering of countenance. This is to offer a soft countenance with a smile to others. The fifth is the oral offering. This is to offer kind and warm words to others. The sixth is the seat offering. This is to offer one's seat to others. The seventh is the offering of shelter. This is to let others spend the night at one's home. These kinds of offering can be practiced by anyone in everyday life.

— THE BUDDHA

Experience, which destroys innocence, also leads one back to it.

— JAMES BALDWIN

CHAPTER FOUR

Facing Fear, Finding Faith

Again and again, throughout the New Testament, we are counseled, "Be not afraid," "Fear not," "Go in peace" (dozens of times in the Gospels alone), and yet fear continues to be a defining aspect of the human condition. It is the source of most of our personal pain and the needless suffering in the world. It has been linked to physical maladies from ulcers to cancers. It lies at the root of greed and aggression, racism and sexism, bigotry, bad blood, and trouble between neighborhoods and nations. We fear not only for ourselves, but for our families, friends, and the world. We fear rejection and loneliness, commitment, failure, and even success. We fear that we won't be able to measure up to the competition or the expectations of others, or even our own expectations of ourselves. We fear that we may be perceived as not smart enough, fine enough, thin enough, Black enough; that our pockets aren't deep enough, or that they are and everyone is trying to get something from us. Even our love of comfort is a kind of fear—a buffer between us and the unpredictability of an ever-changing world. We have so many fears that we have had to borrow words from Greek and Latin to accommodate our more specialized anxieties like claustrophobia, xenophobia, acrophobia, homophobia, even phobophobia (a fear of fear itself).

Our fear may in fact be the very thing that defines us as individual human beings. It is certainly our first experience of the world. As a fetus in the womb, having no concept of "other," we had no concept of "I," no awareness of our own individuality. Then, all at once, terror struck as uterine contractions forced us through a tunnel that was too tight, and coming out the other end we were blinded by light and overwhelmed by a cacophony of sounds. Suddenly we found ourselves flailing about in the relative emptiness of open air, whereas, until that moment, we had known only the security of a warm, snug, watery womb that was all the world to us.

In repeatedly counseling us not to be afraid, Jesus reveals his mission to have been one of compassion—an attempt to alleviate our fears, which he understood to be intrinsic to our sense of separateness. For it is our belief that we are separate, from one another and from God, that is the source of our fear of death, and from that fear comes all the others. Jesus attempted to heal the division—to repair the unity that was split into God and man, life and death, good and evil, and so forth, when, in Judeo-Christian mythology, Adam and Eve ate from the tree of knowledge of good and evil (in other words, the tree of awareness of duality). The reparation or reunion of the human and the divine is in fact the very meaning of the word "religion"—from the Latin *re* (back) and *ligare* (to tie or bind). Religion is that which ties or binds us back to our original oneness. "I and my Father are one," Jesus told his followers, and "Ye [too] are gods." Offering his own life as the example, he attempted to impress upon them the power of their own divinity, and then, by dying, he showed them that death is not final and need not be feared.

As Jon Mundy notes, Old Testament and Koranic passages admonishing us to fear God are more accurately translated as "respect or behold

God." The original Hebrew word for "fear," *pahad*, carried the sense of overwhelming awe in the presence of the divine. The idea of regarding God with fear almost certainly stems from the nature of the experience of transcendent reality, or oneness with God, which Rudolph Otto (in his book *The Idea of the Holy*) described as *mysterium terrible et fascinans*. "It is *terrible*," adds Karen Armstrong in *A History of God*, "because it comes as a profound shock that severs us from the consolations of normality, and *fascinans* because, paradoxically, it exerts an irresistible attraction." "Respect," on the other hand, derives from the Latin *specere*, meaning "to look at," "consider," or "regard" again, or habitually; "to fix one's eyes upon." Preaching and instigating fear of God has only roused a generalized fear of every manifestation of God we mistakenly regard as other—other than ourselves, our family, our group, nation, religion. Historically, the fear-preaching religions were the same that brought you the various religious crusades, jihads, and holy wars. But where God is understood as Love there can be no fear. Where God is One there is no other.

But just as pain has a purpose, fear also has its function. If we were all totally indifferent to death, it's likely that not enough of us would live long enough to accomplish much of anything as cocreators with God or even reproduce our kind. Fear is the engine that has driven not only our intellectual and technological progress, but our evolution as a species. It is a double-edged sword that we have yet to get a handle on: While it has been useful to us in carving out the world we live in, it has also cut up the world, wounded it, and caused us a great deal of pain. We haven't yet figured out how life works, how we can establish peace within and among ourselves. We all wear our masks. We've learned how to convince one another that we feel strong and secure, but secretly we're all fearful and nervous.

There's a better way of living—not without problems, challenges, even occasional catastrophes, but a way of dealing with them from a calm, still, peaceful center we create within ourselves by looking at the world differently. Perception is reality. We literally create the world we live in in our minds and project it outward through the power of the word. Right now, we can begin constructing the world we want by embracing a new paradigm to guide our personal lives. But first, we must have faith; we must believe it is possible.

In my own life, fear has been my call to faith. If not for my fears about being on my own with a small child, with little money and no backup, I might never have known the importance of surrendering to Spirit, might never have put faith so thoroughly to the test. Although I had spent thousands of hours in church and religious instruction, God, for me, was not an inner experience but a remote, stern, and punishing father figure. Fear, on the other hand, was present and very real in my life. It persisted and at times threatened to overwhelm me. When I had no place left to turn, I surrendered. I risked letting go, and with that my heart began to open to the truth that God is the sacred life-giving, life-sustaining energy that flows through us, all of us, all of the time. As I yielded, even to the possibility that this could be true, the fears that blanketed me, blinding my vision, began to lift, revealing a world of light and abundant opportunity. I was blessed to have my daughter, my mother, and friends whom I loved and who loved me. I had my health, my hopes and dreams, and the proud heritage of Black folk who had triumphed over obstacles greater than mine. There was so much to sustain me that I had lost sight of. What is still unfolding for me today is that faith is remembering who you are and Whose you are. I seek confirmation daily in the wisdom of 1 Corinthians 3:16:

"Know ye not that ye are the temple of God, and that the Spirit of God dwelleth in you?"

Choosing faith over fear is really a conscious decision to live in the present, with the understanding that no matter what the circumstances are, no matter what you are experiencing, the present is where God is.

I

Fear

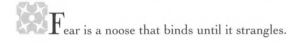Fear is a noose that binds until it strangles.

—JEAN TOOMER

I'll tell you why I highlight Muhammad Ali here, what we saw there, especially given the influence of Malcolm X, was the example of a Black person, in his case, a Black man, who was free from fear and failure. Fear and failure haunt Black people every minute of their lives. . . .

Black people rarely get free from their fear of the White gaze, the fear of Black put-down, the fear of stepping out on their own and being independent. There is a fear of failure deeply ingrained in the Black psyche, because the stereotypical image, which we have largely internalized, is that Black people are always failing. So we have many individuals who fear success, fear that if you are too successful you will be alienated from Black people. Hence we see individuals failing because the anxiety of possible failure after attempted success is so intense.

What I liked about Muhammad Ali was that he was already free in his mind to speak whatever was on his mind, even if he failed, and even if he said something that was controversial. Malcolm X was the same way. And, to that degree, it freed us up. It was empowering for those of us who wanted to be free from fear and failure.

—CORNEL WEST, in dialogue with bell hooks, *Breaking Bread: Insurgent Black Intellectual Life*

We can easily forgive a child who is afraid of the dark; the real tragedy is when men are afraid of the light.

—PLATO

Fear can be a big stopper for many of us: fear of fragility, fear of failure, fear of making a mistake, fear of what others might think, *fear of success*. We may second-guess our next action or word until we talk ourselves out of participating in life.

"But I failed before!" "I can't do it good enough!" "Look at what happened last time!" "What if . . . ?" These statements may disguise fear. Sometimes the fear is disguising shame.

After I finished the first two chapters of a book I was writing, I read them and grimaced. "No good," I thought. "Can't do it." I was ready to pitch the chapters, and my writing career, out the window. A writer friend called, and I told her about my problem. She listened and told me: "Those chapters are fine. Stop being afraid. Stop criticizing yourself. And keep on writing."

I followed her advice. The book I almost threw away became a *New York Times* best-seller.

Relax. Our best is good enough. It may be better than we think. Even our failures may turn out to be important learning experiences that lead directly to—and are necessary for—an upcoming success.

Feel the fear, then let it go. Jump in and do it—whatever it is. If our instincts and path have led us there, it's where we need to be.

—MELODY BEATTIE, *The Language of Letting Go*

Do not be too timid and squeamish about your actions. All life is an experiment. The more experiments you make the better. What if they are a little coarse, and you may get your coat soiled or torn? What if you do fail, and get fairly rolled in the dirt once or twice? Up again; you shall never be so afraid of a tumble.

—RALPH WALDO EMERSON

Many people go through life accomplishing nothing because they are unwilling to do anything for fear of making a mistake. There is no need to be afraid of mistakes or even of failures. Any mistakes which may be made by a person who is obedient to the still small voice will be few, and they will not be sufficiently serious to be irretrievable; he can quickly pick himself up again and soon be wholly immersed in the Spirit. Mistakes are not fatal; not one is forever: Success is forever, but failure is only for a day.

— JOEL S. GOLDSMITH, *Practicing the Presence*

The ego finds the world a dangerous, hostile place, because everything that exists is separate from "I." This is the condition known as duality, and it is a great source of fear — the Veda calls it the only source of fear. As we look "out there," we see every kind of potential threat, all the trauma and pain that life can inflict. The ego's logical defense is to wall itself in with the friendlier things — family, pleasures, happy memories, familiar places and activities. . . . [But] life is a field of unlimited possibilities.

— DEEPAK CHOPRA, *Quantum Healing*

We avoid the things that we're afraid of because we think there will be dire consequences if we confront them. But the truly dire consequences in our lives come from avoiding things that we need to learn about or discover. We must instead learn to be more open and accepting of the things we're afraid of, whether it's exploring our emotions, or learning to balance our checkbook! Acceptance is simply a willingness to look at, confront, and understand something instead of pushing it away.

— SHAKTI GAWAIN, *The Path of Transformation*

They wore their crippleness or blindness like a badge of honor, as though it meant they'd been singled out for some special punishment, were special. Or as though it meant they'd paid some heavy dues and knew, then, what there was to know, and therefore had a right to certain privileges, or were exempt from certain charges, or ought to be listened to at meetings. But way down under knowing "special" was a lie, knowing better all along and feeling the cost of the lie, of the self-betrayal in the joints, in the lungs, in the eyes. Knew, felt the cost, but were too proud and too scared to get downright familiar with the conniption fit getting downright familiar with their bodies, minds, spirits to just sing, "Blues, how do you do? Sit down, let's work it out." Took heart to flat out decide to be well and stride into the future sane and whole. And it took time. —TONI CADE BAMBARA, *The Salt Eaters*

I believe that every single event in life happens as an opportunity to choose love over fear. Everything good in my life has resulted from having chosen love, by which I mean joy, hope and acceptance of the spiritual quest we are born with. Under the heading fear comes the feeling that we're not good enough, not deserving enough; society tells you that fulfillment comes from gaining material goods. But something deep inside you recognizes that there's got to be more to life. And that longing is the longing to love yourself. —OPRAH WINFREY in *More Reflections on the Meaning of Life*

When apparent stability disintegrates,
As it must—
God is Change—
People tend to give in
To fear and depression,
To need and greed.
When no influence is strong enough
To unify people
They divide.
They struggle,
One against one,
Group against group,
For survival, position, power.
They remember old hates and generate new ones,

They create chaos and nurture it.
They kill and kill and kill,
Until they are exhausted and destroyed,
Until they are conquered by outside forces,
Or until one of them becomes
A leader
Most will follow,
Or a tyrant
Most fear.

—OCTAVIA BUTLER, *Parable of the Sower*

Fear cannot be real without a cause. God is the only cause of everything that is real. All else is illusion. For this reason, there is nothing to fear—not even death or the end of the world. Ultimately, everything rests in the arms of God. Though there are passages calling for the fear of God in the Old Testament, God is not the author of fear. What is really being called for is respect for God—which calls for the relinquishing of our egos in favor of guidance from Holy Spirit. The ego is the author of fear, and if there is one thing we are not, it is our egos.

I would like to share a dream I had a long time ago. It was one of those vivid dreams that stays with you. It said more about how love overcomes fear than mere words could ever do.

In the dream I was with two other young men. We were walking and came upon a peninsula with an amusement park on it. On the edge of the park was a tunnel, like a tunnel of love—only this was the *tunnel of fear*. One of the young men was particularly anxious to show us the inside of the tunnel. Though the other young man was very resistant to going through the tunnel, for some reason the two of them went through while I walked around on the outside. When they came out at the other end, the hair of the fellow who had been resistant had turned white. He fell on the ground in a fit, foaming at the mouth.

After a while, the young man recovered and my companions proceeded further onto the peninsula, but I decided to stay behind. I climbed into the top of the tunnel through an attic or loft-like door, much like the one on our barn when I was a boy. It was my intention to expose the inside of this place and show that it was just machinery that had caused my friend to become so fearful.

When I entered the loft, I found that indeed the place was filled with demonic creatures, just as one would see in a book on demonology. I looked at them and proceeded to walk into the room. As I did, they started to back away respectfully. I realized that as long as I was not afraid they were powerless over me. For some reason, however, I was not afraid and kept moving forward. They kept moving back. Finally I stopped, and one of the larger and more human-looking ones approached me. She asked me if I would like to see the devil himself. I said I would, and she led me into a side room.

The devil himself was a little boy sitting in an aluminum lawn chair, with his arms resting regally on the arms of the chair and his head bent down to his chest as though he were pouting about something. I walked over to him, knelt down beside him, put my arms around him and said, "I love you. I love you." As I said that he began to shake violently and started to scream "No. No. You can't say that!" And puff! he disappeared like so much gas. At that very instant, I awoke.

The dream was a clear reminder that in the presence of love, fear is absolutely powerless.

—JON MUNDY, *Awaken to Your Own Call*

Greater than fear is Love.

Love dissolves all fear, casts out all doubt and sets the captive free.

Love, like the River of Life, flows through me and refreshes me with its eternal blessings.

Love cannot be afraid; it is fearless and strong, and is mighty in its works.

It can accomplish all things through the Inner Light of that faith in the All Good,

Which fills my very Being with a Powerful Presence.

Love casts out all fear.

—ERNEST HOLMES, *The Science of Mind*

We have been brought up in a world that does not put love first, and where love is absent, fear sets in. Fear is to love as darkness is to light. It's a terrible absence of what we need in order to survive. Fear is the root of all evil. It's the problem with the world. — MARIANNE WILLIAMSON, *A Return to Love*

Those who love to be feared, fear to be loved, and they themselves are more afraid than anyone, for whereas other men fear only them, they fear everyone. — ST. FRANCIS DE SALES

Never should an aspect of identity that perceived itself as separate from God dictate behavior. — KEN CAREY

Open yourself to your fellow humans. Allow yourself to experience what you feel toward them, and to hear what they feel. Your interactions with them form the basis of your growth. When you fear what you will find in yourself, or what you will find in others, if you allow yourself to hear what others have to say, you turn your back on the opportunities that the Universe is giving you to find the power of your heart, the power of compassion. It is not until you have the courage to engage in human relationships that you grow. — GARY ZUKAV, *The Seat of the Soul*

[W]hen I first had cancer, I had the awesome realization that fear was my master in every area of my life. This was a tremendous feeling of total powerlessness. I knew I had to take charge of my fear because it was destroying my life. But how to do that?

I began to ask God to enter my life at every moment. As I would pick up the phone to make a call, fear would fill my throat and block me. When I answered the door to greet another human being, or had a creative thought or vision, fear would come in and block me from going forward. Fear was my master. Sound familiar?

I began to ask God for help in every way: God, speak through me; God, act through me. I would then let go and trust to the help of God. I didn't know it then, but I was indeed letting go to God in every sense of the word; however, I didn't think of it that way. *It was the only thing that worked.* I asked God for help every moment of the day. I realized that my pride and guilt had prevented me from reaching out for the help and guidance I so desperately needed. I further realized that if we want help with something, we need to ask! This is a necessary part of a successful life. In this manner, we are exercising faith, trust, confidence and humility. God answers all prayers, sometimes not in the form we visualize, but an answer always comes; it is up to us to identify that answer, interpret it and receive it. . . .

—ANGELA PASSIDOMO TRAFFORD, *The Heroic Path: One Woman's Journey from Cancer to Self-Healing*

It was a dark night, early summer, finally turning warm. As Grandpa Joe slipped out of the car, I called to him to ask for his advice. I had been warned that the bears of the mountains were now active especially at night. It was dangerous to walk in the woods in the dark. And furthermore, last summer a bear had actually come and circled the very tipi where I was now living, for it is pitched a good twenty minutes' walk further up the mountain from the other Lama dwellings.

"Grandpa," I asked, "tonight I must walk alone in the dark a long way to get to my tipi. Perhaps I will meet a bear. What should I do? Should I talk to the bear? Should I send it love?"

Grandpa leaned back and we shared a gentle space of silence together. Then he gave me this advice. "No talk to bear. Talk to God!"

—SUNYATA SARASWATI, interdisciplinary healer

Drowning people

Sometimes die

Fighting their rescuers.

—OCTAVIA BUTLER, *Parable of the Sower*

For it is not death or hardship that is a fearful thing, but the fear of hardship and death.

—EPICTETUS

As I approached the mountain, I thought I perceived a monster, but as I came closer, I saw that it was not a monster but a man. And as I came even closer, I saw that he was my brother.

—ANONYMOUS

ANTIDOTES FOR FEAR

Our problem is not to be rid of fear but rather to harness and master it. How may it be mastered?

First, we must unflinchingly face our fears and honestly ask ourselves why we are afraid. This confrontation will, to some measure, grant us power. We shall never be cured of fear by escapism or repression, for the more we attempt to ignore and repress our fears, the more we multiply our inner conflicts. . . .

And let us also remember that, more often than not, fear involves the misuse of the imagination. When we get our fears into the open, we may laugh at some of them, and this is good. One psychiatrist said, "Ridicule is the master cure for fear and anxiety."

Second, we can master fear through one of the supreme virtues known to man: courage. Plato considered courage to be an element of the soul which bridges the cleavage between reason and desire. Aristotle thought of courage as the affirmation of man's essential nature. Thomas Aquinas said that courage is the strength of mind capable of conquering whatever threatens the attainment of the highest good.

Courage, therefore, is the power of the mind to overcome fear. Unlike anxiety, fear has a definite object which may be faced, analyzed, attacked, and, if need be, endured. How often the object of our fear is fear itself! . . .

Courage, the determination not to be overwhelmed by any object, however frightful, enables us to stand up to any fear. . . .

Third, fear is mastered through love. The New Testament affirms, "There is no fear in love; but perfect love casteth out fear." The kind of love which led Christ to a cross and kept Paul unembittered amid the angry torrents of persecution is not soft, anemic, and sentimental. Such love confronts evil without flinching and shows in our popular parlance an infinite capacity "to take it." Such love overcomes the world even from a rough-hewn cross against the skyline. . . .

Hatred and bitterness can never cure the disease of fear; only love can do that. Hatred paralyzes life; love releases it. Hatred confuses life; love harmonizes it. Hatred darkens life; love illuminates it.

Fourth, fear is mastered through faith. A common source of fear is an awareness of deficient resources and of a consequent inadequacy for life. All too many people attempt to face the tensions of life with inadequate spiritual resources.

A positive religious faith does not offer an illusion that we shall be exempt from pain and suffering, nor does it imbue us with the idea that life is a drama of unalloyed comfort and untroubled ease. Rather, it instills us with the inner equilibrium needed to face strains, burdens, and fears that inevitably come, and assures us that the universe is trustworthy and that God is concerned. . . .

Beneath and above the shifting sands of time, the uncertainties that darken our days, and the vicissitudes that cloud our nights is a wise and loving God. This universe is not a tragic expression of meaningless chaos but a marvelous display of orderly cosmos. . . . Any man who finds this cosmic sustenance can walk the highways of life without the fatigue of pessimism and the weight of morbid fears.

Herein lies the answer to the neurotic fear of death that plagues so many of our lives. . . .

This faith transforms the whirlwind of despair into a warm and reviving breeze of hope. The words of a motto which a generation ago were commonly found on the wall in the homes of devout persons need to be etched on our hearts:

> *Fear knocked at the door.*
> *Faith answered.*
> *There was no one there.*

—MARTIN LUTHER KING, JR., *The Strength to Love*

Some of us are timid. We think we have something to lose so we don't try for that next hill or that next rise. The truth is we have nothing to lose—nothing. Shakespeare said that we would "rather bear those ills we have than fly to others that we know not of." Thus, conscience does make cowards of us all because we would rather just stay right here and not dare. Yet the young person who knows and is informed dares enough to understand that life loves the liver of it. Life loves to be taken by the lapel and be told: "I am with you, kid. Let's go."

—MAYA ANGELOU, interviewed in *And Still We Rise* by Barbara Reynolds

**B**e still and know that I am God.

—OLD TESTAMENT

II

Faith

Faith is the substance of things hoped for, the evidence of things not seen. —HEBREWS 11:1

You cannot stay on the summit for ever; you have to come down again . . . So why bother in the first place? Just this: what is above knows what is below, but what is below does not know what is above.

One climbs, one sees. One descends, one sees no longer but one has seen. There is an art to conducting oneself in the lower regions by the memory of what one saw higher up. When one can no longer see, one can at least still know.

—RENÉ DAUMAL, *Mount Analogue*

Speaking of knowing, my primary identity—before that of a religious person—is that of a scientist. We scientists are what are called empiricists. Empiricism holds that the best—not the only, but the best—route to knowledge is through experience. So what do we scientists do but conduct experiments—or controlled experiences—from which we can learn and eventually know? Thus it has been through the experiences of my life—my experiences of grace—that I have come to what little knowledge I have about God.

In this regard, I am very much like Carl Jung, another scientist. Toward the end of his life he submitted himself to a film interview. After many rather prosaic questions, the interviewer finally said, "Dr. Jung, a lot of your writing has a religious flavor. Do you believe in God?"

Old Jung puffed on his pipe. "Believe in God?" he mused out loud. "Well, we use the word 'believe' when we think that something is true but we don't yet have a substantial body of evidence to support it. No. I don't believe in God. I *know* there's a God."

— M. SCOTT PECK, *Further Along the Road Less Traveled*

Faith is personal, individual, nondenominational, stemming from a cosmic respect for the natural order of things—the recognition that there must be systems and balance, law and values, if there is to be purpose, meaning, and success in life.

— AUDREY EDWARDS AND CRAIG K. POLITE, *Children of the Dream*

Faith, as we understand it here . . . means the practical conviction that the universe, between the hands of the Creator, still continues to be the clay in which he shapes innumerable possibilities according to his will. . . . If we do not believe, the waves engulf us, the winds blow, nourishment fails, sickness lays us low or kills us, the divine power is impotent or remote. If, on the other hand, we believe, the waters are welcoming and sweet, the bread is multiplied, our eyes open, the dead rise again, the power of God is, as it were, drawn from him by force and spreads throughout all nature. One must either arbitrarily minimize or explain away the Gospel, or one must admit the reality of these effects not as transient and past, but as perennial and true at this moment. Let us beware of stifling this revelation of a possible vitalization of the forces of nature in God. Let us, rather, place it resolutely at the center of our vision of the world. . . . Under the influence of our faith, the universe is capable, without outwardly changing its characteristics, of becoming more supple, more fully animate. . . .

If we believe, then everything is illuminated and takes shape around us: chance is seen to be order, success assumes an incorruptible plenitude, suffering becomes a visit and a caress of God. But if we hesitate, the rock remains dry, the sky dark, the waters treacherous and shifting. And we may hear the voice of the Master, faced with our bungled lives: "O men of little faith, why have you doubted . . . ?"

— PIERRE TEILHARD DE CHARDIN, *The Divine Milieu*

Our faith is faith in someone else's faith, and in the greatest matters this is most the case.

— WILLIAM JAMES

It is necessary to the happiness of man that he be mentally faithful to himself. Infidelity does not consist in believing, or in disbelieving; it consists in professing to believe what he does not believe.

— THOMAS PAINE

Faith—in Ortega y Gasset's sense of the term, "individual faith"—not faith in what one has been told to believe, or thinks may be propitious to believe—but faith in one's own experience.

— JOSEPH CAMPBELL

Life must be played by ear—which is only to say that we must trust, not symbolic rules and linear principles, but our brains or natures. Yet this must bring one back to the faith that nature makes no mistake. In such a universe a decision which results in one's own death is not a mistake: it is simply a way of dying at the right moment. . . .

As in music, the point of life is its pattern at every stage of its development, and in a world where there is neither self nor other, the only identity is just This—which is all, which is energy, which is God by no name.

— ALAN WATTS, *In My Own Way*

When our reality is truly "faith in God, in God we trust," our fear cannot exist. If you truly have trust and faith in God, then you have no reason to fear anybody or anything in this life. Fear is a strong power, but faith is much stronger. An old saying goes, "Fear knocked at the door. Faith answered. No one was there." Another negative pattern that cannot operate in the presence of faith is excessive worry. Worry is torment; it creates doubts and anxieties to sustain itself, which in turn takes the worrier away from optimism, hope, and faith. . . .

Faith is an inner knowing that takes you beyond belief to a state of oneness with loving trust. Faith is positive energy focused on a desire or conviction that you want to come to pass. Faith is very powerful energy in its raw state. Faith becomes brighter through right action, and loses its glow with inertia. When you declare faith, to keep it working you must make it you—that is, you must become one with it so you are not thinking about it but only guided by it. Your actions and practices will bring about desired outcomes when you unite with your faith. Angels are always there to guard your positive thinking and faith; so when you lose some of your faith, ask for more from God and the angels.

—TERRY LYNN TAYLOR, *Guardians of Hope*

Belief

Initiates and guides action—
Or it does nothing.

—OCTAVIA BUTLER, *Parable of the Sower*

Faith is the prime requisite to success. The degree of one's faith in anything, either positive or negative, causes it to take physical form. It is next to impossible to talk and think one way and experience the opposite.

—DOUG HOOPER, *You Are What You Think*

It is done unto you as you believe.

Jesus proclaimed a law of faith that acts on your belief. . . . At the expense of repetition let us look into this a little more carefully, because it is of such importance. It is this little word *as* that you are to consider the meaning of. Not only is there a law which does something for you (this is easy enough to accept) but in doing so it is limited to *your belief*. This is the important thing to remember.

It is only common sense to recognize that what this law does for you it must, of necessity, do through you. The gift of Life is not complete until it is accepted. If you can believe only in a little good, then the law will be compelled to operate on that little good. Not that the law of itself knows anything about big and little any more than the law of gravitation would know that a mountain is heavier than a marble — it automatically holds everything in place. If you remove a large pile of gravel it will hold this bulk in place. If you dip up but a few thimblefuls it will hold this smaller amount in place with equal impartiality.

Now, shift this whole proposition over into the mental plane, realizing that the mental reproduces the physical, but at a higher level. The law is always a mirror reflecting your mental attitudes. Therefore, if you say, "I can have a little good," it will produce this small amount of good for you, but if you say, "All the good there is is mine," with equal certainty it will produce a larger good. If you believe that wherever you go you will meet with love and friendship, with appreciation and gratitude, then this will become the law of your life.

— ERNEST HOLMES, *This Thing Called You*

Actually, the will of God is the ceaseless desire of the Creator to perfect Himself in that which He has created. It is the healing, guiding, adjusting activity within each individual that has no other work than to "perfect that which concerneth me."

There is nothing uncertain about God's will, nor is it something to be feared. It is wise and practical for any person, faced with a crisis or need, to let go of tension and fear by praying, "Father, let Thy will be done in and through me." For the Father within sees the whole picture, beyond man's limited vision, and knows the solution that is best for him in terms of his highest ultimate good. This activity is so sure and certain that even when it seems that our prayer has not been answered, the very delay itself may very well be the answer.

— ERIC BUTTERWORTH, *Life Is for Living*

His manifestations fill up the world for everyone to see, but only those who have faith notice them. . . . To those who have faith, He offers the opportunity to become one with Him. As this Buddha is the all-inclusive body of equality, whoever thinks of Buddha, Buddha thinks of him and enters his mind freely.

— THE BUDDHA

At the present time, when there is greater and greater insecurity outwardly, there is obviously a yearning for inward security. Since we cannot find security outside, we seek it in an idea, in thought, and so we create that which we call God, and that concept becomes our security. Now a mind that seeks security surely cannot find the real, the true. To understand that which is beyond time, the fabrications of thought must come to an end. Thought cannot exist without words, symbols, images. And only when the mind is quiet, free of its own creations, is there a possibility of finding out what is real. So merely to ask if there is or is not God is an immature response to the problem, is it not? To formulate opinions about God is really childish.

To experience, to realize that which is beyond time, we must obviously understand the process of time. The mind is the result of time, it is based on the memories of yesterday. And is it possible to be free from the multiplication of yesterdays that is the process of time? Surely this is a very serious problem; it is not a matter of belief or disbelief? Believing and disbelieving is a process of ignorance, whereas understanding the time-binding quality of thought brings freedom in which alone there can be discovery. But most of us want to believe because it is much more convenient; it gives us a sense of security, a sense of belonging to the group. Surely this very belief separates us; you believe in one thing and I believe in another. So belief acts as a barrier; it is a process of disintegration.

What is important, then, is not the cultivation of belief or disbelief, but to understand the process of the mind. It is the mind, it is thought that creates time. Thought is time, and whatever thought projects must be of time; therefore, thought cannot possibly go beyond itself. To discover what is beyond time, thought must come to an end, and that is a most difficult thing because the ending of thought does not come about through discipline, through control, through denial or suppression. Thought ends only when we understand the whole process of thinking, and to understand thinking there must be self-knowledge. Thought is the self, thought is the word that identifies itself as the "me" and, at whatever level the self is placed, high or low, it is still within the field of thought.

To find God, that which is beyond time, we must understand the process of thought—that is, the process of oneself. The self is very complex; it is not at any one level, but is made up of many thoughts, many entities, each in contradiction with the others. There must be a constant awareness of them all, an awareness in which there is no choice, no condemnation or comparison; that is, there must be the capacity to see things as they are without distorting or translating them. The moment we judge or translate what is seen, we distort it according to our background. To discover reality or God, there can be no belief because acceptance or denial is a barrier to discovery. We all want to be secure both outwardly and inwardly, and the mind must understand that the search for security is an illusion. It is only the mind that is insecure, completely free from any form of possession that can discover—and this is an arduous task. It does not mean retiring into the woods, or to a monastery, or isolating oneself in some peculiar belief; on the contrary, nothing can exist in isolation. To be is to be related; it is only in the midst of relationship that we can spontaneously discover ourselves as we are. It is this very discovery of ourselves as we are, without any sense of condemnation or justification, that brings about a fundamental transformation in what we are. And that is the beginning of wisdom. —J. KRISHNAMURTI, *On God*

[T]he concept of faith has lost its genuine meaning and has received the connotation of "belief in something unbelievable." . . .

Certainly there is faith in the elevation of the soul above the finite to the infinite, leading to its union with the ground of being. But more than this is included in the concept of faith. And there is faith in the personal encounter with the personal God. But more than this is included in the concept of faith. Faith is the state of being grasped by the power of being-itself. . . . Faith is not a theoretical affirmation of something uncertain, it is the existential acceptance of something transcending ordinary experience. Faith is not an opinion but a state. It is the state of being grasped by the power of being which transcends everything that is and in which everything that is participates. He who is grasped by this power is able to affirm himself because he knows that he is affirmed by the power of being-itself. In this point mystical experience and personal encounter are identical. In both of them faith is the basis of the courage to be. . . .

— PAUL TILLICH, *The Courage to Be*

A faith is something you die for, a doctrine is something you kill for. There is all the difference in the world.

— TONY BENN

Waiting is a window opening on many landscapes. . . . To continue one's journey in the darkness with one's footsteps guided by the illumination of remembered radiance is to know courage of a peculiar kind—the courage to demand that light continue to be light even in the surrounding darkness. To walk in the light while darkness invades, envelops, and surrounds is to wait on the Lord. This is to know the renewal of strength. This is to walk and faint not.

— HOWARD THURMAN, *The Inward Journey*

CHAPTER FIVE

It's All in Divine Order

Everything is in divine order. To what degree and in what detail has divinity fashioned our destinies? There are times when, despite all our efforts in one direction, the current of life seems to take us in another. It's often only in retrospect—weeks or months or years later—that we are able to see the fortuitousness of the turn of events.

The fact that I'm a writer today, living in New York City and happily married to Susan, hinges in part on the fact that in 1975 in Oakland, California, I didn't get the apartment I wanted. It had been rented (or so I was told) just moments before I arrived. Frustrated, I was forced to settle for something else in another neighborhood, and that apartment, it turned out, was situated right above the apartment of a writer, Ilunga Adell, and his wife, Rosalyn (now lifelong friends of mine). It had never crossed my mind that I could make a living as a writer until I met Ilunga. Long story short: He introduced me to television producer Ellis Haizlip, who hired me to work in television in New York City and introduced me to Susan. If things had worked out the way *I'd* wanted them to in 1975, I would probably be leading a very different life.

Call it the hand of God or the organic pattern of the universe, but there is a divine order that serves as the template for all life. We sometimes see hints of its blurred outline when looking back at our lives after the passage of time. But it is most supremely evident in the macrocosm—viewed from the beautiful blue-green oasis we call earth, spinning in the vacuum of space while circling our sun; the sun just one among a hundred billion stars in our galaxy, and our galaxy itself but one in a billion born billions of years ago in the genesis of the Big Bang. And all of it formed virtually from nothing, for in the beginning there was no matter, just electrons, neutrinos, gravity, and light. And in these—the proverbial mustard seeds of an entire universe—were the divine blueprints and patterns for worlds to come, for the rhythms of life and the music of the spheres to arise.

Gravity ignited the stars that shine, and their light in time begat eyes in us to see God's glory. A world of vibrant sound inspired the evolution of ears, and it was the same for scents and the sense of smell. The patterns repeat throughout nature. Animals have mouths for feeding and plants have roots for drawing nutrients from soil and water. All forms of life have systems for transforming matter into energy, growth, and movement. We are the products of a divinely balanced, self-sustaining, self-adjusting universe that to scientists and religious scholars alike is nothing short of miraculous. This divine order is the love, protection, and assurance that God provides.

"Consider the lilies of the field," said Jesus in Matthew 6:28. They neither toil nor spin, but simply are according to their nature. The same laws that govern the universe and protect the lilies of the field also support us. Life is on our side. And this is the truth of the miracle of our being, the reality of our nature.

We human beings find it difficult to relax and just *be*, but when we do we find that the universe is there to support us, and that everything we need at that moment comes together to ensure our success. In these moments we move in perfect harmony with the rhythm of life.

God delights in its manifestation—in the eternal dynamic process of evolving life in infinite variety out of the oneness of its being and then allowing it to resolve back into oneness again, gathering all into its divine embrace. God is One, the beginning and the end, the Alpha and Omega. There is nothing outside of or other than God. Who, then, are we? If you know who you are, and you know from whence you came and where you're going, then you know in fact that you are neither coming nor going; you are here, and there is nowhere for you to go. As an aspect of that divinely ordered universe we call God, you have your existence here in the eternal now of God's being. And right here, right now, there is beauty to be enjoyed and all manner of God's manifestation to take delight in.

Every experience—oneness, individuality, sound, silence, sorrow, joy—has its purpose and is perfect in its time and place in our lives. That we can look back on our lives and see that this is true reassures us that there is a divine order at work. That we can't look forward and see how our challenges will be met and our crises resolved is a blessing. While knowing what the future holds might relieve us of some anxiety, it would also rob us of the excitement of anticipation, the incentive to be creative, and the joy of living. God, being omniscient, may in fact manifest as us in order to enjoy *not* knowing what the future holds, to enjoy being challenged, surprised, anxious, hopeful—all that we experience, including all that we complain about. When you're God, no experience is out of reach. Nor is any too scary, tragic, or sad since, being infinite, you know that they, too, are a part of you, and being omnipotent, nothing can harm you. Remembering who we are helps us to experience all that life has to offer from a higher perspective and more peaceful place.

There is a secret to everything. The seed works underground, sometimes for long periods of time, before it puts forth its green leaf; and throughout its growth its laboratory is still most secret. In the works of men, the mechanism that produces the fair showing is invariably hidden: the works of a watch, the kitchen that produces the banquet, the long hours of practice that produce the virtuoso performance. There is always a secret region of causation.

—ERIC BUTTERWORTH, *Discover the Power Within You*

Always think of the universe as one living organism, with a single substance and a single soul; and observe how all things are submitted to the single perceptivity of this one whole, all are moved by its single impulse, and all play their part in the causation of every event that happens. Remark the intricacy of the skein, the complexity of the web. . . .

All things are interwoven with one another; a sacred bond unites them; there is scarcely one thing that is isolated from another. Everything is coordinated, everything works together in giving form to the one universe. The world-order is a unity made up of multiplicity: God is one, pervading all things; all being is one, all law is one . . . and all truth is one.

—MARCUS AURELIUS, *Meditations*

The world is not to be put in order, the world is order. It is for us to put ourselves in unison with this order.

—HENRY MILLER

Here is an affirmation that has been a help and an influence in my life on countless occasions: *"God's law of adjustment regulates all the affairs of my life, and all things are in divine order."* In the face of injustice, indecision, inharmony, or the insecurity of great change, speak this word of Truth. Affirm it again and again—not to make it true or to stir God into action, but to let the activity of that which is true be established "in earth, as *it is* in heaven (A.V.)."

There are no impossibilities in God, only the divine possible which is God's answer before we call. In God, under divine law, there is neither big nor little. It takes no more effort for gravity to hold a mountain steadfast than to hold the tiniest wisp of a feather. It is only in the mind of man that problems appear big or little, hard or easy. That which we seek to do is done according to our attitude of mind, our expectation. It becomes difficult if we believe it will be. It might even be impossible of solution, if we accept it in that light. However, at any moment faith may lay hold of the divine possible, even if it takes what the human mind calls a miracle, and the desired good will be established.

There is a sense in which we are closer to God in times of trouble than at other times. Of course in actuality there can be neither closeness or distance in relation to God, for God is omnipresent and omniactive. But wherever a problem appears, there is a force field set up around it which is the activity of the divine law of adjustment seeking to resolve the problem into a pattern that is good.

—ERIC BUTTERWORTH, *Life Is for Living*

I am convinced that the universe is under the control of a loving purpose, and that in the struggle for righteousness man has cosmic companionship. Behind the harsh appearance of the world there is a benign power.

—MARTIN LUTHER KING, JR.

The fact that our experiences are results of our actions is not a system of punishment and reward. When a flower grows from a seed, it's neither a reward nor a punishment of the seed. It's merely a result. Similarly, when our actions bring our future experiences, these are results of our actions, not their rewards or punishments. . . . We don't say it's unfair that an object falls down and not up, for we know that no one invented gravity. Gravity isn't due to someone's favoritism. It's simply the way things naturally function. Similarly, no one made the rule that if we harm others now, we'll have problems in the future. This is simply the natural result arising from that cause.

—THUBTEN CHODRON, *Open Heart, Clear Mind*

It's difficult enough, day by day, to try to envision and understand God's overall plan for us. It's especially hard when tragedies occur, or when we must face major disappointments. How can we learn to accept and deal with unfolding events that are not always to our liking? How can we gain increasing trust in God's sometimes seemingly mysterious ways?

What helps me is to try to change my perspective of myself, acknowledging first that I am but one of millions upon millions of God's children. I stand back and try to see myself and the things that happen in my life as an infinitesimal part of God's limitless and ever-changing universe.

When I get into that meditational frame of mind, I then visualize myself as a small tile—a single tile in a splendid and beautiful mosaic of God's creation.

If I come in really close, focusing only on myself, all I can see is the single tile. However, if I step back and broaden my field of vision, I am able to imagine the entire mosaic in all its glory and perfection. When I can do this, it invariably helps me again to accept myself and what occurs in my life as a necessary part of God's larger plan.

You are only one part, but an integral part, of God's glorious mosaic.

—ANONYMOUS, *A New Day: 365 Meditations for Personal and Spiritual Growth*

"The elements of all things," she began, "whatever their mode,
observe an inner order. It is this form
that makes the universe resemble God.
In this the higher creatures see the hand
 of the Eternal Worth, which is the goal
 to which these norms conduce, being so planned.

All Being within this order, by the laws
 of its own nature is impelled to find
 its proper station round its Primal Cause.

Thus every nature moves across the tide
 of the great sea of being to its own port,
 each with its given instinct as its guide.

This instinct draws the fire about the moon.
 It is the mover in the mortal heart.
 It draws the earth together and makes it one.

Not only the brute creatures, but all those
 possessed of intellect and love, this instinct
 drives to their mark as a bow shoots forth its arrows.

The Providence that makes all things hunger here
 satisfies forever with its light
 the heaven within which whirls the fastest sphere."

   —DANTE ALIGHIERI, *The Divine Comedy: Paradiso* (voice of Beatrice, Dante's angel guide)

WHAT IS SOCIAL SECURITY?

I was awakened in the morning before any exposure to sun rays by the noise from people gathering up the few scattered articles we had used the evening before. I was told the days gained in heat, so we would walk during the cooler morning hours, rest, and then resume our journey into the later night. I folded the dingo hide and handed it to a man who was packing. The hides were left easily accessible, because during the peak heat of the day, we would find shelter, build a *wiltja,* or temporary brush shelter, or use our sleeping skins to construct shade.

Most of the animals do not like the glaring sun. Only the lizards, spiders, and bush flies are alert and active at one hundred plus degrees. Even snakes must bury themselves in the extreme heat, or they become dehydrated and die. It is hard sometimes to spot snakes as they hear us coming and peek their heads out of the sandy soil to find the source of the vibration. I am grateful that at the time I was not aware there are two hundred different types of snakes in Australia, and more than seventy are poisonous.

I did learn that day, however, the remarkable relationship the Aborigines have with nature. Before we started walking for the day, we formed a close-knit semicircle, all of us facing the east. The Tribal Elder moved to the center and started chanting. A beat was established and carried through by each person clapping their hands, stomping their feet, or hitting their thighs. It lasted about fifteen minutes. This was routine each morning, and I discovered that it was a very important part of our life together. It was morning (prayer, centering, goal setting, whatever you want to call it). These people believe everything exists on the planet for a reason. Everything has a purpose. There are no freaks, misfits, or accidents. There are only misunderstandings and mysteries not yet revealed to mortal man.

The purpose of the plant kingdom is to feed animals and humans, to hold the soil together, to enhance beauty, to balance the atmosphere. I was told the plants and trees sing to us humans silently, and all they ask in return is for us to sing to them. My scientific mind immediately translated this to mean nature's oxygen–carbon dioxide exchange. The primary purpose of the animal is not to feed humans, but it agrees to that when necessary. It is to balance the atmosphere, and be a companion and teacher by example. So each morning the tribe sends out a thought or message to the animals and plants in front of us. They say, "We are walking your way. We are coming to honor your purpose for existence." It is up to the plants and animals to make their own arrangements about who will be chosen.

The Real People tribe never go without food. Always, the universe responds to their mind-talk. They believe the world is a place of abundance. Just as you and I might gather to listen to someone play the piano, and honor that talent and purpose, they sincerely do the same thing with everything in nature. When a snake appeared on our path, it was obviously there to provide our dinner. The daily food was a very important part of our evening celebration. I learned that the appearance of food was not taken for granted. It was first requested, always expected to appear, and did appear, but was gratefully received and genuine gratitude was always given. The tribe begins each day by saying thank you to Oneness for the day, for themselves, their friends, and the world. They sometimes ask for specifics, but it is always phrased "If it is in my highest good and the highest good for all life everywhere." . . .

The tribe carried no provisions. They planted no crops; they participated in no harvest. They walked the blazing Australian Outback, knowing each day they would receive bountiful blessings of the universe. The universe never disappointed them. — MARLO MORGAN, *Mutant Message Down Under*

If you would find the highest, the fullest, and the richest life that not only this world but that any world can know, then do away with the sense of the separateness of your life from the life of God. . . . Then it will be yours, without fears or forebodings, simply to do today what your hands find to do, and so be ready for tomorrow when it comes, knowing that tomorrow will bring tomorrow's supplies for the mental, the spiritual, and the physical life. Remember, however, that tomorrow's supplies are not needed until tomorrow comes. — RALPH WALDO TRINE, *In Tune with the Infinite*

In some way which you know not of, through some process which never reveals its face, Life has entered into you and with it the irresistible impulse to create. Divine Intelligence has willed it so, nor you, nor any other person, nor all the wit, science or philosophy of man, nor the inspiration of saints or sages, can change one bit of it any more than man can arrest the eternal circuits of time, the revolutions of the planets or the desire of the fledgling to leave its nest, to soar and sing.

Create or perish is the eternal mandate of nature. Be constructive or become frustrated, is an equal demand. You cannot escape the conclusion that whatever this thing is which is seeking expression through everything, it can find satisfactory outlet only through constructive and life-giving creativeness. You may call this process good or evil, right or wrong, God or the devil, heaven or hell. Would it not be more simple to say that finally things work out for the best only when they are life-giving.

We are all some part of a universal order. The very urge for personal gratification is incomplete until it finds a universal outlet. This is the cause back of all upheavals in human history. The pattern is trying to fit the pieces into greater and greater units as though it could not accomplish its purpose through anything other than a democracy of Spirit, a union of all. — ERNEST HOLMES, *This Thing Called You*

Dancing symbolizes the rhythmic, patterned movements of life itself. Music and dance amplify and make manifest to our senses the unheard tones and unseen waves that weave together the matter of existence. Even when we are sitting most still or resting in deepest sleep, the atoms, molecules, cells, tissues, organs, and systems of our bodies dance in astounding harmony and exchange the ambient energies from air, water, food, and invisible electromagnetic radiation. — YAYA DIALLO, *The Healing Drum*

There is a thing confusedly formed

Born before heaven and earth

Silent and void

It stands alone and does not change,

Goes round and does not weary.

It is capable of being the mother of the world.

I know not its name
So I style it "the way."

— LAO-TZU

At first glance, life appears meaningless, futile, full of contradictions and absurdities. But a deeper, meditating look uncovers beauty, order and harmony, revealing life as a supreme accomplishment of eternal wisdom. From the atom to the galaxy, a master design is at work and at play, created by a master builder unequaled in his attributes and grace. All of creation is an act of love and providence, a drama imbued with meaning: the flower sprouting from the bud, the child emerging from the womb, the human race evolving from the furthest branch of the tree of existence. When we discover that there are tens of thousands of species of botanic life, when we are stunned by the variations of human DNA, fingerprints and lip prints — we understand that this infinite variation is deliberate, created by a superior will, a superior ego. This realization is not a thought or a theory; it is a feeling, a sense, in one's heart, of the presence of God.

The march of life from bacterium to Shakespeare, from bushman to the Prophet, has been a steady advance. We have a natural inclination to walk in step with this march, i.e., to improve ourselves and upgrade our standards as we open the sleeping flower within us. This is actually the essence of all religions. In simple words: Life is a mission of awareness and awakening and deep enlightenment. We are here to sense this divine presence beyond all phenomena. We are here to recognize a deep urge in our hearts to act in harmony, in conformity and in love with these divinities.

— MUSTAPHA MAHMOUD in *More Reflections on the Meaning of Life*

My religion consists of a humble admiration of the illimitable superior spirit who reveals himself in the slight details we are able to perceive with our frail and feeble minds. That deeply emotional conviction of the presence of a superior reasoning power, which is revealed in the incomprehensible universe, forms my idea of God.

— ALBERT EINSTEIN

The universe is the harmonious interaction of all the elements that create balance and harmony. The word universe literally means "one song" *(uni:* one; *verse:* song). In this song, in this harmony, there is peace, laughter, joy, and bliss.

—DEEPAK CHOPRA, *Creating Affluence: Wealth Consciousness in the Field of All Possibilities*

SCIENCE OF THE SACRED

In the beginning, say theoreticians, there was neither time, nor space, nor matter. All that existed were the laws of physics, identical to those that reign today. These laws, even absent any supernatural agency, were sufficient to create something from nothing. Astronomer Carl Sagan says this means there was "nothing left for a Creator to do." But to other thinkers, the existence of the laws outside time and space, and their ability to create the world, imbue them with aspects of the sacred.

—SHARON BEGLY, *Newsweek*, November 28, 1994

All is a miracle. The stupendous order of nature, the revolution of a hundred millions of worlds around a million of stars, the activity of light, the life of all animals, all are grand and perpetual miracles.

—VOLTAIRE

CHAPTER SIX

Relationships:
Looking in the Mirror

Susan and I draw inspiration from couples who have remained happily married for many years. And so it was a particular joy for us to spend an afternoon and evening with Ossie Davis and Ruby Dee talking about their relationship, a conversation that eventually became an article for *Essence* magazine. Speaking of their forty-something-year marriage, Ruby, in her wise and poetic way, noted, "The wedding is a fact; the marriage is a process, and it's ongoing."

Tapping into an older, more significant meaning of the word "marriage," Ruby contrasts the ritual of the event—the marriage ceremony—with the ongoing work of integrating two lives into a whole that is greater than the sum of its parts. We've seen this in couples who can finish each other's sentences, who know each other so intimately they seem to think each other's thoughts, who even begin to look alike. The process that results in such a union of two souls is a paradigm for the ultimate union of every soul in God and is a step toward that union. And it is for that reason that marriage has been regarded as sacred by all cultures throughout time, and that ceremonies solemnizing the event have invoked the gods to witness our commitments to love—that is, to sacrifice for, do for, and think of someone other than ourselves.

Our intimate relationships are also mirrors in which we can see ourselves clearly if we are willing to look. They reflect the best in us—our gentle, kind, loving nature—as well as the areas where we have more inner work to do. These emotionally charged unions show us where we may be in emotional trouble and where our fears and insecurities lie. They call up within us the inner conflicts that make us impatient, demanding, judgmental; reveal unhealed wounds from former unions that cause us to behave in ways that make us miserable or incapable of sustaining a healthy union.

I'd been yearning for a loving marriage long before Khephra and I started dating, yet three years into our romance, despite the fact we'd become great friends and I was deeply in love with him, each time he would talk about us getting married, I'd find an excuse. I wanted to wait for my daughter to graduate from high school, then I needed some time alone. . . . In retrospect, although Khephra and I had grown closer than I'd been to any lover, I feared the deeper levels of self-revelation and intimacy that building an enduring love relationship demands. But despite my fear, I married Khephra and now each day I thank God I did.

Love is the most powerful force in the universe. It is also one of the most frightening, because it involves tearing down the walls we build around ourselves, walls we create to protect us, but which, over time, only make us feel separate and alone. Our love relationships are our greatest opportunities to experience intimacy—the feeling of oneness we all long for. We mistake this longing for union as a need for someone else's love, but a relationship with another person can't fully satisfy that visceral desire. Our longing for union is a longing for something greater than that. It is a hunger for union with God, which the ecstasies of our intimate relationships only hint at.

The process of awakening to our innate wholeness is solitary work.

Preachers can preach and gurus can guide, but we must undertake the search ourselves. We must open ourselves to a greater awareness of our relationship to God, embrace the divinity within, and appreciate the myriad manifestations of divinity without and all around us. Awakening to that wholeness is key to building a loving, healthy relationship with oneself and others. We are called by Love to love, for love is the wellspring of all existence. When you are loving, you feel yourself in harmony with life, at one with God. Giving love is a fundamental way of being that begins with self. Our partnerships have their best chance of thriving if we come to them feeling happy and whole and understanding that no one can fill the void we feel when we don't practice loving ourselves.

A marriage should function like a wise teacher, challenging us to expand the sphere of our love beyond self and awaken us to an awareness of our deeper identity. Our perfect partner is not someone whose physical attributes match some arbitrary standard set for us by others, nor someone who is rich and powerful enough to give us the material things we want. It's not someone we can control or someone who will never disagree with us. The perfect partner is one who is respectful of our individuality and who we can trust to challenge and stretch us in ways that help us grow.

We become the perfect partner when we feel comfortable within ourselves and feel safe revealing who we are.

I found my perfect complement in Susan. For just as Dante in *Paradiso* was guided by his beloved Beatrice through the higher spheres of God-consciousness, so Susan, by example, continues to show me how to love. But it is the relationship itself that is somehow wiser than either of us. As a teacher, it is less didactic than artful; it does not instruct as much as lead us to discover.

When we finally agreed to marry, Susan was quite candid about the issue of children: She wasn't having any more. I, on the other hand, having grown up with two sisters and a brother—all close in age and closely knit—wanted children very much. But Susan confessed that being a single mother to Nequai had been her greatest challenge. By the time we married, four years later, Nequai had graduated from high school and was on her way to college. Susan, celebrating a job well done, had even less desire to revisit the years of struggle and restricted movement that parenting inevitably represent. For me, having a child of our own offered another opportunity to love and to help create and shape a world. I confess I was briefly haunted by a vague dread of not following through on nature's design and of being judged accordingly by the ancestors for failing to heed the commandment to make of us twain "one flesh." But there is no shortage of opportunities to love, and a passage from a book by a Catholic priest, Father Eugene Kennedy, which an old schoolmate, Horace Mansfield, sent me, confirmed what I already knew but was nonetheless thankful to be reminded of:

"Men have always wanted to leave something lasting of themselves behind. Only the mighty or the highly gifted have the chance to do this through history or the arts. Everyone, however, leaves something that outlasts the greatest fame or accomplishment when he reaches out, even for a few moments, in loving another." And it doesn't matter who we love.

I remember Khephra saying, "One of us will make the sacrifice: Either you will make the sacrifice, and we will have a child, or I will make the sacrifice, and we won't." And I never felt any pressure from him. As it turned out in time, after our relationship grew deeper, stronger, and more joyous than I could ever have envisioned, I, too, began hungering for our child and threw away my diaphragm. But it was not meant to be — we weren't blessed with a child of our own. Still, as Khephra often says, we are so blessed to have Nequai and our beautiful nieces and nephews, Sabrina, Michael, Nicholas, and Sahara.

An enduring relationship requires a willingness to see and to be seen; to communicate in the most open, truthful, and self-revealing way; and to guard against being judgmental so that our partner feels safe in revealing him- or herself. When we are ready to relate to another person soul-to-soul, we find that our soul mate, our divine right partner, is no stranger, but someone with whom the marriage begins, naturally, even before the wedding and, hopefully, continues throughout a lifetime.

These ideas and more are echoed in the range and variety of writings we have excerpted for this section, from the ancient wisdom of the Upanishads and a traditional Sufi tale about the wise fool Nasrudin, to contemporary writers like Shakti Gawain, who offers insight on the meaning of conflict in our relationships; Emmanuel, who sees erotic love as the longing for reunion with the Oneness of God; Marianne Williamson and Iyanla Vanzant, who discuss the need to heal ourselves of our own dysfunctional behavior before seeking a relationship with another whom we expect also to be whole; and a moving haiku by Sonia Sanchez. We share their inspirational words in the hope that they will help you in your own unfolding relationships.

Each soul and spirit, prior to its entering into this world, consists of a male and female united into one being. When it descends on this earth the two parts separate and animate two different bodies. At the time of marriage, the Holy One, blessed be He, who knows all souls and spirits, unites them again as they were before, and they again constitute one body and one soul, forming as it were the right and left of one individual.

—THE ZOHAR

Mulla Nasrudin was sitting in a tea shop when a friend came excitedly to speak with him. "I'm about to get married, Mulla," his friend stated, "and I'm very excited. Mulla, have you ever thought of marriage yourself?" Nasrudin replied, "I did think of getting married. In my youth in fact I very much wanted to do so. I waited to find for myself the perfect wife. I traveled looking for her, first to Damascus. There I met a beautiful woman who was gracious, kind, and deeply spiritual, but she had no worldly knowledge. I traveled farther and went to Isphahan. There I met a woman who was both spiritual and worldly, beautiful in many ways, but we did not communicate well. Finally I went to Cairo and there, after much searching, I found her. She was spiritually deep, graceful, and beautiful in every respect, at home in the world and at home in the realms beyond it. I felt I had found the perfect wife." His friend questioned further, "Then did you not marry her, Mulla?" "Alas," said Nasrudin as he shook his head. "She was, unfortunately, waiting for the perfect husband."

—TRADITIONAL SUFI TALE

"One of the commitments we have, beside telling the truth and truly being oneself, is to take care of ourselves separately. Somebody told me that a long time ago and I had no idea what they were talking about. It took ten years to figure out what she meant: if you truly love someone, the highest gift you can give them is to take care of yourself. I think that's a forgotten piece in marriage. People marry so that someone else will take care of them. That's dangerous. There's a me and there's a him and there's something higher, which is us, that is not maintained unless I stay as a me and he stays as a him. . . ."

—JANMARIE SILVERA in Cathleen Rountree's *The Heart of Marriage*

No one can give us what we don't already have. Mr. or Ms. Right cannot be to us what we are not. If we are unhappy, unfulfilled, not pleased about who we are, we owe it to ourselves to stop looking. We have to ask ourselves: Would I marry me? Am I doing my best, giving my all, being the best I can be to myself? If not, why are we pawning ourselves off on someone else. We need to take time to do some homework on self-love, self-esteem and self-confidence. When we can pass the test of self-acceptance, the perfect someone who will complement all that we already are will walk right through the door.

—IYANLA VANZANT, *Acts of Faith*

JUST DON'T NEVER GIVE UP ON LOVE

Don't never go looking for love, girl. Just wait. It'll come. Like the rain fallin' from the heaven, it'll come. Just don't never give up on love.

—SONIA SANCHEZ

When a relationship isn't working, it means that the partners are preoccupied with "I": "What I want is . . ." or "This isn't right for me. . . ." And all weak relationships reflect the fact that somebody wants something for himself or herself. . . . I've heard about a way of designing houses at the beach, where big storms can flood houses: when they are flooded, the middle of the house collapses and the water, instead of taking down the whole house, just rushes through the middle and leaves the house standing. A good relationship is something like that. It has a flexible structure and a way of absorbing shocks and stresses so that it can keep its integrity, and continue to function. But when a relationship is mostly

"I want," the structure will be rigid. When it is rigid, it can't take pressure from life and so it can't serve life very well. Life likes people to be flexible so it can use them for what it seeks to accomplish.

—CHARLOTTE JOKO BECK, *Everyday Zen*

But, alas, our soul is, in effect, driving us onward through the gates of earthly experience to enrich its own repertoire. Its plan to hook us up with any other souls must always be suspect to motives of its own that will always include "teachings." These other souls, then, become the vehicle through which we are taught. All too often our blessed soul is bent on teaching us such things as compassion, surrender, and detachment, by means of emotional experiences so difficult or heart-wrenching that we have great difficulty claiming any participation or knowledge of it ourselves. Who takes the brunt? Who turns the screw? Who does the deed? Our soul-mate! Our accomplice in growth. Not the one who takes us to dizzying heights of ecstasy, but the one who makes us swallow the bitter medicine—all for our highest good!

—CHRIS GRISCOM, *The Healing of Emotion*

Married life is not a joke. It is something that should be taken seriously. Relationships can become a path to God, a path to eternal freedom and peace, provided you have the right attitude. Don't automatically consider separation each time you feel uncomfortable. Strive to be adaptable. Try to be patient, not once or twice, but many times.

—SRI SRI MATA AMRITANANDAMAYI, *Awaken, Children!*

Oftentimes we find ourselves attracted to our opposites—people who have developed opposite qualities from the ones we most identify with. In these relationships, we are unconsciously seeking to become whole, drawn to people who express those energies that are undeveloped in our own personalities. On some level, we recognize that they have the potential to help us become more balanced.

People who express our opposite aspects can be our most powerful teachers if we allow them to be. But first we must acknowledge that they express what we want and need to develop in ourselves. Early in a relationship, we often sense that the other person is bringing us exactly what we need. It is, in fact, their differentness that is so attractive to us. However, unless we are able to acknowledge that this person is offering us a reflection of something we need to see in ourselves, the differentness that drew us to them can actually become a source of conflict. After a while, we may begin to resent them for the ways they are different and begin trying to change them to be more like us!

[I]t's important in any relationship to learn constructive ways to communicate honestly about our needs, our likes and dislikes, and so forth. However, along with letting the other person know our feelings, including ways we might wish they would change, we need to remind ourselves that we brought them into our lives to teach and inspire us to develop new aspects of ourselves. Our challenge, then, is to be open to discovering the parts of ourselves that they mirror for us, and to learn how we can express those parts of ourselves more in our own lives. —SHAKTI GAWAIN, *The Path of Transformation*

All struggles
Are essentially
power struggles.
Who will rule,
Who will lead,
Who will define,
refine,
confine,
design,
Who will dominate.
All struggles
Are essentially
power struggles,
And most
are no more intellectual

than two rams

knocking their heads together.
— OCTAVIA BUTLER, *Parable of the Sower*

If we are ever to know love without limits, there can be no range to our giving. To want something from another is to utterly misunderstand his role in our happiness. Another person is our opportunity to extend what we **are.** ... Whoever understands this at the moment must assume responsibility for whatever is occurring in the marriage. One person, making the effort to forgive completely what is happening and to replace his own anxiety and criticisms with a gentle lightheartedness and limitless goodwill, will become the governing factor in any relationship he is part of.

It is not necessary to encourage our spouse to talk about what we judge to be wrong with the marriage or to talk about anything at all. It is not necessary to pressure our spouse to take responsibility for his part or to confess his mistakes. It is not necessary to force compromises or to formulate a joint plan of external response to future problems. Nothing is really necessary except that we remind ourselves alone that we are not in this relationship by accident and that all that occurs **can** be seen in love. A kind vision is always a possibility. It will occur when one person pauses long enough to recall his heartfelt thanks for how central a role the other person has played in his spiritual growth, whether the other person consciously intended this effect or not.
— HUGH PRATHER, *The Quiet Answer*

In Tantrism, enlightenment is sought through a profound experience of sensual love in which each is both.
— FRITJOF CAPRA

To be sensual ... is to respect and rejoice in the force of life, of life itself, and to be present in all that one does, from the effort of loving to the breaking of bread.

— JAMES BALDWIN, *The Fire Next Time*

According to this mysticism of sexual love, the ultimate experience of love is a realization that beneath the illusion of two-ness dwells identity: "each is both." This realization can expand into a discovery that beneath the multitudinous individualities of the whole surrounding universe—human, animal, vegetable, even mineral—dwells identity; whereupon the love experience becomes cosmic, and the beloved who first opened the vision is magnified as the mirror of creation.

—JOSEPH CAMPBELL ON PLATO'S *Symposium, The Hero with a Thousand Faces*

She is a friend of mind. She gather me, man. The pieces I am, she gather them and give them back to me in all the right order. It's good, you know, when you got a woman who is a friend of your mind.

—TONI MORRISON, *Beloved*

And they twain shall be one flesh: so then they are no more twain, but one flesh.   —MARK 10:8

There's a funny smell in a bachelor's house.

—OLD NEGRO SAYING

We bring into our marriage a host of romantic expectations. We may also bring visions of mythic sexual thrills. And we may impose on our sex life many more expectations, more "shoulds," than the average everyday act of love can fulfill. The earth should move. Our bones should sing. Fireworks should explode. Consciousness—self—should burn on the pyre of love. We should achieve either paradise or a reasonable facsimile thereof. We will be disappointed. . . . Such sexual shoulds transform the sex act into a test of performance and into proof of the state of our mental health, intimidating and shaming—and yes, disappointing—the husbands and wives who can't achieve apocalyptic orgasm. But even when passion is fever-pitch and all the systems are go, it is difficult to sustain such peaks of excitement. . . . Now to say all this is not to deny that we can have sexual moments as remarkable as any fantasist's dream, moments in which the coming together—whether or not it involves perfectly synchronized orgasms—involves a mutual wedding of passion and love. Nor does an absence of storybook sex mean that we cannot achieve what analyst Kernberg calls "multiple forms of transcendence," where—through acts of sexual love—we cross and erase the boundaries that separate self from other, woman from man, love from aggression and the present from the future and the past. . . . But for many—perhaps most—couples such moments are extraordinary and rare. Or they succumb to custom, and custom stales. For although in sexual love we may strive to continue with our body the connections we have made with our heart and our mind, there are times when the leap from love to ecstasy fails. There are times—there are plenty of times—when what we will have to settle for are imperfect connections.

—JUDITH VIORST, *Necessary Losses*

Sexual attraction is possibly the most important love indicator for most couples. If two people are only sexually attracted to one another, the odds are that the relationship will be short-lived. Such understanding is critically important for the young, who have not developed fully emotionally and often confuse sexual attraction and/or sexual satisfaction with love. It is imperative to understand that good sex is possible without love. Therefore, every sexual encounter may not be with the person that one truly loves or needs to love.

For example, one partner may be a balloon head and the other a dried-up pea head. A balloon head and a pea head may have a great time in bed for the first six months of their togetherness, but beyond that what do balloon heads and pea heads talk about other than that which is mundane or mediocre? What is created from their union other than baby balloon/pea heads? My point is that two people, if it is written in their minds and hearts and if they are intelligent in their quest, will grow into love, friendship, and sexual fulfillment.

Marriage is not a vacation or a prolonged holiday. Eighty percent of a marriage is work, compromise, adaptations, changes, intimate conversations, laughter, sexual sharing, confusion, joy, smiles, tears, pain, crises, reeducation, community, apologies, mistakes, more mistakes, new knowledge, and love. If children are involved, include parenting and repeat everything above twice for each year of the marriage. If the marriage lasts more than fifteen years, the couple should add wisdom. What about the other twenty percent? I presume that even in the most successful of marriages, the couple will sleep.

—HAKI R. MADHUBUTI, *Claiming Earth*

The need for intimacy springs from that portion of you that has been cast from Oneness. It remembers what Oneness feels like and is trying to find its way Home. . . .

In relationship you are moving close to the miracle of bringing Oneness into the illusion of duality. Yet how insistently duality tugs at your coattails!

Since love is the entire issue that is to be explored, lived out, and ultimately to be honored in your planet, then love must be the center of the focus. There is no rule that says if a heart has moved, if a consciousness has grown, the human being must remain faithful to something that no longer holds them in the name of society's definition of the meaning of love. — PAT RODEGAST AND JUDITH STANTON, *Emmanuel's Book II* (Emmanuel speaking through Pat Rodegast)

After the bloom of romance fades
and the differences begin to emerge
the opportunity is open
for real love.

Now is the time
to make a conscious choice
to devote your energy
to the nurturing of your beloved
and yourself.

It is time
to face the differences between you
with courage (and even interest),
to learn from each other,
to be open
and determined
to maintain a heart space.

Unconditional love
doesn't mean
you have to like everything
your partner says or does.

Your partner is not
his or her actions —
any more than you are
what you say or do.

You can allow yourself
to appreciate the actor or actress
even if you don't like
the role
s/he is playing
in this movie.

Both you and your partner
are always lovable
even when you act
unkindly or unwisely —
just as a child
is lovable
even when
s/he is noisy
or mischievous.

—KEN KEYES, JR., *Your Heart's Desire*

The moral law begins in the relationship between man and woman, but ends in the vast reaches of the universe.

— CONFUCIUS

You are an individual soul that is connected to the whole, but you are not the relationship to that whole. Your identification with your relationship provides you with great frustration because every time there is a glitch in it, as there always will be, you find yourself feeling worthless.

Remember that you are eternal, that which is changeless. You are in a great number of relationships, all of which have validity, but they come and go just like your life here in form comes from no-where and goes to now-here and then back to no-where. It is a relationship of coming and going, and thus it changes.

Dropping your personal history means dropping the belief that a failed relationship makes you a failure. There are no failed relationships. Every person who enters and exits your life does so in a mutual sharing of life's divine lessons. Some have longer roles to play than others, but ultimately, you will return to your relationship to the absolute.

— WAYNE W. DYER, *Your Sacred Self*

In the failure of a relationship we resolve never to make the same mistakes again. We get toughened to some extent and perhaps become a little wiser. But love itself is eternally young and always manifests some of the folly of youth. So, maybe it is better not to become too jaded by love's suffering and dead ends, but rather to appreciate that emptiness is part of love's heritage and therefore its very nature. It isn't necessary to make strong efforts to avoid past mistakes or to learn how to be clever about love. The advance we make after we have been devastated by love may be to be able simply to enter it freely once again, in spite of our suspicions. . . .

— THOMAS MOORE, *Care of the Soul*

HAIKU

There are things sadder
than you and I. some people
do not even touch.

— SONIA SANCHEZ

The only beloved who can always be counted on is God. The ultimate partner is a divine one, an experience of ourselves that is totally supportive and forgiving. Until we know this, we keep seeking sustenance from men that they cannot give us. Most men and women today are wounded. The search for someone who isn't in pain is unreasonable until we ourselves are healed of our own dysfunctions. Until then, we will be led to people as wounded as we are in order that we might heal and be healed together. What this means is that no partner can save us, deliver us, or give meaning to our lives. The source of our salvation, deliverance, and meaning is within us. It is the love we give as much as it is the love we get. The passion we most need to feed is our relationship to God. This is ultimately our relationship to ourselves.

— MARIANNE WILLIAMSON, *A Woman's Worth*

CHAPTER SEVEN

Only Love

*S*ome of my earliest recollections of Susan are of seeing her at various cultural affairs around New York City. She was always open and giving, always ready to smile and to greet folks warmly. As we grew closer, I discovered that the person she appeared to be initially is genuinely the person she is. And, what's more, she is open and giving despite the hurt she's endured. She is forgiving—more so than I'm inclined to be—and in this she continues to be my teacher.

Stevie Wonder, in his song "As," sings of the assurance of knowing he is loved because he has given himself away in love and through love. It's a philosophy that Susan shares as well. They both know that love is healing, that it banishes our fears, gives us peace of mind, and, ultimately, ensures our immortality. And so Stevie sings confidently that even if tomorrow death makes him part of the past, he will live on in the impact the love he has given will continue to have in the world.

It would seem the simplest and most natural thing in the world to do—to "love and be loved in return," as Nat "King" Cole sang in Eden Ahbez's "Nature Boy." And yet it is often our most difficult challenge. We are born open to giving and receiving love, but in time, the push and pull of living— the stresses, the disappointments, and abuse we endure, and the fear we are taught along the way—make us feel insecure and untrusting. In time, we forget the truth of who we are. Feeling belittled, we attack one another and even ourselves. We become judgmental rather than compassionate. We shun communicating, soul to soul, because it means risking revealing ourselves, making ourselves vulnerable. But the courage to love is always inside us, and as we grow in the awareness of its presence and trust it to guide our every thought, word and deed, the daunting layers of life's painful experiences are peeled away.

I often tell Khephra, that, of God's many blessings, it is the renewing power of love that I am most grateful for. Even from the depths of despair,

I've been able to renew myself and make a fresh start by opening my heart to God and allowing love to guide my thoughts and actions. By choosing love rather than doubt and fear, you step into the unlimited flow of life where there are no boundaries. Under the influence of love, our doubt, fear, anger, loneliness, and, very often, illness, too, evaporate. Love is our secret talisman: It increases in our lives as we live it and give it away.

There is no pain in our lives or in the world that love cannot heal. Where there is suffering, there are also beacons of light calling us to love. And there is no one we cannot love. We have been called by Jesus to love even our enemies, and for two thousand years have found this a particularly difficult challenge. How do you begin to love people whose sole purpose in life seems to be to frustrate your every endeavor? Dr. Martin Luther King, Jr., tells us we can begin with the kind of love the Greeks called *agape,* the intent of harboring in our hearts only goodwill toward all people, a love of humanity. This requires us to take a larger view of life—one that allows us greater compassion and forgiveness for human weakness and folly. But by holding on to the idea of wishing all people well, we can begin to extend the practice of love beyond the boundaries of our current circle of loved ones. Rather than wishing those who cause pain and suffering reciprocal pain and suffering, we can wish instead that they be healed of the sickness and circumstances at the root of their behavior and even begin to do something to bring about a change.

Love is a verb; it's something you do, not just something you feel or profess in moments of infatuation. Love is the act of doing for others. It's what you give, not what you seek to get. Love is an act of self-sacrifice. It is the willful sacrifice of some part of oneself—one's own momentary desires or time and energy so that that time and energy or those resources may be put to use to benefit others. This is what God does. God is eternally giving Him/Her/Itself away to all. This is the act of Creation. And this is why we say God is Love.

Our desire for love is a desire to be part of something bigger than ourselves, to be embraced, to be included. Ultimately, it is a desire for union with Love Itself. The close physical, emotional, and spiritual bonds we feel with others are like a subtle gravity, drawing all of us inexorably into union with one another and with God. When we give of ourselves, we act out of our divine nature and are more truly ourselves than at any other time, because we are Love made manifest. We are love manifesting as channels through which ever more love may flow and find expression. In the oneness of God, in the interrelationship of all to all, love is the link that binds each of us to all others. Love tells us what we must do and what we must be in order to experience oneness. If you would know God, love. Commit random acts of kindness. Love without reservation, even as the Christ does.

Malidoma Somé, the Dagara shaman from Burkina Faso, describes an encounter with pure Love during his initiation into adulthood. The experience is so emotionally overwhelming, he says, that no human being could stand it for long: "You would have to be dead or changed into something capable of handling these unearthly feelings . . ." This is what Kahlil Gibran meant when he wrote, "For even as Love crowns you so shall he crucify you." But even as Love crucifies you, so shall it resurrect you.

The greatest thing you'll ever learn
is just to love and be loved
in return.

—EDEN AHBEZ, "Nature Boy"

There is a mystery in love because it breaks down walls and topples over fences. . . . It enlarges us and moves us always forward. . . . It does not confine itself to one relationship or one style of relationship.

—EUGENE KENNEDY, *The Pain of Being Human*

Love is what we were born with. Fear is what we learned here. The spiritual journey is the relinquishment, or unlearning, of fear and the acceptance of love back into our hearts. Love is the essential existential fact. It is our ultimate reality and our purpose on earth. To be consciously aware of it, to experience love in ourselves and others, is the meaning of life.

We came here to cocreate with God by extending love. Life spent with any other purpose in mind is meaningless, contrary to our nature, and ultimately painful. —MARIANNE WILLIAMSON *A Return to Love*

LOVING YOUR ENEMIES

The meaning of love is not to be confused with some sentimental outpouring. Love is something much deeper than emotional bosh. Perhaps the Greek language can clear our confusion at this point. In the Greek New Testament are three words for love. The word *eros* is a sort of aesthetic or romantic love. In the Platonic dialogues *eros* is a yearning of the soul for the realm of the divine. The second word is *philia,* a reciprocal love and the intimate affection and friendship between friends. We love those whom we like, and we love because we are loved. The third word is *agape,* understanding and creative, redemptive goodwill for all men. An overflowing love which seeks nothing in return, *agape* is the love of God operating in the human heart. At this level, we love men not because we like them, nor because their ways appeal to us, nor even because they possess some type of divine spark; we love every man because God loves him. . . . Now we can see what Jesus meant when he said, "Love your enemies." We should be happy that he did not say, "Like your enemies." It is almost impossible to like some people. "Like" is a sentimental and affectionate word. How can we be affectionate toward a person whose avowed aim is to crush our very being and place innumerable stumbling blocks in our path? How can we like a person who is threatening our children and bombing our homes? That is impossible. But Jesus recognized that love is greater than like. When Jesus bids us to love our enemies, he is speaking neither of *eros* nor *philia;* he is speaking of *agape,* understanding and creative, redemptive goodwill for all men. . . .

Agape is love seeking to preserve and create community. It is insistence on community even when one seeks to break it. *Agape* is a willingness to go to any length to restore community. . . . The cross is the eternal expression of the length to which God will go in order to restore broken community. The resurrection is a symbol of God's triumph over all the forces that seek to block community. The Holy Spirit is the continuing community creating reality that moves through history. He who works against community is working against the whole of creation. Therefore, if I respond to hate with a reciprocal hate I do nothing but intensify the cleavage in broken community. I can only close the gap in broken community by meeting hate with love. . . .

In the final analysis, *agape* means a recognition of the fact that all life is interrelated. All humanity is involved in a single process, and all men are brothers.

— MARTIN LUTHER KING, JR., *Stride Toward Freedom*

Or maybe the purpose of being here, wherever we are, is to increase the durability and the occasions of love among and between peoples. Love, as the concentration of tender caring and tender excitement, or love as the reason for joy. . . . [L]ove is the single, true prosperity of any moment and that whatever and whoever impedes, diminishes, ridicules, opposes the development of loving spirit is "wrong"/hateful.

— JUNE JORDAN, in *Revolutionary Petunias* BY ALICE WALKER

If the community is in trouble, a man must not say, "I will go to my house, and eat and drink, and peace shall be with thee, O my soul." But a man must share in the trouble of the community, even as Moses did. He who shares in its troubles is worthy to see its consolation.

— THE TA'ANIT, 11A

There is no need to mention the great difference between the amount of satisfaction there is in just oneself being happy and the amount of satisfaction there is in an infinite number of people being happy.

If even one person cannot stand suffering, what need is there to mention how all people can't stand suffering? Therefore, it is a mistake if one uses others for one's own purpose; rather, one should use oneself for others' welfare. Thus one should use whatever capacities of body, speech, and mind one has for the benefit of others: That is right. Thus it is necessary to generate an altruistic mind and wish that the welfare of others is increased through their achievement of happiness and through their getting rid of suffering.

—THE DALAI LAMA, *Ocean of Wisdom*

Love must be the first law. Love is the action of being in the same space with other beings, which means that love is real, as real as we are. Love is not a limited idea, it is something we do, ultimately with our whole selves.

—THADDEUS GOLAS

Those of you whose work it is
to wake the dead, get up!
This is a work day.

—JALAL AL-DIN RUMI

To live to benefit mankind is the first step.

—HELENA PETROVNA BLAVATSKY

God is our Selfhood, and . . . anything of an erroneous or negative nature which emanates from any individual has power only in the degree that we ourselves give it power. So it is that whatever of good or of evil we do unto others, we do unto the Christ of our own being. "Inasmuch as ye have done it unto one of the least of these my brethren, ye have done it unto me." In that realization, we shall see that this is the truth about all men, and that the only road to a successful and satisfying life is to understand our neighbor to be our Self.

The Master has instructed us specifically as to the ways in which we can serve our fellow man. He emphasized the idea of service. His whole mission was the healing of the sick, the raising of the dead, and the feeding of the poor. The moment that we make ourselves avenues for the outflow of divine love, from that very moment, we begin serving each other, expressing love, devotion, and sharing, all in the name of the Father.

— JOEL S. GOLDSMITH, *Practicing the Presence*

Tsze-kung asked, saying, "Is there one word which may serve as a rule of practice for all one's life?" The Master said, "Is not Reciprocity such a word? What you do not want done to yourself, do not do to others."

— CONFUCIUS, the Analects

THE GOLDEN RULE

Christianity: "All things whatsoever ye would that men should do to you, do ye even so to them: for this is the Law and the Prophets."

— MATTHEW 7, 12

Judaism: "What is hateful to you, do not to your fellow man. That is the entire Law; all the rest is commentary."

— THE TALMUD, THE SHABBAT, 31A

Brahmanism: "This is the sum of duty: Do naught unto others which would cause you pain if done to you."

— THE MAHĀBHĀRATA, 5, 1517

Buddhism: "Hurt not others in ways that you yourself would find hurtful."

—THE UDANA-VARGA, 5,18

Confucianism: "Surely it is the maxim of loving-kindness: Do not unto others that you would not have them do unto you."

—THE ANALECTS, 15, 23

Taoism: "Regard your neighbor's gain as your own gain and your neighbor's loss as your own loss."

—T'AI SHANG KAN YING P'IEN

Zoroastrianism: "That nature alone is good which refrains from doing unto another whatsoever is not good for itself."

—DADISTAN-I-DINIK, 94, 5

LOVE THY NEIGHBOR AS THYSELF

At the heart of this injunction lies the realization that we are not separate from our neighbor. Therefore, loving one's self is loving one's neighbor and vice versa. So the assignment is simply, learn to love. Love is not a thing but an act of being. Love as a meditation practiced as continuously as possible is different from love as a set of prescribed behaviors or as a pleasure response. Love as a meditation allows us to soften our ego-boundaries a little—to permit our neighbor's consciousness into our awareness once in a while. With patience and perseverance, love does happen within us. And that love—not externally imposed or derived forms of behavioral love—is what transforms our behavior and touches our neighbor.

—AMIT GOSWAMI, *The Self-Aware Universe*

If two men claim thy help, and one is thy enemy, help him first.　　—THE BABA METZIA, 32B

Sometimes you may think that you hate mankind. You may consider people insane, the individual creatures with whom you share the planet. You may rail against what you think of as their stupid behavior, their bloodthirsty ways, and the inadequate and shortsighted methods that they use to solve their problems. All of this is based upon your idealized concept of what the race should be—your love for your fellow man, in other words. But your love can get lost if you concentrate upon those variations that are less than idyllic.

When you think you hate the race most, you are actually caught in a dilemma of love. You are comparing the race to your loving idealized conception of it. In this case however you are losing sight of the actual people involved.

—JANE ROBERTS, *The Nature of Personal Reality* (Seth speaking through Jane Roberts)

Sometimes we need to act on love even if it is entirely contrary to the way we are feeling about some certain person or situation. I wish I could picture for you some of the hundreds of times I have seen this work out in the lives of men and women. When love is introduced into a situation, the floodgates are opened and the alchemy of love begins. Every sort of healing in mind, body and affairs follows after the door of the heart has been opened to God's love.

—JACK AND CORNELIA ADDINGTON, *How to Love and Be Loved*

There is no greater invitation to love than loving first.　　—ST. AUGUSTINE OF HIPPO

Love has no awareness of merit or demerit; it has no scale by which its portion may be weighed or measured. It does not seek to balance giving and receiving. Love loves; this is its nature.

—HOWARD THURMAN, *Meditations of the Heart*

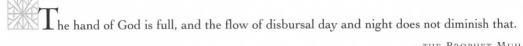
THE HAND OF GOD

The hand of God is full, and the flow of disbursal day and night does not diminish that.

—THE PROPHET MUHAMMAD

The sage does not hoard.

    Having bestowed all he has on others, he has yet more;

    Having given all he has to others, he is richer still.

The way of heaven benefits and does not harm; the

way of the sage is bountiful and does not contend.

—LAO-TZU

There are those who give little of the
much which they have—and they give it
for recognition and their hidden desire
makes their gifts unwholesome.

    And there are those who have little and
give it all.

    These are the believers in life and the
bounty of life, and their coffer is never
empty.

    There are those who give with joy, and
that joy is their reward.

    And there are those who give with pain,
and that pain is their baptism.

    And there are those who give and know
not pain in giving, nor do they seek joy,
nor give with mindfulness of virtue;

They give as in yonder valley the myrtle
breathes its fragrance into space.

Through the hands of such as these God
speaks, and from behind their eyes He
smiles upon the earth.

—KAHLIL GIBRAN, *The Prophet*

Love is not an emotion that begins in us and ends in the positive response of another. Love is a divine energy that begins in God and has no end.

—ERIC BUTTERWORTH

Know thou of a certainty that Love is the secret of God's holy Dispensation, the manifestation of the All-Merciful, the fountain of spiritual outpourings. Love is heaven's kindly light, the Holy Spirit's eternal breath that vivifieth the human soul. Love is the cause of God's revelation unto man, the vital bond inherent, in accordance with the divine creation, in the realities of things. Love is the one means that ensureth true felicity both in this world and the next. Love is the light that guideth in darkness, the living link that uniteth God with man, that assureth the progress of every illumined soul. Love is the most great law that ruleth this mighty and heavenly cycle, the unique power that bindeth together the divers elements of this material world, the supreme magnetic force that directeth the movements of the spheres in the celestial realms. Love revealeth with unfailing and limitless power the mysteries latent in the universe. Love is the spirit of life unto the adorned body of mankind, the establisher of true civilization in this mortal world, and the shedder of imperishable glory upon every high-aiming race and nation.

—ABDU'L-BAHA, Sufi mystic

The universe is truly in love with its task of fashioning whatever is next to be; and to the universe, therefore, my response must be, "As thou lovest, so I too love."

—MARCUS AURELIUS, Roman emperor and philosopher

Man and the universe are an outpouring of love. The very being of each creature is God abandoning himself for love. . . .

— ALAN WATTS

No matter what . . . it is with God. He is gracious and merciful. His way is through love in which we all are. It is truly — A Love SUPREME.

— JOHN COLTRANE

What is essentially involved in both love and religion is the repairing of unities broken by experience, and beyond that the retrieval of a Unity both all-encompassing and sempiternal . . . in a word, love discovers theology (as Christianity still supposes). Put another way, before the mind has grown sufficiently abstract to imagine divinities, love alone must minister to the fear of death. Its inadequacy in this regard must surely have been a principal stimulus to the development of religious imagination.

— DUDLEY YOUNG, *Origins of the Sacred*

God enters the love we have for each other, stays there, and will not leave to go to any so-called "house of God," *kaaba,* temple, church, or sacred grove.

— JALAL AL-DIN RUMI

For even as Love crowns you so shall he crucify you.

— KAHLIL GIBRAN, *The Prophet*

Out of nowhere, in the place where the tree had stood, appeared a tall woman dressed in black from head to foot. She resembled a nun, although her outfit did not seem religious. Her tunic was silky and black as the night. She wore a veil over her face, but I could tell that behind this veil was an extremely beautiful and powerful entity. I could sense the intensity emanating from her, and that intensity exercised an irresistible magnetic pull. To give in to that pull was like drinking water after a day of wandering in the desert.

My body felt like it was floating, as if I were a small child being lulled by a nurturing presence that was trying to calm me by singing soothing lullabies and rocking me rhythmically. I felt as if I were floating weightless in a small body of water. My eyes locked on to the lady in the veil, and the feeling of being drawn toward her increased. For a moment I was overcome with shyness, uneasiness, and a feeling of inappropriateness, and I had to lower my eyes. When I looked again, she had lifted her veil, revealing an unearthly face. She was green, light green. Even her eyes were green, though very small and luminescent. She was smiling and her teeth were the color of violet and had light emanating from them. The greenness in her had nothing to do with the color of her skin. She was green from the inside out, as if her body were filled with green fluid. I do not know how I knew this, but this green was the expression of immeasurable love.

Never before had I felt so much love. I felt as if I had missed her all my life and was grateful to heaven for having finally released her back to me. We knew each other, but at the time I could not tell why, when, or how. I also could not tell the nature of our love. It was not romantic or filial; it was a love that surpassed any known classifications. Like two loved ones who had been apart for an unduly long period of time, we dashed toward each other and flung ourself into each other's arms.

The sensation of embracing her body blew my body into countless pieces, which became millions of conscious cells, all longing to reunite with the whole that was her. If they could not unite with her, it felt as if they could not live. Each one was adrift and in need of her to anchor itself back in place. There are no words to paint what it felt like to be in the hands of the green lady in the black veil. We exploded into each other in a cosmic contact that sent us floating, adrift in the ether in countless intertwined forms. In the course of this baffling experience, I felt as if I were moving backward in time and forward in space.

While she held me in her embrace, the green lady spoke to me for a long time in the softest voice that ever was. She was so much taller than I was that I felt like a small boy in her powerful arms. She placed her lips close to my left ear and she spoke so softly and tenderly to me that nothing escaped my attention. I cried abundantly the whole time, not because what she told me was sad, but because every word produced an indescribable sensation of nostalgia and longing in me.

Human beings are often unable to receive because we do not know what to ask for. We are sometimes unable to get what we need because we do not know what we want. If this was happiness that I felt, then no human could sustain this amount of well-being for even a day. You would have to be dead or changed into something capable of handling these unearthly feelings in order to live with them. The part in us that yearns for these kinds of feelings and experiences is not human. It does not know that it lives in a body that can withstand only a certain amount of this kind of experience at a time. If humans were to feel this way all the time, they would probably not be able to do anything other than shed tears of happiness for the rest of their lives—which, in that case, would be very short.

Human beings never feel that they have enough of anything. Ofttimes what we say we want is real in words only. If we ever understood the genuine desires of our hearts at any given moment, we might reconsider the things we waste our energy pining for. If we could always get what we thought we wanted, we would quickly exhaust our weak arsenal of petty desires and discover with shame that all along we had been cheating ourselves.

Love consumes its object voraciously. Consequently, we can only experience its shadow.

—MALIDOMA SOMÉ, *Of Water and the Spirit*

I seem to have loved you in numberless forms, numberless times, in life after life, in age after age forever.

—RABINDRANATH TAGORE

Unconditional love not only means I am with you, but also I am for you, all the way, right or wrong. . . . Love is indescribable and unconditional. I could tell you a thousand things that it is not, but not one that it is. Either you have it or you haven't, there's no proof of it.

—DUKE ELLINGTON, *Music Is My Mistress*

The grand dais of God-realization, reached when a disciple goes beyond the beautiful stage of self-realization, is completely inexpressible in human tongue. For even the stage of self-realization cannot be adequately explained to one who has never experienced it. It defies human expression, for it is a stage when we go beyond words, beyond mind, and become what we truly are—God. We no longer speak the human language, rather we love, and that is what there is in everything we see for the rest of our lives and in eternity. —BAMBI BAABA, *Redeemer of the New Age*

Take it for granted that everybody in creation, everything in creation loves you, because everything has come out of love and goes back to love and remains in love. Then you are with the flow of the current. You are with the flow of the river. . . .

The whole creation is moving towards love. It is in love. But the one who is swimming against the current is not in love.

Oneness with existence is intimacy.

In true intimacy all modes and all moods are involved, are included. What I mean by love is not always goody-goody and saying nice things. It is sometimes saying unpleasant things, too. That is also love. Getting angry sometimes is also love. Love is fighting, too. It is all modes. . . .

True intimacy is recognizing the flow of the current and joyfully floating with it. The current is there. You don't have to stroke. You don't have to move your hands and feet. It carries you and you float. Effortlessly. Taking everything for granted is true intimacy. —SRI SRI RAVI SHANKAR, *Bang on the Door*

What I see with my body's eyes alone is not happening. What I see with love is real. As a lampshade surrounds a light, so things appear to encircle spirit, and words imprison thought. But that appearance of limitation is only imagined. Spirit is invisible to the body's eyes and cannot be heard with ears alone, and yet sounds and objects begin to brighten as I focus my spiritual sight. I simply say, "I love you," to everything, and mean it, and all the gauzy lampshades on earth begin to vanish before a world of immeasurable beauty and light. —HUGH PRATHER, *The Quiet Answer*

As the sun spreads vital rays of light, I will spread rays of hope in the hearts of the poor and forsaken, and kindle a new strength in the hearts of those who think that they are failures.

— PARMAHANSA YOGANANDA, *Metaphysical Meditations*

MAKE LOVE YOUR AIM

If I speak in the tongues of men
and of angels,
but have not love,
I am a noisy gong
or a clanging cymbal.
And if I have prophetic powers,
and understand all mysteries
and all knowledge,
and if I have all faith
so as to remove mountains,
but have not love,
I am nothing. . . .

   Love is patient and kind;
love is not jealous or boastful,
it is not arrogant or rude.
Love does not insist on its own way;
it is not irritable or resentful;
it does not rejoice at wrong,
but rejoices in the right.
   Love bears all things,

believes all things,

hopes all things,

endures all things.

   Love never ends. . . .

So faith, hope, and love abide,

these three;

but the greatest of these is love.

Make love your aim.

—1 CORINTHIANS 13 (NIV)

I will greet this day with love in my heart.

   And how will I do this? Henceforth will I look on all things with love and I will be born again. I will love the sun for it warms my bones; yet I will love the rain for it cleanses my spirit. I will love the light for it shows me the way; yet I will love the darkness for it shows me the stars. I will welcome happiness for it enlarges my heart; yet I will endure sadness for it opens my soul. I will acknowledge rewards for they are my due; yet I will welcome obstacles for they are my challenge.

—OG MANDINO, The Greatest Salesman in the World

Recently, I reread an old myth. It concerned a child who was willing to sacrifice himself to conserve the life of his king and country. He convinced his parents to consent to his act and, as he was about to be sacrificed to the demon, he laughed joyously. In response, those witnessing the sacrifice stopped and assumed an attitude of prayer. I believe that when you know why the boy laughed, you know the meaning of life.

   The Bible tells us that the Son of Man came not to be served but to serve and to ransom his life for the good of the many. The boy knew he was achieving immortality in the only way possible—through love, in his case an unconditional love that expressed itself in sacrifice for the good of many others. In his short life, he was doing all that anyone could hope to do. That realization brought him true joy. He was also laughing at the attachment the others had to their bodies, something he has transcended. . . .

We must find our own particular way of loving the world and put our energy into it. Decide your way of loving and you will be rewarded. —BERNIE SIEGEL in *More Reflections on the Meaning of Life*

By the accident of fortune a man may rule the world for a time, but by virtue of love he may rule the world forever. —LAO-TZU

Men have always wanted to leave something lasting behind themselves. Only the mighty or the highly gifted have the chance to do this through history or the arts. Everyone, however, leaves something that outlasts the greatest fame or accomplishment when he reaches out, even for a few moments, in loving another. He touches the ways of all men and their destiny when he can love one man with deep responsibility. He becomes an instrument of life, ever-increasing life, when he truly loves. His name may be forgotten, but the presence of the Spirit survives in the love he leaves behind.

—EUGENE KENNEDY, *The Pain of Being Human*

As

As today I know I'm living but tomorrow
Could make me the past but that I mustn't fear
For I'll know deep in my mind
The love of me I've left behind
Cause I'll be loving you always. —STEVIE WONDER

The conclusion is always the same: love is the most powerful and still the most unknown energy of the world.

—PIERRE TEILHARD DE CHARDIN

CHAPTER EIGHT

The Journey Toward Enlightenment

Enlightenment is the purpose of our challenging, often baffling, and sometimes painful journey from birth to death; a journey on which we are meant to discover the divinity within ourselves and honor it in one another and all life. Our quest is always for more light and greater clarity. We yearn for insight and illumination and think of those who possess them as divinely inspired, radiant. We sing "This Little Light of Mine" with an intuition that whispers we are all sparks of that one divine light.

The ultimate reality—our oneness with God—is available to each of us at any moment. It is there, right in front of us, within us and all around us, but we feel our way around it, bit by bit in the dark, trying to get a mental picture of it. And we are only in the dark because our eyes are not open. Once they are, we are fairly blinded by the light, just as Paul was blinded on the road to Damascus, as Moses would have been on Mount Sinai had he not shielded himself in the crevice of a rock.

Suggesting, however, that we only need to open our metaphysical "eyes" is like asking us to open our physical eyes if we'd been born unaware that we *have* eyes. We would need help, perhaps someone to come along and open them for us, allowing the light to come rushing in. Then we would suddenly perceive the world in a startling new way. And even if we only saw it for a minute before our vision faded, we would be forever changed. Even in our world of darkness, we would remember what reality looked like.

Our great work along the journey is to open our eyes, to be diligent about expanding our awareness and understanding of the multidimensional nature of our existence. As a famous proverb states, the first step—and perhaps the only one we need to take—is to "know thyself." In knowing self—our true self—we are filled with compassion for others, knowing that they are not *other*, but are ourself as well.

The continuing suffering in our world is dependent on us not having a clear vision of who we are. When we fail to recognize our own divinity, we fail to recognize our connection to one another and to all life on the planet. We build a wall around the light that radiates from the center of our being and that otherwise reaches into the limitless universe, mingling as one with the divine light that radiates from every other being. They are us, and we are them; respect for others is self-respect and vice versa.

As an African American male confronted at every turn by ubiquitous, unrelenting, and unrepentant racism, the temptation to separate humanity into a Black-White duality is ever-present. But such divisions, once begun, are never-ending. And I have often thought that a good working definition of "insanity" is a sense of complete separateness—total isolation to the point that one is unable to function cooperatively, empathize, or even communicate with others. Similarly, to the enlightened, our notion of ourselves as individuals with separate identities to promote and defend must look like insanity as well, if only of a higher order. Intuitively, we sense this and seek the balm of community, the unity that makes us feel strong, whole, and healthy. And it is in fact the emphasis in the last two decades on "doing our own thing" and "getting mine" that has led to the disintegration of our communities. The fallout from our fragmented way of being—the lack of reverence for the dignity and sanctity of life, the tangle of our disorganized and stressful lives, our inability to communicate with one another, and our growing tendency toward violence—differs only in degree from symptoms exhibited by individuals we say are psychotic.

Such a separated sense of self is a vortex drawing us ever downward, clouding our vision and distracting us with a thousand separate things. But "When thine eye is single," as Jesus said cryptically—that is, when we see the truth of the unity of all life—then "thy whole body is full of light." "Thy whole body" is not just *your* body, healed and made whole; it is the Body of Christ, the body (meaning the group) comprised of all creatures animated by the living Light. When our eye is single, we are focused on the larger picture—the unified whole—and are clear about the critical work we were created to do, that of transforming our world and bringing to an end the senseless pain and suffering around us.

The journey toward enlightenment is what I write about each month in my *Essence* editorial, "In the Spirit." For me, enlightenment is a feeling of wholeness, of oneness with all in creation, and the knowledge that we are loved and protected. This assurance doesn't guarantee there won't be times when we feel afraid, sad, or overwhelmed. But it is the deeper knowledge that no matter what life brings you this day, you have every-thing needed—the wisdom, creativity, and strength—to see it through or see through it. It is knowing that no matter what you've done or where you are on your path, you are at the divine right place and are no more nor less than any other aspect of God. We are at once human and divine. Heaven and earth meet in us. To be enlightened is to be fully present to this truth, not just during prayer, meditation, or worship service, but during times of upheaval and pain, for these, too, are God's invitations to grow, to broaden our vision of what we are capable of mastering, and to deepen our faith that we are forever in God's care.

There's an old axiom that says "perception is reality"—that how we see the world, as Susan often says, determines our experience of it. Seeing is what enlightenment is all about. Ask a Zen master how to become en-lightened and you may be told, "Become seeing." See, as God sees, your oneness with the whole of life, judging not, but experiencing its wonder. And once you have seen you cannot help but be filled with compassion for all life.

Usually, our flashes of insight and illumination are brief and fleeting, even though their impact on our lives may be lasting. But the experience of enlightenment is not an accomplishment in the same sense as receiving a diploma. It doesn't certify us as spiritually transformed the way passing the bar certifies one as licensed to practice law. We're not enlightened once and for all time. Enlightenment is an awakening; remaining awake is another matter. And it's only through constant remembering and conscious effort that we gradually shift our identity from the ego-centered self to the All of creation. But it is then that we know there is no one and nothing to fear, that all love is self love, and that love of self is love of all.

Your teachers
Are all around you.
All that you perceive,
All that you experience,
All that is given to you
or taken from you.
All that you love or hate,
need or fear
Will teach you —
If you will learn.
God is your first
and your last teacher.
God is your harshest teacher:
subtle,

demanding.

Learn or die.

— OCTAVIA BUTLER, *Parable of the Sower*

I always think that we live, spiritually, by what others have given us in the significant hours of our life. These significant hours do not announce themselves as coming, but arrive unexpected.

— ALBERT SCHWEITZER, *The Light Within Us*

A lightbulb is nothing more than that unless it is turned on. When the connection is made with electrical energy, it becomes a radiant source of light and warmth. Man is a spiritual being, a child of God, heir to all the infinite potential that inheres in all God's creation, including Love, the strongest single force in existence. But, in reality, the fulfilling of the power of our divinity comes only when we are attuned to the Father and are expressing His love, light, and power.

At any time, under any circumstances, we can turn on the light, and the infinite energy of love will dissolve darkness, heal broken relationships, and become a veritable protecting presence. Man is a creature of light. When his light is shining brightly in all directions and in all situations, he is imperturbable, indefatigable, and undefeatable. "Nothing shall be impossible unto him."

How we frustrate this potential of light! Consider this practical illustration. If you were to walk into a room full of people who were being hampered in their work by lack of light, and if you had a bright lamp in your hands, would you turn your lamp down in reaction to the dim light of the room? No, you would bring as much light as you possibly could. But if you walk into a room of hostile people, what is your reaction? Normally, you meet their hostility with hostility of your own and walk away saying, "What an unfriendly bunch of people!"

You may say, "But I am only human." This is the understatement of your life. You are not only human—you are also divine in potential. The fulfillment of all your goals and aspirations in life depends upon stirring up and releasing more of that divine potential. And there is really nothing difficult about letting this inner light shine. All we must do is correct the tendency to turn off our light when we face darkness.

— ERIC BUTTERWORTH, *Discover the Power Within You*

The light of heaven's sun is a hundred in relation to the courtyards of houses.

But all their lights are one when you remove the walls from between. — JALAL AL-DIN RUMI

[A] light is revealed in which you do not see anything other than yourself. In it a great rapture and deep transport of love seize you, and in it you find bliss with God that you have not known before. All that you saw previously becomes small in your eyes, and you sway like a lamp.

— IBN 'ARABI, *Journey to the Lord of Power*

Enlightenment is any experience of expanding our consciousness beyond its present limits. We could also say that perfect enlightenment is realizing that we have no limits at all, and that the entire universe is alive.

The difficulty in writing about it, and in all efforts to tell how to achieve it, comes of trying to use limited terms to talk about going beyond limits. To be enlightened is to be in a state of flexible awareness, an open mind. Enlightenment is the very process of expanding, not of arriving at a different set of limits.

— THADDEUS GOLAS, *The Lazy Man's Guide to Enlightenment*

Spiritual understanding is not like intellectual understanding. Chemistry requires intellectual understanding. You need to know the formula and the elements of the formula. You need to know which formulas you can mix together and which you cannot. With that knowledge, you are probably pretty well equipped to make new formulas. Spiritual understanding requires courage, trust, and faith. On the spiritual path, understanding often comes after a test of faith. Your willingness, commitment, level of trust and belief in the principles of Spirit are going to be tested by your experiences in life. Once you make it through the faith test, you have a greater awareness of your connection to God. You develop a greater sense of wellness and well-being. The experiences and the tests take on meaning. It is then that you develop understanding.

— IYANLA VANZANT, *The Spirit of a Man*

If we make contact with the kingdom of God within us, we shall be living through God the rest of our days. Then spiritual sonship—God expressing Itself as individual Selfhood—will be revealed on earth. God formed us to manifest Itself on earth, to show forth Its glory, and that is our destiny. God planted His infinite abundance in the midst of us. Nothing need come to you or to me, but everything must flow out from us. And by what means? By that Presence, that Presence which heals, supplies, multiplies, and teaches. That Presence will perform every legitimate function of life, but It is only active in our life as we dedicate and consecrate ourselves to periods of meditation.

— JOEL S. GOLDSMITH, *Practicing the Presence*

For the Minianka, silence, *fiaga*, is the principal condition of the inner life. Fiaga is the mother of the word, or *diomon*. . . . To keep silent is to cultivate one's interior dimension. The Minianka learn how to sit quietly. Many sayings reflect various aspects of silence: "Silence hides a person's way of being, the word discloses it"; "Silence is reflective, the word thoughtless"; "Silence has delimited the paths, the word has jumbled them"; "Silence has given birth to seriousness, the word to diversion"; "The secret belongs to the one who knows how to keep silent."

— YAYA DIALLO, *The Healing Drum*

Mystics and visionaries in every spiritual tradition speak with reverence of aloneness. Being alone is regarded as a sacred space and time; it is the birthplace of vision, renewal and creativity. Being alone is a transformative time, a time of willingly shedding the props of our goals and ambitions, our identities and habits, our assumptions and conclusions, and resting in a fertile inner openness which is the home of guidance, vision and revelation. Spiritual stories abound of shamans and saints who seek seclusion in deserts and on mountains, tales of the countless people who follow the ancient path of going forth into homelessness, not as a rejection of the world but as a way of exploring the richness and joy of inner solitude. Being alone is an invitation to strip ourselves of knowing and to explore the mystery of the unknown. Learning to be at ease in our aloneness, surrendering the desire to discover fulfilment and definition outside of ourselves, is essential to awakening. No one can substitute for us on this

journey to awakening, no one can provide us with the peace, wisdom and oneness our hearts yearn for. We need to be willing to be alone, to return to ourselves, to take up the invitation of inner solitude. It is a quest to find ourselves and in finding ourselves discovering a quality of profound communion that bonds us with all life. . . .
— CHRISTINA FELDMAN, *The Quest of the Warrior Woman*

The power of quiet is great. It generates the same feelings in everything one encounters. It vibrates with the cosmic rhythm of oneness. It is everywhere, available to anyone at any time. It is us, the force within that makes us stable, trusting, and loving. It is contemplation contemplating us. Peace is letting go—returning to the silence that cannot enter the realm of words because it is too pure to be contained in words. This is why the tree, the stone, the river, and the mountain are quiet.
— MALIDOMA SOMÉ, *Of Water and the Spirit*

Pure consciousness is our spiritual essence. Being infinite and unbounded, it is also pure joy. Other attributes of consciousness are pure knowledge, infinite silence, perfect balance, invincibility, simplicity, and bliss. This is our essential nature. . . .

The ego . . . is not who you really are. The ego is your self-image; it is your social mask; it is the role you are playing. Your social mask thrives on approval. It wants to control, and it is sustained by power, because it lives in fear.

Your true Self, which is your spirit, your soul, is completely free of those things. It is immune to criticism, it is unfearful of any challenge, and it feels beneath no one. And yet, it is also humble and feels superior to no one, because it recognizes that everyone else is the same Self, the same spirit in different disguises. . . .

[I]f you want to make full use of the creativity which is inherent in pure consciousness, then you have to have access to it. One way to access the field is through the daily practice of silence, meditation, and non-judgment. Spending time in nature will also give you access to the qualities inherent in the field: infinite creativity, freedom, and bliss.

Practicing silence means making a commitment to take a certain amount of time to simply *Be*. Experiencing silence means periodically withdrawing from the activity of speech. It also means periodically withdrawing from such activities as watching television, listening to the radio, or reading a book. If you never give yourself the opportunity to experience silence, this creates turbulence in your internal dialogue.

—DEEPAK CHOPRA, *The Seven Spiritual Laws of Success*

Silence is also speech.

—FULFULDE PROVERB

Silence is something extraordinary; it's not the silence between two noises. Peace is not between two wars. Silence is something that comes naturally when you are watching, when you are watching without motive, without any kind of demand, just to watch, and see the beauty of a single star in the sky, or to watch a single tree in a field, or to watch your wife or husband, or whatever you watch. To watch with a great silence and space. Then in that watching, in that alertness, there is something that is beyond words, beyond all measure. . . .

If you listen, learn, watch, be totally free from all the anxieties of life, then only is there a religion that brings about a new, totally different culture. . . .

The ending of the self, the "me": to be nothing. . . . To have no image of any kind, no illusion, to be absolutely nothing. The tree is nothing to itself. It exists. And in its very existence it is the most beautiful thing, like those hills: they exist.

—J. KRISHNAMURTI, *On Nature and the Environment*

In the split second where you understand a joke you experience a moment of "enlightenment." It is well known that this moment must come spontaneously, that it cannot be achieved by explaining the joke, i.e., by intellectual analysis. Only with a sudden intuitive insight into the nature of the joke do we experience the liberating laughter the joke is meant to produce. The similarity between a spiritual insight and the understanding of a joke must be well known to enlightened men and women, since they almost invariably show a great sense of humor. Zen, especially, is full of funny stories and anecdotes, and in the Tao-te Ching we read, "If it were not laughed at, it would not be sufficient to be Tao."

— FRITJOF CAPRA, *The Tao of Physics*

"Wisdom is not communicable. The wisdom which a wise man tries to communicate always sounds foolish."

"Are you jesting?" asked Govinda.

"No, I am telling you what I have discovered. Knowledge can be communicated, but not wisdom. One can find it, live it, be fortified by it, do wonders through it, but one cannot communicate and teach it. I suspected this when I was still a youth and it was this that drove me away from teachers."

— HERMANN HESSE, *Siddhartha*

The instant you speak about a thing you miss the mark.

— ZEN SAYING

The tao that can be told
is not the eternal Tao.
The name that can be named
is not the eternal Name.

The unnameable is the eternally real.
Naming is the origin
of all particular things.

Free from desire, you realize the mystery.
Caught in desire, you see only the manifestations.

Yet mystery and manifestations
arise from the same source.
This source is called darkness.

Darkness within darkness.
The gateway to all understanding.   — LAO-TZU

Which of you by taking thought can add one cubit unto his stature?   — JESUS OF NAZARETH

If it could be talked about, everybody would have told his brother.   — CHUANG-TZU

Thinking is more interesting than knowing, but less interesting than looking.

— JOHANN WOLFGANG VON GOETHE

Standing on the bare ground . . . a mean egotism vanishes. I become a transparent eyeball; I am
nothing; I see all; the currents of the Universal Being circulate through me; I am part or particle of God.

— RALPH WALDO EMERSON

Behead yourself! Dissolve your whole body into Vision, become seeing, seeing, seeing!

— JALAL AL-DIN RUMI

The whole of life lies in the verb *seeing*.   — PIERRE TEILHARD DE CHARDIN

CREATOR OF ABSENCE AND PRESENCE

Human beings live in three spiritual states. In the first, we pay no attention to God. We notice only the stones and the dirt of the world, the wealth, the children, the men and the women. In the second, we do nothing but worship God. In the third, most advanced state, we become silent. We don't say, "I serve God," or "I don't serve." We know that God is beyond being present or absent. The creator of absence and presence! And other than both.

These opposites that generate each other are not qualities of God. There are no likenesses. God did not create God. When you reach this point, stop! At the edge of the ocean, footprints disappear.

— JALAL AL-DIN RUMI

Lighten up! Your higher self demands nothing of you. You do not have to prove yourself to God. You were created as an extension of the highest spiritual force, the very essence of the universe. You did not arrive in now-here incomplete in any way. You do not have to strive to prove anything. . . .

When you stop striving and start knowing that you are on a divine mission, and that you are not alone, you will be guided to the experience of arriving. That experience will introduce you to the bliss of being in the realm of spirit, where there is no worry or guilt. Being fully in the now means that you will experience heaven on earth because you are completely absorbed in the soul of the holy instant.

— WAYNE W. DYER, *Your Sacred Self*

The grand dais of God-realization, reached when a disciple goes beyond the beautiful stage of self-realization, is completely inexpressible in human tongue. For even the stage of self-realization cannot be adequately explained to one who has never experienced it. It defies human expression, for it is a stage when we go beyond words, beyond mind, and become what we truly are—God. We no longer speak the human language, rather we love, and that is what there is in everything we see for the rest of our lives and in eternity.

— BAMBI BAABA, *Redeemer of the New Age*

The meaning of life is rooted in each person's search for happiness. Happiness is not something one has to go anywhere to find: The nature of life *is* happiness. Life knows this about itself, not through analysis or investigation but simply by virtue of being.

Beneath the shroud of problems and suffering, each of us is infinite, unbounded. Unlimited intelligence, freedom and power are at our disposal—if only people would learn to live on the ground of infinity rather than the ground of problems! . . .

Physics has discovered the edge of infinity; the wisdom of the ages takes us across the border, which is nowhere but in us. When each person rejoins the stream of evolution that upholds the galaxies and sweeps life forward on the wave of eternity, human existence will cease to contain any suffering, and our real purpose in living—to create heaven on earth—will be realized.

—MAHARISHI MAHESH YOGI in *More Reflections on the Meaning of Life*

With one mindful step . . . we enter the *dharmadhatu* and are surrounded by light. We are everything else, there is no discrimination. Everything we do for ourselves is for others, everything we do for others is for us.

—THÍCH NHÂT HANH, *Touching Peace*

The attainment of wholeness requires one to stake one's whole being. Nothing less will do; there can be no easier conditions, no substitutes, no compromises.

—CARL GUSTAV JUNG

"Most of our energy goes into upholding our importance. . . . If we were capable of losing some of that importance, two extraordinary things would happen to us. One, we would free our energy from trying to maintain the illusory idea of our grandeur; and two, we would provide ourselves with enough energy to . . . catch a glimpse of the actual grandeur of the universe."

—CARLOS CASTANEDA, *The Art of Dreaming* (voice of Don Juan)

The practice of nonattachment gives value and significance to even the most ordinary incidents of the dullest day. It eliminates boredom from our lives. And, as we progress and gain increasing self-mastery, we shall see that we are renouncing nothing that we really need or want, we are only freeing ourselves from imaginary needs and desires. In this spirit, a soul grows in greatness until it can accept life's worst disasters, calm and unmoved. Christ said, "For my yoke is easy and my burden is light"—meaning that the ordinary undiscriminating life of sense-attachment is really much more painful, much harder to bear, than the disciplines which will set us free. We find this saying difficult to understand because we have been trained to think of Christ's earthly life as tragic—a glorious, inspiring tragedy, certainly—but ending nevertheless upon a cross. We should rather ask ourselves: "Which would be easier—to hang on that cross with the enlightenment and nonattachment of a Christ, or to suffer there in the ignorance and agony and bondage of a poor thief?" And the cross may come to us anyway, whether we are ready and able to accept it or not.

—SWAMI PRABHAVANANDA AND CHRISTOPHER ISHERWOOD,

How to Know God: The Yoga Aphorisms of Patanjali

Light has come into the world, and every man must decide whether he will walk in the light of creative altruism or the darkness of destructive selfishness.

—MARTIN LUTHER KING, JR., *The Strength to Love*

If you surrendered to the air, you could *ride* it. —TONI MORRISON, *Song of Solomon*

All is never said. —IBO PROVERB

CHAPTER NINE

The Oneness of God

"God and you *is* one," as Unity leader Olga Butterworth has said so often. And in the depths of our souls we know it's true. It's the one truth we need embrace to find lasting inner peace and joy, but the very one we have the greatest difficulty staying mindful of, especially since our egos tell us constantly that we are two. And so we live in a world of illusion, a world of twoness or duality: a world of up and down, right and left, life and death, male and female, you and me, us and them, God and humankind. But in reality All is One and One is All.

There is a single divine Intelligence in the universe. It is omnipresent and omnipotent, the power behind everything in Creation and beyond comprehension. It *is* Creation and comprehension. It is One, infinite and eternal, complete unto Itself. There is nothing other than or outside of it. Not you, not us. It beats our hearts, breathes for us, sees for us, is us, and there is ultimately nothing that we can call yours or mine, not even our selves.

We are Spirit manifesting as individual physical beings in bodies that are absolute marvels of temporary housing, each complete with its own live-in gatekeeper, our ego. The ego is very protective of its beautiful accommodations because if anything should happen to the body, making it unfit for habitation by the Spirit—a fatal accident, for instance—the mortal ego would die as well. Always mindful of its inevitable demise and threatened by anything that might cause it pain, the ego has put up walls around the indwelling Spirit, creating an isolated, illusory thing we call our "self." Our ego works hard at providing our self with a false sense of identity. It drives us out each day to seek our good fortune, knowledge, and the approval of others. It wants us to be competitive, to be right, to be winners, to be adored, and to feel secure if not superior. It encourages us to "go for self."

But the greatest misperception we have about life is that each of us is a separate entity—separate from others and separate from God. It is this illusion of separateness that is the source of all of our pain and suffering. Because of it, we often feel alone and vulnerable, defensive, fearful, or angry. As we begin to see through the illusion of our separate self and strive to maintain an awareness of our oneness with God, we invest less and less time and effort in defending the self. We reign in our ego, watch it carefully, and keep spirit in charge. We remind ourselves to be present here and now, with *this* breath, in *this* holy moment, the only moment we can know oneness with God. To do this we have to break through the walls that imprison us in the world of duality. Our true Self has no limits. The real you, the you at the core of your being, the you that was before it acquired a name or titles or memories, the you that preceded your proudest accomplishments, misdeeds, and most deeply held secrets—that you is One. In all the universe, there is *only* one, and it is the same one that we all share. That you, that divine Self, is God.

We're like the soap bubbles of a child's toy, lifted aloft on the wind; each bubble formed of a single breath drawn from the infinite and expansive air, with only a thin soapy film—the ego—separating it from its true identity. Within and without, it is one, a fact it only discovers when the bubble bursts in the experience of enlightenment.

We are linked in what Dr. Martin Luther King, Jr., described as an inescapable web of mutuality. This all-encompassing reality connects everything in the cosmos through the divine principles of unity, harmony, justice, and love. As infants we are instinctively at home in the safety of this truth. As children we trust it. But in time we forget our true identity and learn to discriminate between ourselves and others. We learn to fear. And increasingly, we feel alone and unprotected, in need of walls, fences, and defenses. So we clutch and cling to ideas, things, and people. We reach for boundaries rather than horizons.

Our challenge is to become selfless—to risk letting go until we are freed from the tenacious grip of the ego and able, at last, to see past our illusory self to our true identity in the One Self which is God. In striving to see ourselves in every stranger's face, we will create a shift in consciousness and will want only the best for all. We will no longer feel the need to be right or perfect or adored, but will know that we *are* Love. Like

Ntozake's colored girls, we will have found God in our Self and will love her fiercely.

In this section of *Confirmation*—the largest in the book—sages, saints, mystics, and seers speak passionately and powerfully about the transcendent experience of selflessness and the Oneness of God. It is a universal experience, and for us, these visions and revelations, spanning more than three thousand years, and the wisdom and insights drawn from them represent the heart of this work. It is from such direct experiences of the divine that most of the concepts expressed in *Confirmation* derive, and so, many of these ideas naturally overlap the subject areas of other sections of the book—certainly, universal love, communion with the divine, divine order, forgiveness, and enlightenment.

Vivid accounts of encounters with the divine can be found in the sacred texts and oral traditions of every religion and culture. Each has evolved its own rituals, prayers, meditations, and other practices to help bring us to a realization of our divinity. With that realization, everything we do becomes worship; working, eating, breathing, all become a confirmation and celebration of that ultimate reality. God is One. As we strive to embrace this truth, we embrace all others.

I
Selflessness

The realization of nothingness is the first act of being.

—JEAN TOOMER

For the one
who
standing in the sun
does not cast a shadow

—JUNE JORDAN

We've never been so self-conscious about our selves as we seem to be these days. The popular magazines are filled with advice on things to do with a self: how to find it, identify it, nurture it, protect it, even, for special occasions, weekends, how to lose it transiently. There are instructive books, best-sellers on self-realization, self-help, self-development. Groups of self-respecting people pay large fees for three-day sessions together, learning self-awareness. Self-enlightenment can be taught in college electives.

You'd think, to read about it, that we'd only just now discovered selves. Having long suspected that there was something alive in there, running the place, separate from everything else, absolutely individual and independent, we've celebrated by giving it a real name. My self.

It is an interesting word, formed long ago in much more social ambiguity than you'd expect. The original root was *se* or *seu*... used to indicate something outside or apart, hence words like "separate," "secret"....

—LEWIS THOMAS, *The Medusa and the Snail*

"I," "me," and "mine" are products of our thinking. My friend Larry Rosenberg, of the Cambridge Insight Meditation Center, calls it "selfing," that inevitable and incorrigible tendency to construct out of almost everything and every situation an "I," a "me," and a "mine," and then to operate in the world from that limited perspective which is mostly fantasy and defense. Hardly a moment passes that this doesn't happen, but it is so much a part of the fabric of our world that it goes completely unnoticed, much as the proverbial fish has no knowledge of water, so thoroughly is it immersed in it. You can see this for yourself easily enough whether you are meditating in silence or just living a five-minute segment of your life. Out of virtually any and every moment and experience, our thinking mind constructs "my" moment, "my" experience, "my" child, "my" hunger, "my" desire, "my" opinion, "my" way, "my" authority, "my" future, "my" knowledge, "my" body, "my" mind, "my" house, "my" land, "my" idea, "my" feelings, "my" car, "my" problem.

If you observe this process of selfing with sustained attention and inquiry, you will see that what we call "the self" is really a construct of our own mind, and hardly a permanent one, either. If you look deeply for a stable, indivisible self, for the core "you" that underlies "your" experience, you are not likely to find it other than in more thinking. You might say you are your name, but that is not quite accurate. Your name is just a label. The same is true of your age, your gender, your opinions, and so on. None are fundamental to who you are.

When you inquire in this way as deeply as you can follow the thread into who you are or what you are, you are almost sure to find that there is no solid place to land. If you ask: "Who is the I who is asking who am I?", ultimately you come to, "I don't know." The "I" just appears as a construct which is known by its attributes, none of which, taken singly or together, really makes up the whole of the person. Moreover, the "I" construct has the tendency continually to dissolve and reconstruct itself, virtually moment by moment. It also has a strong tendency to feel diminished, small, insecure, and uncertain, since its existence is so tenuous to begin with. This only makes the tyranny and suffering associated with unawareness of how much we are caught up in "I," "me," and "mine" that much worse.

Then there is the problem of outside forces. The "I" tends to feel good when outside circumstances are supporting its belief in its own goodness, and bad when it runs into criticism, difficulties, and what it perceives as obstacles and defeats. Here perhaps lies a major explanation for diminished self-esteem in many people. We aren't really familiar with this constructed aspect of our identity process. This makes it easy for us to lose our balance and feel vulnerable and inconsequential when we are not propped up and reinforced in our need for approval or for feeling important. We are likely to continually seek interior stability through outside rewards, through material possessions, and from others who love us. In this way, we keep our self-construct going. Yet in spite of all this self-generating activity, there may still be no sense of enduring stability in one's own being, nor calmness in the mind. Buddhists might say that this is because there is no absolute separate "self" in the first place, just the process of continual self-construction or "selfing." If we could only recognize the process of selfing as an ingrained habit and then give ourselves permission to take the day off, to stop trying so hard to be "somebody" and instead just experience being, perhaps we would be a lot happier and more relaxed.

—JON KABAT-ZINN, *Wherever You Go, There You Are*

I feel myself a soul as immense as the world, truly a soul as deep as the deepest rivers, my chest has the power to expand without limit. I am a master and I am advised to adopt the humility of the cripple. Yesterday, awakening to the world, I saw the sky turn upon itself utterly and wholly. I wanted to rise, but the disemboweled silence fell back upon me, its wings paralyzed. Without responsibility, straddling Nothingness and Infinity, I began to weep.

—FRANTZ FANON, *Black Skin, White Masks*

If you gaze for long into the abyss, the abyss also gazes into you.

—FRIEDRICH WILHELM NIETZSCHE

The awakening of consciousness is not unlike the crossing of a frontier—one step and you are in another country.

—ADRIENNE RICH

Along with a physicist friend, I made my way up from Katmandu, the capital, to be nearer the Himalayas. We found a beautiful alpine lake, which Nepalese princes once favored as a summer retreat.

For less than a dollar, we rented a boat and pushed out onto the water. It was a windy day with clearing skies, a perfect day to fly kites. I had bought one at the bazaar, painted a fierce red and built for acrobatics. I stood up, and it jumped out of my hand as I let it loose on the wind.

The tiny kite floated up into the high, thin air. I stood looking up toward the great mountains around us. Though they hid their heads in the clouds, they gave off an aura of grandeur and peace. As I watched, the clouds lifted all at once. I was absolutely in awe. What I had taken for mountains were only foothills! Beyond them, like ancient gods, rose the true Himalayas, unbelievably mighty and majestic.

We could hardly speak, so much power and beauty was concentrated in that breathtaking scene. The sense of having a small, isolated self disappeared, and in its place was the delicious sensation of flowing out into everything I beheld. I felt a sense of complete fullness contained in my own silence. Fittingly, the tallest peak before us was Annapurna, whose name means "fullness of life."

Standing there on the lake, I saw directly into the reality where time really is timeless. The same power that reared these mountains was flowing through me. If I wanted to find the source of time and space, I only needed to place my fingers over my heart. The single adequate word to describe my sensations at that moment is *bliss*. —ROBERT KEITH WALLACE, Nepal, India, 1974

In self-abandonment the self is abandoned, which is to say the perimeters of self and other are disregarded, and one feels oneself expand even as the sense of self is fading away. . . . "Ecstasy," from the Greek *ekstasis*, literally means "standing outside oneself." —DUDLEY YOUNG, *Origins of the Sacred*

The birds have vanished into the sky,
and now the last cloud drains away.

We sit together, the mountain and me,
until only the mountain remains.

—LI PO, Chinese poet

THE PROPHET

Parched with the spirit's thirst, I crossed
An endless desert sunk in gloom,
And a six-winged seraph came
Where the tracks met and I stood lost.
Fingers light as dream he laid
Upon my lids; I opened wide
My eagle eyes, and gazed around.
He laid his fingers on my ears
And they were filled with roaring sound:
I heard the music of the spheres,
The flight of angels through the skies,
The beasts that crept beneath the sea,
The heady uprush of the vine;
And, like a lover kissing me,
He rooted out this tongue of mine
Fluent in lies and vanity;
He tore my fainting lips apart
And, with his right hand steeped in blood,
He armed me with a serpent's dart;
With his bright sword he split my breast;
My heart leapt to him with a bound;
A glowing livid coal he pressed
Into the hollow of the wound.
There in the desert I lay dead,
And God called out to me and said:
"Rise, prophet, rise, and hear, and see,

And let my works be seen and heard
By all who turn aside from me,
And burn them with my fiery word."

—ALEXANDER PUSHKIN

My heart was split, and a flower
   appeared; and grace sprang up;
   and it bore fruit for my God.
You split me, tore my heart
   open, filled me with love.
You poured your spirit into me;
   I knew you as I know myself.

—THE ODES OF SOLOMON

My soul has been carried away, and usually my head as well, without my being able to prevent it.

—ST. TERESA

Why are you here? You are here to take the curriculum. You can use your own "case" (your negativity, anger, lust, fear, and so on) as a stepping-stone. . . . You move from somebodiness to nobodiness; when you are nobody you are free to be everybody and everything.

—BABA RAM DASS

What actually happened was something absurdly simple and unspectacular: I stopped thinking. A peculiar quiet, an odd kind of alert limpness or numbness, came over me. Reason and imagination and all mental chatter died down. For once, words really failed me. Past and future dropped away. I forgot who and what I was, my name, manhood, animalhood, all that could be called mine. It was as if I had been born that instant, brand-new, mindless, innocent of all memories. There existed only the

Now, that present moment and what was clearly given in it. To look was enough. And what I found was khaki trouser legs terminating downwards in a pair of brown shoes, khaki sleeves terminating sideways in a pair of pink hands, and a khaki shirtfront terminating upwards in—absolutely nothing whatever! Certainly not in a head.

It took me no time at all to notice that this nothing, this hole where a head should have been, was no ordinary vacancy, no mere nothing. On the contrary, it was very much occupied. It was a vast emptiness vastly filled, a nothing that found room for everything—room for grass, trees, shadowy distant hills, and far above them snowpeaks like a row of angular clouds riding the blue sky. I had lost a head and gained a world.

—D. E. HARDING, *On Having No Head*

When thine eye is single, thy whole body is full of light.

—JESUS OF NAZARETH

THE PRAEPARATIVE

Before I knew these Hands were mine,
Or that my Sinews did my Members join;
　When neither Nostril, Foot, nor Ear,
As yet could be discern'd or did appear;
　I was within
A House I knew not; newly clothed with Skin.

Then was my Soul my only All to me,
　A living, endless Eye,
　Scarce bounded with the Sky,
Whose Power, and Act, and Essence was to see;
　I was an inward Sphere of Light,

Or an interminable Orb of Sight,

    Exceeding that which makes the Days. . . .

— THOMAS TRAHERNE

Lo, I am with you always, means when you look for God,

God is in the look of your eyes,

in the thought of looking, nearer to you than your self,

or things that have happened to you.

There's no need to go outside.

Be melting snow.

Wash yourself of yourself.

A white flower grows in the quietness.

Let your tongue become that flower.

— JALAL AL-DIN RUMI

THE MIND OF ABSOLUTE TRUST

The Great Way isn't difficult

    for those who are unattached to their preferences.

Let go of longing and aversion,

    and everything will be perfectly clear.

When you cling to a hairbreadth of distinction,

    heaven and earth are set apart.

If you want to realize the truth,

    don't be for or against.

The struggle between good and evil

    is the primal disease of the mind.

Not grasping the deeper meaning,
    you just trouble your mind's serenity.
As vast as infinite space,
    it is perfect and lacks nothing.
But because you select and reject,
    you can't perceive its true nature.
Don't get entangled in the world;
    don't lose yourself in emptiness.
Be at peace in the oneness of things,
    and all errors will disappear by themselves.

If you don't live the Tao,
    you fall into assertion or denial.
Asserting that the world is real,
    you are blind to its deeper reality;
denying that the world is real,
    you are blind to the selflessness of all things. . . .
Step aside from all thinking,
    and there is nowhere you can't go. . . .

All at once you are free,
    with nothing left to hold on to.
All is empty, brilliant,
    perfect in its own being.
In the world of things as they are,
    there is no self, no nonself.
If you want to describe its essence,
    the best you can say is "Not-two."

In this "Not-two" nothing is separate,
    and nothing in the world is excluded.
The enlightened of all times and places
    have entered into this truth.
In it there is no gain or loss;
    one instant is ten thousand years.
There is no here, no there;
    infinity is right before your eyes. . . .

Being is an aspect of nonbeing;
    nonbeing is no different from being.
Until you understand this truth,
    you won't see anything clearly.
One is all; all
    are one. When you realize this,
    what reason for holiness or wisdom?
The mind of absolute trust
    is beyond all thought, all striving,
is perfectly at peace, for in it
    there is no yesterday, no today, no tomorrow.

                                          — SENG-TS'AN, Zen master

The Golden God, the Self, the immortal Swan
leaves the small nest of the body, goes where He wants.
He moves through the realm of dreams; makes numberless forms;
delights in sex; eats, drinks, laughs with His friends;
frightens Himself with scenes of heart-chilling terror.

But He is not attached to anything that He sees;

and after He has wandered in the realms of dream and awakeness,

has tasted pleasures and experienced good and evil,

He returns to the blissful state from which He began.

As a fish swims forward to one riverbank then the other,

Self alternates between awakeness and dreaming.

As an eagle, weary from long flight, folds its wings,

gliding down to its nest, Self hurries to the realm

of dreamless sleep, free of desires, fear, pain.

As a man in sexual union with his beloved

is unaware of anything outside or inside,

so a man in union with Self knows nothing, wants nothing,

has found his heart's fulfillment and is free of sorrow.

Father disappears, mother disappears, gods

and scriptures disappear, thief disappears, murderer,

rich man, beggar disappear, world disappears,

good and evil disappear; he has passed beyond sorrow.

— THE UPANISHADS

Within man is the soul of the whole; the wise silence; the universal beauty, to which every part and particle is equally related; the eternal ONE. And this deep power in which we exist and whose beatitude is all accessible to us is not only self-sufficing and perfect in every hour, but the act of seeing and the thing seen, the seer and the spectacle, the subject and the object, are one. We see the world piece by piece, as the sun, the moon, the animal, the tree; but the whole, of which these are the shining parts, is the soul. . . . Every man's words who speaks from that life must sound vain to those who do not dwell in the same thought on their own part. I dare not speak for it. My words do not carry its august sense; they fall short and cold. Only itself can inspire whom it will. . . . As I have said, it contradicts all experiences.

In like manner, it abolishes time and space. The influence of the senses has in most men overpowered the mind to that degree that the walls of time and space have come to look real and insurmountable; and to speak with levity of these limits is, in the world, the sign of insanity.

—RALPH WALDO EMERSON, *The Best of Ralph Waldo Emerson*

I have been in that Heaven of His most light,
and what I saw, those who descend from there
lack both the knowledge and the power to write.

For as our intellect draws near its goal
it opens to such depths of understanding
as memory cannot plumb within the soul.

—DANTE ALIGHIERI, *The Divine Comedy: Paradiso*

It is no merely human joy to lose oneself like this, so to be emptied of oneself as though one almost ceased to be at all; it is the bliss of heaven . . . to become thus is to be deified. . . . How otherwise could God be "all in all" if anything of man remained in man?

—ST. BERNARD, *On the Love of God*

God, whose love and joy
are present everywhere,
can't come to visit you
unless you aren't there.

—ANGELUS SILESIUS, German priest and poet

Midnight. No waves,
no wind, the empty boat
is flooded with moonlight.

—DŌGEN, Zen master

We shape clay into a pot, but it is the emptiness inside that holds whatever we want.

—LAO-TZU, Tao-te Ching

Those who realize true wisdom,
rapt within this clear awareness,
see me as the universe's
origin, imperishable.

All their words and all their actions
issue from the depths of worship;
held in my embrace, they know me
as a woman knows her lover.

Creatures rise, creatures vanish;
I alone am real, Arjuna,
looking out, amused, from deep
within the eyes of every creature.

I am the object of all knowledge,
father of the world, its mother,
source of all things, of impure and
pure, of holiness and horror.

I am the goal, the root, the witness,
home and refuge, dearest friend,
creation and annihilation,
everlasting seed and treasure.

I am the radiance of the sun, I
open or withhold the rain clouds,
I am immortality and
death, am being and nonbeing.

I am the Self, Arjuna, seated
in the heart of every creature.
I am the origin, the middle,
and the end that all must come to.

Those who worship me sincerely
with their minds and bodies, giving
up their whole lives in devotion,
find in me their heart's fulfillment.

Even those who do not know me,
if their actions are straightforward,
just, and loving, venerate me
with the truest kind of worship.

All your thoughts, all your actions,
all your fears and disappointments,
offer them to me, clear-hearted;
know them all as passing visions.

Thus you free yourself from bondage,
from both good and evil karma;

through your nonattachment, you
embody me, in utter freedom.

I am justice: clear, impartial,
favoring no one, hating no one.
But in those who have cured themselves of
selfishness, I shine with brilliance.

Even murderers and rapists,
tyrants, the most cruel fanatics,
ultimately know redemption
through my love, if they surrender
to my harsh but healing graces.
Passing through excruciating
transformations, they find freedom
and their hearts find peace within them.

I am always with all beings;
I abandon no one. And
however great your inner darkness,
you are never separate from me.

Let your thoughts flow past you, calmly;
keep me near, at every moment;
trust me with your life, because I
am you, more than you yourself are.

— THE BHAGAVAD GITA

i found god in myself / and i loved her fiercely.

—NTOZAKE SHANGE

My body is God's, my mind is God's, my being itself is God's, all on loan to nothing and no one. But if I'm not here, I know Who is!

—ALAN WATTS

Who *is* the Potter, pray, and who the Pot?

—OMAR KHAYYÁM, *The Rubá'iyát*

Man lives in God, and the circumference of life cannot be rightly drawn until the center is set.

—BENJAMIN MAYS

When he was about eighteen, Allan had accidentally stumbled into the trance called Shivadar-shana, in which the universe, having been perceived in its totality as a single phenomenon, independent of space and time, is then annihilated. This experience had determined the whole course of his life. His one object was to get back into that state.

—ALEISTER CROWLEY, *The Confessions of Aleister Crowley*

Attachment to things, identification with things, keep alive a thousand useless "I's" in a man. These "I's" must die in order that the big "I" may be born.

—GEORGE IVANOVICH GURDJIEFF

GOD HAS STOLEN MY "I" FROM ME

God has stolen my [illusory] "I" from me and has brought me near to my [real] "I," and the disappearance of the earth has brought the disappearance of heaven. The whole and the part have merged. The vertical and the horizontal are annihilated. . . . The voyage has reached its end and everything other than Him has ceased to exist.

— AMIR 'ABD AL-KADER

With God, two "I's" cannot find room. You say "I" and He says "I." Either you die before Him, or let Him die before you; then duality will not remain. But it is impossible for Him to die, either subjectively or objectively, since He is the Living God, the Undying. He possesses such Gentleness that were it possible, He would die for you so that duality might vanish. But since it is impossible for Him to die, you die, so that He may manifest Himself to you and duality may vanish.   — JALAL AL-DIN RUMI

God . . . when he has just decided to launch upon his work of creation is called *He*. God in the complete unfolding of his Being, Bliss and Love, in which he becomes capable of being perceived by the reasons of the heart . . . is called *You*. But God, in his supreme manifestation, where the fullness of His Being finds its final expression in the last and all-embracing of his attributes, is called *I*.

— MOSES DE LEÓN, Spanish Kabbalist

My father and I are one.

— JESUS OF NAZARETH

[T]he sole purpose of your incarnation is the crucifixion of the ego . . . to grow in love, to expand that love, and to merge with God and this is best done through service.

— SATHYA SAI BABA, Indian mystic

The Master shows you the best and natural way of coming closer and closer to God, until you merge into Him and become One with Him so that your individual identity is totally absorbed in God-hood. Then you no longer live, but God lives, and nothing is, but God is. You have become Love. You are Love. You are your Master. You are the lover and the beloved. You are Eternity.

— BAMBI BAABA, *Redeemer of the New Age*

One should get rid of a selfish mind and replace it with a mind that is earnest to help others. An act to make another happy inspires the other to make still another happy, and so happiness is born from such an act.

Thousands of candles can be lighted from a single candle, and the life of the candle will not be shortened. Happiness never decreases by being shared. — THE BUDDHA

I must not ignore the wounded man on life's Jericho Road, because he is a part of me and I am a part of him. His agony diminishes me, and his salvation enlarges me. — MARTIN LUTHER KING, JR.

Our physical consciousness is the loud voice in each of us. This voice guides us every waking moment. However, there is another level of intelligence that many of us never visit. The inner voice, the quiet side, a shared intelligence found in all life, a peacefulness that goes beyond fear and rejection. It is an inner intelligence that does not have a defined limit. It is a stillness that is always there wanting to be activated, to be called upon. It is the intelligence within the intelligence: our spirit or the spiritual self in us. The seeker.

The quality of our lives, and the real beauty in our days is determined by the spirit in each of us and how we share it with others. — HAKI R. MADHUBUTI, *Claiming Earth*

It is this indwelling divine intelligence that we must identify as our Self. . . . Imagine having this indwelling intelligence that knows how to run the machinery of your body, running your career, education, your marriage, your nation, and so on.

— RA UN NEFER AMEN, *Metu Neter*

II

Oneness

I am that I am.

— OLD TESTAMENT

Here's the thing, say Shug. The thing I believe. God is inside you and inside everybody else. You come into the world with God. But only them that search for it inside find it. And sometimes it just manifest itself even if you not looking, or don't know what you looking for. Trouble do it for most folks, I think. Sorrow, lord. Feeling like shit.

It? I ast.

Yeah, It. God ain't a he or a she, but a It.

But what do it look like? I ast.

Don't look like nothing, she say. It ain't a picture show. It ain't something you can look at apart from anything else, including yourself. I believe God is everything, say Shug. Everything that is or ever was or ever will be. And when you can feel that, and be happy to feel that, you've found It. . . .

She say, My first step from the old white man was trees. Then air. Then birds. Then other people. But one day when I was sitting quiet and feeling like a motherless child, which I was, it come to me: that feeling of being part of everything, not separate at all. I knew that if I cut a tree, my arm would bleed. And I laughed and I cried and I run all around the house. I knew just what it was. In fact, when it happen, you can't miss it. It sort of like you know what, she say, grinning and rubbing high up on my thigh.

Shug! I say.

Oh, she say. God love all them feelings. That's some of the best stuff God did. And when you know God loves 'em you enjoys 'em a lot more. You can just relax, go with everything that's going, and praise God by liking what you like.

God don't think it dirty? I ast.

Naw, she say. God made it. Listen, God love everything you love—and a mess of stuff you don't. But more than anything else, God love admiration.

You saying God vain? I ast.

Naw, she say. Not vain, just wanting to share a good thing. I think it pisses God off if you walk by the color purple in a field somewhere and don't notice it.

What it do when it pissed off? I ast.

Oh, it make something else. People think pleasing God is all God care about. But any fool living in the world can see it always trying to please us back.

Yeah? I say.

Yeah, she say. It always making little surprises and springing them on us when us least expect.

You mean it want to be loved, just like the bible say.

Yes, Celie, she say. Everything want to be loved. Us sing and dance, make faces and give flower bouquets, trying to be loved. You ever notice that trees do everything to git attention we do, except walk?

— ALICE WALKER, *The Color Purple*

God is not a person residing in a certain place, though it is possible to have a personal God-experience within the self. For *the only place God can be looked for and found is within,* not in any other place. God's existence can be deduced outside of the self from the beauty of Creation, from the manifestations of nature, from the wisdom collected by philosophers and scientists. But such observations become an experience of God only when God's presence is felt first within. The inner experience of God is the greatest of all experiences because it contains all desirable experiences.

— EVA PIERRAKOS, *The Pathwork of Self-Transformation*

People see God every day, they just don't recognize him.

— PEARL BAILEY

In the faces of men and women I see God, and in my own face in the glass;
I find letters from God dropped in the street, and every one is signed by God's name. . . .

— WALT WHITMAN, *Leaves of Grass*

A Course in Miracles tells us that all human conflicts stem from the fact that we do not recognize ourselves, our brothers, or even God. We make them strangers by misperceiving them. And having turned them into "the other," we attack our brothers. Such judgment always involves rejection; the choice to judge our brother rather than to know him causes loss of peace.

Let's begin, then, to know ourselves, to get clear on who we are.

— SONDRA RAY, *Loving Relationships II*

The thing is to see all faces as the masks of God, all characters as his roles.   — ALAN WATTS

I take a totally different view of God and Nature from that which the later Christians usually entertain, for I hold that God is the immanent, and not the extraneous, cause of all things. I say, All is in God; all lives and moves in God.

— BENEDICT (BARUCH) SPINOZA

ALL

Through many incarnations, the ALL has brought about,
the message of the ONENESS we all must soon find out,

Hari Rama, Hari Krishna, Allah and Buddha too,
Jehovah and Jesus Christ, just to name a few.

The final realization that everything is ONE
will take a bit of doing, but yet it must be done.
Spirit, ALL is spirit, spirit is all there is,
no matter what form it takes, be it yours, hers or his.

ALL time is now.
ALL space is here.
ALL life is endless.
ALL love is near.

ALL minds relate.
ALL souls evolve.
ALL forms are changing.
ALL thoughts resolve.

ALL words take shape.
ALL will directs.
ALL deeds are binding.
ALL faith protects.

ALL ears are deaf.
ALL eyes are blind.
ALL things are spirit.
ALL is in mind.

The father, son and mother of all the universe
is power, presence, knowledge, for which we all do search.
Through the mind, through the body, shining right through the soul,
the spirit that is within, tries to make us whole.

However long it takes me, wherever I may go,
I must become the master of body, mind and soul.
All the persons, all the places, the things that I might see,
the spirit is there within, yearning to be free.

— HORACE SILVER

Once you become aware of this force for unity in life, you can't ever forget it. It becomes part of everything you do.

— JOHN COLTRANE

Creation exists in finding unity, finding likenesses, finding pattern. . . . Nature is chaos. It is full of infinite variety . . . [but] there comes a moment when many different aspects suddenly crystallize in a single unity. You have found the key; you have found the clue; you have found the path that organizes the material. You have found what Coleridge called "unity in variety." That is the moment of creation.

— JACOB BRONOWSKI, *A Sense of the Future*

. . . The birth and dissolution of the cosmos itself take place in me. There is nothing that exists separate from me, Arjuna. The entire universe is suspended from me as my necklace of jewels.

. . . I am the taste of pure water and the radiance of the sun and moon. I am the sacred word and the sound heard in air, and the courage of human beings. I am the sweet fragrance in the earth and the radiance of fire; I am the life in every creature and the striving of the spiritual aspirant.

My eternal seed, Arjuna, is to be found in every creature. I am the power of discrimination in those who are intelligent, and the glory of the noble. In those who are strong, I am strength, free from passion and selfish attachment. I am desire itself, if that desire is in harmony with the purpose of life.

. . . I am the true Self in the heart of every creature, Arjuna, and the beginning, middle, and end of their existence.

. . . I am death, which overcomes all, and the source of all beings still to be born. I am the feminine qualities: fame, beauty, perfect speech, memory, intelligence, loyalty, and forgiveness.

I am the seed that can be found in every creature, Arjuna; for without me nothing can exist, neither animate nor inanimate.

But of what use is it to you to know all this, Arjuna? Just remember that I am, and that I support the entire cosmos with only a fragment of my being.

—THE BHAGAVAD GITA

I was sitting by the ocean one late summer afternoon, watching the waves rolling in and feeling the rhythm of my breathing, when I suddenly became aware of my whole environment as being engaged in a gigantic cosmic dance. Being a physicist, I knew that the sand, rocks, water and air around me were made of vibrating molecules and atoms, and that these consisted of particles which interacted with one another by creating and destroying other particles. I knew also that the Earth's atmosphere was continually bombarded by showers of "cosmic rays," particles of high energy undergoing multiple collisions as they penetrated the air. All this was familiar to me from my research in high-energy physics, but until that moment I had only experienced it through graphs, diagrams and mathematical theories. As I sat on that beach my former experiences came to life; I "saw" cascades of energy coming down from outer space, in which particles were created and destroyed in rhythmic pulses; I "saw" the atoms of the elements and those of my body participating in this cosmic dance of energy; I felt its rhythm and I "heard" its sound, and at that moment I knew that this was the Dance of Shiva, the Lord of Dancers worshipped by the Hindus.

— FRITJOF CAPRA, *The Tao of Physics*

O hidden Life,
   vibrant in every atom,
O hidden Light,
   shining in every creature,
O hidden Love,
   embracing all in oneness,
May all who feel themselves
   as one with thee
Know they are therefore one
   with every other.

— ANNIE BESANT, English theosophist

Suddenly my perceptions changed, turning inside out in an instant. . . . I felt as if everything around me, other than the strangely immobile fire and my companions, had come to life—a strange life. . . . All around me and underneath me I could feel life pulsating, down to the smallest piece of dirt on the ground. . . . Everything seemed alive with meaning. . . . Each person was like the sum total of all the emanations taking place. The people, however, were not in charge of the operation of the universe around them—they were dependent on it and they were useful to it as well. . . . Without being able to put it into words, I understood what was happening, for at that stage of consciousness there is no difference between meaning and being. Things had become their meaning. . . . All I could do was to feel and honor the effects of the subtle invisible world breaking through my own blindness and preempting my perceptions. How acquiescent one becomes when face-to-face with the pure universal energy!

— MALIDOMA SOMÉ, *Of Water and the Spirit*

...I am aware that all the race, in some very meaningful sense, breathes through me—that I am a part of the very pulsating rhythm of existence. —HOWARD THURMAN, *Meditations of the Heart*

The universe is elegantly simple in times of lucidity, but we clutter up our lives with such senseless structures in an effort to make scientific thought work, to make logic seem logical and valuable. We blind ourselves and bind ourselves with a lot of nonsense in our scramble away from simple realities like the fact that everything is one in this place, on this planet. We and everything here are extensions of the same consciousness, and we are co-creators of that mind, will, thought.

—TONI CADE BAMBARA, a dialogue with Claudia Tate, *Black Women Writers at Work*

[T]here is indeed a great force in the world, a force spiritual and able to shape the physical universe, but that force is not something cut off, not something separate from ourselves. It is an energy in us, strongest in our working, breathing, thinking together as one people; weakest when we are scattered, confused, broken into individual, unconnected fragments.

—AYI KWEI ARMAH, *Two Thousand Seasons*

All are caught in an inescapable network of mutuality, tied in a single garment of destiny. Whatever affects one directly, affects all indirectly. I can never be what I ought to be until you are what you ought to be, and you can never be what you ought to be until I am what I ought to be.

—MARTIN LUTHER KING, JR.

Where I wander—You!
Where I ponder—You!
Only You everywhere, You, always You.
You, You, You.
When I am gladdened—You!

And when I am saddened—You!
Only You, everywhere You!
You, You, You.
Sky is You!
Earth is You!
You above! You below!
In every trend, at every end,
Only You, everywhere You!

—LEVI YITZCHAK OF BERDICHEV

The world is no more than the Beloved's single face;
In the desire of the One to know its own beauty, we exist.

—GHĀLIB, Indian poet

I am reality without beginning, without equal. I have no part in the illusion of "I" and "you," "this" and "that." I am Brahman, one without a second, bliss without end, the eternal, unchanging truth. . . . I dwell within all beings as the soul, the pure consciousness, the ground of all phenomena, internal and external. I am both the enjoyer and that which is enjoyed. In the days of my ignorance, I used to think of these as being separate from myself. Now I know that I am All.   —SHANKARA, Hindu mystic

In the everlasting Presence, you are the Witness and the Witnessed!   —JALAL AL-DIN RUMI

Our soul is oned to God,
unchangeable goodness,
and therefore

between God and our soul
there is neither wrath nor forgiveness
because
there is no between.

— DAME JULIAN OF NORWICH

There is no time, no place, no state where God is absent. — MARIANNE WILLIAMSON

[T]he evils of this world are evil only in the consciousness that accepts them as such. Wherever there is an acceptance of the universal belief in two powers, there are two powers; and there, two powers operate. Wherever a person rises in spiritual consciousness to a place where he recognizes that the Omnipotence of God—and I now give you that word *Omnipotence* to ponder—makes any other so-called power no power, he discovers that there cannot be Omnipotence *and* another power, there cannot be All-power *and* another power. He either deals with Omnipotence as Omnipotence by being convinced of the nonpower of any other appearance or condition, or he merely pays lip service to it and then sings hymns to God Almighty, but "pass the ammunition." — JOEL S. GOLDSMITH, *The Contemplative Life*

The nature of God is a circle of which the center is everywhere and the circumference is nowhere. — EMPEDOCLES

You are He manifesting as you. You are as legitimate as He is. If you are a part of God then He is also a part of you, and in denying your own worth you end up denying His as well. I do not like to use the term "He," meaning God, since All That Is is the origin of not only all sexes but of all realities.

— JANE ROBERTS, *The Nature of Personal Reality* (Seth speaking through Jane Roberts)

Know One, know all.

—THE KATHA UPANISHAD

All the beliefs which are professed about Him are for Him just different names. Now, the multiplicity of names does not imply multiplicity of the Named! He has a Name in all languages, which are infinite in number, but that does not affect His unicity. . . .

He is—may He be exalted!—the essential reality of everything whose existence is conceivable, imaginable or perceived by the senses, the One who does not multiply Himself or divide Himself. He is at the same time all things that are contrary and all things that are alike; and there is nothing other than that in the universe. He is at the same time "the First and the Last, the Apparent and the Hidden" (Kor. 57:3); and there is nothing other than that in the universe. The places where He manifests Himself do not limit Him, the opinions and the beliefs of the ancients or the moderns do not contain Him. . . . He conforms to the opinion which each believer has of Him and with what the tongue of each speaker says of Him, for the opinion and the speech are His creations. Every representation which is made of Him is really Him, and His presence in this representation does not cease if the one who represented Him in this way later represents Him otherwise: He will be equally present in this new representation. He is limited for someone who believes and represents Him to be limited, absolute for someone who believes Him absolute. He is substance or accident, transcendent or immanent, He is pure concept; or He resides in the heavens, or on the earth, and so on, in conformity with each of the innumerable beliefs and doctrines.

This is why someone has said, "Each time that something comes to your mind regarding Allah—know that He is different from that!" This saying is rich in meaning in the order of essential truths. . . . Its true meaning is that God is not contained in any one particular belief or doctrine but that He is, in a certain respect, whatever someone says who speaks of Him or whatever each believer believes. Whatever comes to your mind regarding Allah, His essence and His attributes, know that He is that and that He is other than that! . . . Allah is not limited by what comes to your mind—that is to say, your creed—or enclosed in the doctrine you profess. . . .

If what you think and believe is the same as what the people of the Sunna say, know that He is that—and other than that! If you think and believe that He is what all the schools of Islam profess and believe—He is that, and He is other than that! If you think that He is what the diverse communities believe—Muslims, Christians, Jews, Mazdeans, polytheists and others—He is that and He is other than that! And if you think and believe what is professed by the Knowers par excellence—prophets, saints and angels—He is that! He is other than that! None of His creatures worships Him in all His aspects; none is unfaithful to Him in all His aspects. No one knows Him in all His aspects; no one is ignorant of Him in all His aspects.

—AMIR 'ABD AL-KADER

I, Isis, am all that has been, all that is or shall be, and no mortal man has ever unveiled me.

—INSCRIPTION ON THE TEMPLE OF ISIS

Blessed are the pure in heart:
for they shall see God.

We are told, "No man hath seen God at any time" (John 1:18). . . . God is not to be seen with the physical eyes, for God is a whole of which man is a part. Every part is a manifestation of God. . . . So every part contains the essence, and thus the potential of the whole. If man is conscious of the whole within himself, then he *is* whole. . . . When you are pure in heart, when you are unalterably convinced that "There is only one presence and one power, God, the good, omnipotent," then you see God everywhere, you see good everywhere . . . you are seeing things, not as they are, but as you are.

If you want to change the world, or to be an influence for such a change, you must begin within yourself by changing the way you see the world.　　—ERIC BUTTERWORTH, *Discover the Power Within You*

Nurturing our own inner awareness is essential to a deepening of our vision of oneness. It is the beginning of our spiritual life. Such nurturing is more than an act of compassion for ourselves; it is an act of compassion towards our world. To learn to connect with and honor our own spirit and dignity is the beginning of learning to honor the spirit and dignity of all life.

—CHRISTINA FELDMAN, *Woman Awake*

Whatever is, is sacred.

—JEAN TOOMER

If you are a poet, you will see clearly that there is a cloud floating in this sheet of paper. Without a cloud, there will be no rain; without rain, the trees cannot grow; and without trees, we cannot make paper. The cloud is essential for the paper to exist. If the cloud is not here, the sheet of paper cannot be here either. So we can say that the cloud and the paper *inter-are*. "Inter-being" is a word that is not in the dictionary yet, but if we combine the prefix "inter-" with the verb "to be," we have a new verb, *inter-be*. Without a cloud, we cannot have paper, so we can say that the cloud and the sheet of paper inter-are.

If we look into this sheet of paper even more deeply, we can see the sunshine in it. If the sunshine is not there, the forest cannot grow. In fact, nothing can grow. Even we cannot grow without sunshine. And so, we know that the sunshine is also in this sheet of paper. The paper and the sunshine inter-are. And if we continue to look, we can see the logger who cut the tree and brought it to the mill to be transformed into paper. And we see the wheat. We know that the logger cannot exist without his daily bread, and therefore the wheat that became his bread is also in this sheet of paper. And the logger's father and mother are in it too. When we look in this way, we see that without all of these things, this sheet of paper cannot exist.

Looking even more deeply, we can see we are in it too. This is not difficult to see, because when we look at a sheet of paper, the sheet of paper is part of our perception. Your mind is in here and mine is also. So we can say that everything is in here with this sheet of paper. You cannot point out one thing that is not here—time, space, the earth, the rain, the minerals in the soil, the sunshine, the cloud, the river, the heat. Everything coexists with this sheet of paper. That is why I think the word "inter-be" should be in the dictionary. "To be" is to inter-be. You cannot just *be* by yourself, alone. You have to inter-be with every other thing. This sheet of paper is, because everything else is.

—THÍCH NHÂT HANH, *The Heart of Understanding*

Lift the stone and you will find me; cleave the wood and I am there.   —JESUS OF NAZARETH

And if you would know God be not
therefore a solver of riddles.

Rather look about you and you shall see
Him playing with your children.

And look into space; you shall see Him
walking in the cloud, outstretching His arms
in the lightning and descending in rain.

You shall see Him smiling in flowers,
then rising and waving His hands in trees.

—KAHLIL GIBRAN, *The Prophet*

Not long ago I joined up with some cousins and paid a visit to the old homestead, which had been sold to a man who wanted the land only for hunting. We found that the barn had fallen to the ground and was now completely hidden by brush; even the house was no longer visible among the tall grasses that had grown up around its foundation. But a piece of the orchard was still visible, and the chestnut trees had not lost their nobility and kindliness. My cousins and I talked about those trees and some of the people who had sat under them on hot summer days telling tall tales and innumerable stories about the past. I remembered an uncle making a slanted cut on a small twig from the tree, showing me the marks of horseshoe nails in the cross-section—his explanation of why the tree was called a horse chestnut.

If someone thinking of widening the road or building a new house should ever come to cut down those chestnut trees, it would be a painful loss for me and many members of my family, not just because the trees are symbols of time past, but because they are living beings filled with beauty and surrounded by a huge aura of memory. In a real sense they are part of the family, bound to us as individuals of another species but not another community.

— THOMAS MOORE, *Care of the Soul*

As Sendivogius, an alchemist, said, "The greater part of the soul lies outside the body." *Mens sana in corpore sano* today means "the body of the world"; if it is not kept healthy, we go insane. The neglect of the environment, the body of the world, is part and parcel of our personal "insanity." The world's body must be restored to health, for in that body is also the world's soul. I don't think spiritual disciplines take the world enough into account; they're always set on transcending, that is, denying it with spiritual practices.

— JAMES HILLMAN, *We've Had a Hundred Years of Psychotherapy—And the World's Getting Worse*

Teach your children what we have taught our children, that the earth is our mother. Whatever befalls the earth, befalls the children of the earth. If we spit upon the ground, we spit upon ourselves. This we know. The earth does not belong to us; we belong to the earth. One thing we know, which the white man may one day discover, our God is the same God. You may think now that you own Him as you wish to own our land, but you cannot. He is the God of all people, and His compassion is equal for all. This earth is precious to God, and to harm the earth is to heap contempt on its Creator. . . . So love it as we have loved it. Care for it as we have cared for it. And with all your mind, with all your heart, preserve it for your children, and love it . . . as God loves us all. . . .

Every part of this earth is sacred to my people. Every shining pine needle, every sandy shore, every mist in the dark woods, every clearing and humming insect is holy in the memory and experience of my people. . . . We are part of the earth and it is part of us. The perfumed flowers are our sisters; the deer, the horse, the great eagle, these are our brothers. The rocky crests, the juices of the meadows, the body heat of the pony, and man all belong to the same family. . . . What is man without the beasts? If all the beasts were gone, men would die from a great loneliness of spirit. For whatever happens to the beasts, soon happens to man. All things are connected. —CHIEF SEATTLE, *Chief Seattle's Testimony*

I was seeing in a sacred manner the shapes of all things in the spirit, and the shape of all shapes as they must live together like one being. And I saw that the sacred hoop of my people was one of many hoops that made one circle, wide as daylight and as starlight, and in the center grew one mighty flowering tree to shelter all the children of one mother and one father. And I saw that it was holy.

—BLACK ELK, holy man of the Oglala Sioux

Trees and animals, humans and insects, flowers and birds: these are active images of the subtle energies that flow from the stars throughout the universe. Meeting and combining with each other and the elements of the Earth, they give rise to all living things. The superior person understands this, and understands that her own energies play a part in it. Understanding these things, she respects the Earth as her mother, the heavens as her father, and all living things as her brothers and sisters.

Those who want to know the truth of the universe should practice . . . reverence for all life; this manifests as unconditional love and respect for oneself and all other beings. —LAO-TZU

Do not think you can love God
and despise creation.
The two are at root One.

—RABBI CHANINA

THE ONE, THE OTHER, THE DIVINE, THE MANY
IN ZULU TRADITIONAL RELIGION OF SOUTHERN AFRICA

One becomes aware that one did not create the universe; one found the universe already created. This awe-inspiring universe with its boundless spaces and measureless forces occasions God-consciousness.

The Zulu notion of God-consciousness . . . says that God lives in, through, and beyond everything and everyone, but that God is most clearly apprehended through those spirits who are always around, below, above, and in them. . . . When the Zulus see the Deity in every place and all the time, they are acknowledging the ubiquitous nature of God as well as their constant sojourn within the realm of the divine presence.

— LIZO DODA JAFTA

The spiritual is real and permeates all existence so that the ancestral spirits, the living dead, are all around us, concerned to promote the well-being of those who are bound together with them in the bundle of life. They are the guardians of morality to ensure the essential harmony of the community remains intact. And so before you partake of a drink you spill a little as a libation to acknowledge the presence of this ever-present cloud of witnesses surrounding the living and yet to be born.

— DESMOND TUTU, *The African Prayer Book*

For the raindrop, joy is in entering the river.

— GHĀLIB

God is the source of a mighty stream of substance, and you are a tributary of that stream, a channel of expression.

— CHARLES FILLMORE

He felt that he had now completely learned the art of listening. He had often heard all this before, all these numerous voices in the river, but today they sounded different. He could no longer distinguish the different voices—the merry voice from the weeping voice, the childish voice from the manly voice. They all belonged to each other: the lament of those who yearn, the laughter of the wise, the cry of indignation and groan of the dying. They were all interwoven and interlocked, entwined in a thousand ways. And all the voices, all the goals, all the yearnings, all the sorrows, all the pleasures, all the good and evil, all of them together was the world. All of them together was the stream of events, the music of life. When Siddhartha listened attentively to this river, to this song of a thousand voices; when he did not listen to the sorrow or laughter, when he did not bind his soul to any one particular voice and absorb it in his self, but heard them all, the whole, the unity; then the great song of a thousand voices consisted of one word: Om—perfection.

—HERMANN HESSE, *Siddhartha*

CHAPTER TEN

Forgive and Be Forgiven

"To err is human, to forgive divine," we are told. And with that we seem to have relinquished the work of forgiveness to a God somewhere outside of ourselves. After all, we confess in rare but convenient moments of humility, we're "only human." We forget that we are human *and* divine, fully qualified to forgive all who have trespassed against us. On the other hand, when we are advised to forgive and forget, too often our grudging response is that we may forgive, but we'll never forget. We sometimes continue to withhold our forgiveness even after we've forgotten the details of the incident we're angry about. But this is just the sort of selected memory—remembering to be angry but forgetting we are also divine—that makes forgiving *and* forgetting possible.

Rather than being present in each moment as it unfolds, most of us live our lives as a collection of moments. Just as a movie is comprised of moments captured on a celluloid filmstrip, we view each experience much like a frame in our own real-life drama. But unlike film, the scenes that don't fit the picture we think our lives should be are not so easily edited out. In life, nothing is left on the cutting room floor; every frame counts, and every take is a good one. How we view them is up to us. But every person in our experience whom we have not forgiven for hurting us is a frame in our film, a part of our life, like it or not. The choice is ours, but if we could see our lives from the divine perspective, we would see each one as perfect and every hurt and misfortune as an integral part of the whole. Kenneth Wapnick, a psychotherapist and author, uses the film metaphor to show how we unconsciously project our feelings of guilt on others, as if they were our movie screen. In playing this blame game, he says, we shift our own shortcomings to others and give ourselves opportunities to forgive the faults we can't bear to look at in ourselves.

Life shows us how to live and love by example. But it also teaches by sending us relationships that challenge us to be loving. Our most difficult relationships offer us our greatest opportunities to grow in wisdom and openheartedness. If we could only see this, we would be grateful to the "teachers" and "task masters" Spirit sends our way. This is the point Wayne W. Dyer makes in the excerpt we've included from his book *Your Sacred Self*. Dyer insists that such "petty tyrants," as he calls them, may turn out to be some of the most important people in your life.

The difficulty we have forgiving is underscored by the fact that we often would rather feel bad than forgive some people. As kids, we used to say, "You make me sick," whenever we became angry at one another. Fortunately, as kids we could be mad one minute and playing together in the next. Adults are not as flexible emotionally. We hold on to our hurts as if they were a set of credentials. But bitterness, like love, creates after its kind. When we criticize and condemn others, we wound ourselves, and not only emotionally and spiritually, but physically as well. And our resentment rarely disturbs the person who offended us. Rather, it destroys the host; it literally makes us sick. But forgiveness is a pain reliever, says sister Iyanla Vanzant. It frees those who forgive, and it is the forgiver who benefits most.

There are certainly acts in our own lives for which we would like to be forgiven. In moments of quiet reflection and reminiscence they come back to haunt us. But these private pangs of conscience are self-inflicted. Ultimately, we are either willing to forgive or we are not, and until we are able to forgive others, totally, we won't be able to forgive ourselves. "Judge not and condemn not," we read in Matthew 7:1 in the New Testament, "For with what judgment ye judge, ye shall be judged." And farther on, in Matthew 25:40, God the King says, "Inasmuch as ye have done it unto one of the least of these my brethren, ye have done it unto me," and "Inasmuch as ye did it not . . . ye did it not to me."

There is a beautiful symmetry in the workings of divine justice. Jesus is saying whatever you do or don't do—whether you judge or judge not, forgive or withhold your forgiveness—you do or fail to do the same unto the Body of Christ, which is only ourselves—all of us, as communicants in the oneness of God. Jesus taught we must do unto others as we would have them do unto us. But the deeper truth is that those "others" *are* us, and we are them. Forgive them as you forgive yourself is what the wisdom of the ages counsels.

We all have our regrets—some secret guilt or private embarrassment we have carried around inside, often for years. It may be something we said or did to someone we have long since lost touch with, someone who today remembers us as the person we were, unaware of how much we have grown and the kind of person we've become. Likewise, those we are still angry with because of their past transgressions are not who they were. They, too, have changed.

The wisest way is always to choose love, for love heals everything in its path. When we feel anger toward someone, rather than allowing it to settle in us or lashing out at the person, we should ask Spirit what we are to learn about ourselves and about life from the experience. Staying in the light, even in the face of anger and pain, is the key to self-mastery. It was a challenge even for Jesus. When he uttered, "Father, forgive them, for they know not what they do," he was speaking to God within himself. For he knew that, as we forgive, so are we forgiven.

I seek your forgiveness for all the times I talked when I should have listened; got angry when I should have been patient; acted when I should have waited; feared when I should have delighted; scolded when I should have encouraged; criticized when I should have complimented; said no when I should have said yes and said yes when I should have said no. I did not know a whole lot about parenting or how to ask for help. I often tried too hard and wanted and demanded so much, and mistakenly sometimes tried to mold you into my image of what I wanted you to be rather than discovering and nourishing you as you emerged and grew.

— MARIAN WRIGHT EDELMAN, *The Measure of Our Success: A Letter to My Children and Yours*

THE HASTY WORD

We see as if by a flash of blinding light the meaning of something which we have done; the hasty word, the careless utterance, the deliberate act by which another was injured or confused, the decision to do what even at the time we felt was neither the right thing nor the thing which we were willing to back with our lives. All of these things crowd in upon us, our Father. We want to be sure that what we say in Thy presence and what we feel in Thy presence will be honest and clear and sincere. As we look at this aspect of our lives, there is only one moving request which we make and that is for forgiveness. . . .

— HOWARD THURMAN

Let all bitterness, and wrath, and
anger, and clamor, and evil
speaking, be put away from you,
with all malice:

And be ye kind one to another,
tenderhearted, forgiving one
another, even as God for Christ's
sake hath forgiven you.

— EPHESIANS 4:31, 32

Then came Peter to him, and said, Lord, how oft shall my brother sin against me, and I forgive him? till seven times?

Jesus saith unto him, I say not unto thee, Until seven times: but, Until seventy times seven.

—MATTHEW 18:21–22

[Christ] wasn't concerned with the arithmetic here. He was indicating infinity. Forgiveness must be perpetual, a state of consciousness and not just an occasional gesture. Why? Because unforgiveness is a price that man cannot afford to pay. . . .

The man who forgives is no more saintly than one who insists upon keeping clean. In reality, the act of forgiveness constitutes a mental bath—letting go of something that can only poison us within.

We may have a perfect justification for our bitterness and anger. We may be completely righteous in our indignation. But we will have to pay the price of the broken connection of the divine circuits. The power that goes with our divinity is only ours when we act the part. We can have our unforgiveness and bitterness and anger if we so choose, but we will also have our stomach ulcers and nervous tension and heart trouble, and mental and physical breakdowns. Turn on the light—not so much for the benefit of others, but for you. "Forgive and you shall be forgiven."

—ERIC BUTTERWORTH, *Discover the Power Within You*

[F]orgiveness is not a matter of quantity, but of quality. A man cannot forgive up to four hundred and ninety times without forgiveness becoming a part of the habit structure of his being. Forgiveness is not an occasional act; it is a permanent attitude. —MARTIN LUTHER KING, JR.

O, foolish one and blind, what do you know about virtue? Has your life always been beyond reproach? Have you never fallen short of the divine calling? Who are you to point the finger of scorn at your brother? The man who feels self-righteousness rise from his petty virtues, lives a life of self-delusion.

Know this: Virtue does not know that it is virtuous, and could it know, it would immediately become vicious. Virtue is sweet as the morning dew, soft as the evening star, and brilliant as the noonday sun. Could the dew tell why it is sweet, the star say why its light is soft, or the sun say why it shines? When we learn to put away our petty virtues with our petty vices, then shall we see clearly—not what either virtue or vice is—but what Truth is!

— ERNEST HOLMES, *The Science of Mind*

The process of forgiveness—indeed, the chief reason for forgiveness—is selfish. The reason to forgive others is *not* for their sake. They are not likely to know that they need to be forgiven. They're not likely to remember their offense. They are likely to say, "You just made it up." They may even be dead. The reason to forgive is for our own sake. For our own health. Because beyond that point needed for healing, if we hold on to our anger, we stop growing and our souls begin to shrivel.

— M. SCOTT PECK, *Further Along the Road Less Traveled*

Forgiveness is the key to inner peace because it is the mental technique by which our thoughts are transformed from fear to love. . . .

Forgiveness is "selective remembering"—a conscious decision to focus on love and let the rest go. . . .

The decision to let go our grievances against other people is the decision to see ourselves as we truly are, because any darkness we let blind us to another's perfection also blinds us to our own. . . .

Forgiveness is the choice to see people as they are now. When we are angry at people, we are angry because of something they said or did before this moment. But what people said or did is not who they are. Relationships are reborn as we let go perceptions of our brother's past. By bringing the past into the present, we create a future just like the past. By letting the past go, we make room for miracles. . . .

As extensions of God, we are ourselves the spirit of compassion, and in our right minds, we don't seek to judge but to heal. We do this through forgiveness. When someone has behaved unlovingly—when they yell at us, or lie about us, or steal from us—they have lost touch with their essence. They have forgotten who they are. But everything that someone does . . . is either love or a call for love. If someone treats us with love, then of course love is the appropriate response. If they treat us with fear, we are to see their behavior as a call for love.

— MARIANNE WILLIAMSON, *A Return to Love*

Whatever stands between you and that person, stands between you and yourself.

—JEAN TOOMER

[W]e should be grateful for every single person in our lives, especially those with whom we have the most trouble. The ones that we hate the most, that we find the most disagreeable, the most uncomfortable to be with, are the very ones that the Holy Spirit has "sent" to us and can use to show us that we can make another choice about the person we first were tempted to project our guilt onto. If they had not been on the film and screen of our lives, we would not know that this guilt is really in us. Therefore, we would not have the opportunity of letting it go. The only chance we ever have to forgive our guilt and to be free from it is to see it in someone else and to forgive it there.

—KENNETH WAPNICK, *A Talk Given on "A Course in Miracles"*

Compassion and forgiveness make reconciliation possible. Compassion combines the capacity to empathize with another's distress and the will and desire to ease that distress. As black women learn how to ease the distress we feel, our ability to generously give to others (not as self-sacrificing martyrs) will be strengthened. We will then have no need to control and bind others to us by always reminding them about what we have done on their behalf. Rather than seeing giving care as diminishing us, we will experience the kind of caregiving that enriches the giver. When we feel like martyrs, we cannot develop compassion. For compassion requires that we be able to stand outside ourselves and identify with someone else. It is fundamentally rooted in the ability to empathize. . . .

Judging others, presuming to know why they are doing what they are doing, blocks our capacity to know compassion. Often black women judge each other harshly. Cultivating our capacity to empathize would deepen our bonds with one another.

—BELL HOOKS, *Sisters of the Yam*

Forgiveness is the spiritual pain reliever. Without making anyone wrong or beating up on yourself, you can forgive. Most of us believe that when we forgive others, we are excusing their behavior. In some way we think that to forgive is to admit that what has happened is all right. Quite the contrary. Forgiveness moves you out of the way and opens the way for divine justice to prevail. It takes the responsibility from your shoulders, particularly when the focus of your anger is no longer around. Spirit can find anybody, anywhere that person happens to be. When you forgive, you clear your mental and emotional airwaves so that you can get on with your life. God knows who is accountable for what, and in the end, no matter what they did to you, they will not have to answer to you for it. . . .

Forgiveness is not what you do for someone else. It is what you must do to free yourself from distorted perceptions and judgments that create fear, anger, and hatred. It is what you must do to eliminate internal confusion and conflict. I know how hard it is to be angry at a parent. I know the pain and confusion it causes in your life when you carry a broken heart and wounded ego into relationships, into a career, and into the role of being a parent. These toxic emotions create patterns of behavior and cycles of fear that are handed down generation to generation until somebody finds the strength and the courage to say, "Enough! No more! The pain stops here!" Forgiveness stops the pain, breaks the pattern, and ends the cycle of psychological and emotional dysfunction. Forgiveness, like surrender, calls upon the divine wisdom of Spirit. The difference between the two is that surrender is an internal state of stillness that creates an external manifestation, while forgiveness is an external course of action that creates an internal state of stillness.

— IYANLA VANZANT, *The Spirit of a Man*

Everyone who comes into your life in any capacity is valuable. The petty tyrants in your life are just as divine as those who provide you with encouragement and support. Emerson put this important lesson like this: "The whole course of things goes to teach us faith." The *whole course*. This means everything that comes your way. . . .

The bully in your life, pushing your fear and panic buttons, might just be God in disguise, teaching you how to rely on your own wits and transcend this petty tyrant's behavior. The thief who cons you out of your money could represent a divine lesson teaching you to let go and not be attached to your things. The drug pusher may be teaching you how to experience addiction and down-in-the-gutter depression so that you will transcend this reliance on external substances for your highs in life.

All people, and I do mean *all*, are in your life to teach you valuable lessons. Don't ignore those lessons.

Get the message and bless them, and move on. When you ignore them, or simply dismiss them as evil, you fail to understand the truth Emerson knew: Truly, "The whole course of things goes to teach us faith."

—WAYNE W. DYER, *Your Sacred Self*

The unforgiving mind is full of fear, and offers love no room to be itself; no place where it can spread its wings in peace and soar above the turmoil of the world. The unforgiving mind is sad, without the hope of respite and release from pain. It suffers and abides in misery, peering about in darkness, seeing not, yet certain of the danger lurking there.   —FOUNDATION FOR INNER PEACE, *A Course in Miracles*

Be innocent of judgment, unaware
of any thoughts of evil or of good
that ever crossed your mind of anyone.
Now do you know him not. But you are free
to learn of him, and learn of him anew.
Now is he born again to you, and you
are born again to him, without the past
that sentenced him to die, and you with him.
Now is he free to live as you are free,
because an ancient learning passed away,
and left a place for truth to be reborn.

—FOUNDATION FOR INNER PEACE, *Choose Once Again*

Though you have heard "Don't judge," judgment comes unavoidably in day-to-day life. By the actions and behaviors of people, you either approve or disapprove. But always remember that everything is changing, and do not hold on to the judgment. Otherwise your judgment gets solidified like a rock. It brings misery for you and for others.

If judgments are lighter like air, like a breeze, they bring in fragrance, then move away. They could bring a foul smell, then move away. They should not stay there forever.

Judgments are so subtle that you are not even aware of their existence. Judging or labeling someone as judgmental is also a judgment. Only in the state of Being when you are full of love and compassion can you ever be free from all judgments.

Yet the world cannot move without judgments. Until you judge something as good or bad, you cannot do any actions. If you see rotten apples in the market, you say, "No good." Good ones you buy. If someone lies to you ten times, you think next time it also could be a lie. A judgment happens automatically.

—SRI SRI RAVI SHANKAR, *The Way of Grace*

Where there is unforgivingness from past relationships, new relationships may also be filled with mistrust.

We cannot create positive relationships, ones that are whole and totally loving, until we have healed the unhealed relationships from the past. To learn again how to trust, we need to learn to let go of any emotional investments we still have in our hurtful past.

We can trust in the present only when we have truly forgiven the past. This means letting go of the many perceptions we learned very early in our lives. For instance, it means being willing to stop listening to the voice of the ego, telling us never to forgive or forget old hurts because history will surely repeat itself and we might get hurt again. . . .

As we choose the belief system of love, rather than the belief system of the ego, we once again discover that happiness is our natural inheritance and our natural state of being.

How do we transform ourselves? How do we let go of the ego's belief system and begin to accept the belief system of love? The answer is simple, but our egos may try to tell us that it is too difficult.

The answer can be found in the "Bridge of Forgiveness." The foundation for this bridge is built on the very soil of love, where no one can do anything that is unforgivable. As we cross this bridge we discover that everyone is deserving of our total love, and we can learn to let go of the blocks of our ego perceptions so that we can once again love each other, ourselves, and the source of all life unconditionally.

To walk across the Bridge of Forgiveness is to walk the most important Bridge in the Universe, the bridge that can lead us to love, peace, and happiness beyond our wildest dreams. Though our egos will do their very best to distract us from seeing it, the Bridge of Forgiveness is always there, inviting us to cross it, guaranteeing us that in so doing, our relationships will become healed and we will experience more love and peace than we have ever before imagined.

— GERALD G. JAMPOLSKY AND DIANE V. CIRINCIONE, *Love Is the Answer*

[An] immediate necessity is to forgive yourself. It is imperative to say: "I did what I knew to do and it was stupid, but that's all I could do. So now that I have forgiven myself I'll make a change. And it's all right." You are the only person who can forgive yourself. Once that forgiving has taken place, you can then console yourself with the knowledge that a diamond is the result of extreme pressure. Less pressure is crystal, less pressure than that is coal, less than that is fossilized leaves, or just plain dirt. The pressure can make you into something quite precious, quite wonderful, quite beautiful and extremely hard.

— MAYA ANGELOU, interviewed in *And Still We Rise* by Barbara Reynolds

Forgiveness truly is the key to happiness, to simple liking, to heartfelt contentment, and to the certainty we will exist forever in freedom. Just forgive, merely let go of dislike and "justified" resentments, simply forget grievances and bleak anticipations, set all things free of memories and cruel expectations, let loose, let go, let be, and the earth cannot help but sing and your heart dance with it. *Forgive and be happy.* That is the ancient secret, the inner teaching, the hidden answer, the lost knowledge, the only message of the still, quiet voice, the only wisdom ever to be attained.

— HUGH PRATHER, *The Quiet Answer*

CHAPTER ELEVEN

The Many Paths to God

From the time when our most ancient forebears gazed into the night sky with wonder, witnessed the miracle of birth, were haunted by the silence of death, such awe-inspiring phenomena have encouraged the contemplation of the mysteries of life and eternity. And because, as Kahlil Gibran writes, our ears "thirst for the sound" of what our hearts know in silence, we have in every age and culture attempted to put the infinite and inexpressible into words and have used the words to establish diverse religions and spiritual paths. Often the religion we practice is not one we have chosen, but is the religion of our parents, grandparents, and culture that has been handed down to us. More than likely, it is a religion that they were born into as well. And it may very well be one that does not encourage us to ask questions or seek enlightenment, but rather accept religious doctrine on the church's authority. What they offer in return is comfort.

As a young man, I found no comfort in the religion I was baptized into, but then, I was not in pain—either spiritually or existentially—or in need of comforting. In 1970 I had a spiritual awakening. (I can't call it a religious experience; since the experience itself transcended words, it necessarily transcended religion also.) Since then, the raft of my religion has been one of my own making, with planks borrowed from Christianity, Zen Buddhism, Hinduism, Jainism, Judaism, Islam, science, ancestor worship, and anywhere else that offers support for my own experience. It is not comfort but confirmation that delights me, even though it comes only with the discomfort of questioning, always questioning. And I sometimes think that Christianity, for example, forgets that Jesus came not to bring peace but a sword.

In my ongoing effort to puzzle out a picture of reality that most closely resembles my own experience of it, I have separated out into a huge pile the pieces that just don't fit: the hellfire-and-damnation piece, the threatening vengeful-God piece, the Satan piece, the creationist piece, and the one-and-only-true-religion piece, to name a few.

If salvation is what is at stake, then mine is far too important for me to relinquish responsibility for it to any individual minister, book, doctrine, or institution. I once imagined myself standing at the mythical Pearly Gates pleading to St. Peter: "But the Church told me . . ." or "The Bible said . . ." only to have Pete admonish: "God gave you a brain and a deeply seated, intuitive understanding of what's what. You could have used these, but you were lazy and decided it would be easier to accept what somebody else said about God than to embark upon the search yourself." For me, heaven and hell are only metaphors for different states of mind. There is no eternal damnation from which we must be saved, since God is One, and all manifestation must ultimately return to its source, the oneness of God. But there is a hell of a lot of suffering we could be delivered from right here on earth.

Like Khephra, the ritual and rule of my early religious training offered me little in the way of comfort, but unlike him, I needed it. I needed solace from the hurt of feeling isolated and alienated from my family. My parents weren't mean or abusive, they were just removed. Never openly displaying any affection toward each other or us children, Babs and Lawrence were fiercely private, circumspect, cool—if not cold—in the manner that their Victorian upbringing has shaped many African Caribbeans of their generation. I doubt that Mommy or Daddy had even the slightest inkling that I hungered for their love and affection, or how I longed to feel that I was their precious little girl and not a bother or a pest. I yearned to be known and liked in my deepest self and to see myself loved in my parents' eyes. These were such powerful feelings, too powerful for me to ignore.

Early on I was aware that something vital to my happiness was missing. And I've never been shy or reticent about seeking the love I need— even if, at times, I sought it in the wrong places. For a time, I took the route too many young women take—one that is a mindless, meandering search for love and identity. But all of life's roads lead us to wisdom and truth. Some of us travel the long, more difficult way home. For Khephra, illumination came in a blinding flash along the way. He's blessed. I believe most of us travel through the canyons of emptiness and despair to awakening. Some of us find our way to God walking the gauntlet of drug or alcohol addiction. For others it may be the experience of abuse, losing our sense of self-worth, or battling a life-threatening illness. There is no "only way" to truth. Whether we walk consciously or unconsciously, all paths lead to God. It took some time before I recognized there was a spiritual dimension to my longings, that we need much more than our parents' or a lover's affection to sustain and nourish our lives, that on this soul journey nothing can bring us peace but discovering a deeper Self.

Each of us is an individual expression of all that God is. To gain the highest wisdom and insight we must have absolute faith in the divine within ourselves. Wiser souls, philosophies, and theologies can inform and inspire us, but no person or institution can tell us who we are or how we should be. We must learn to listen inwardly and trust what is true for us, the truth that is often drowned out by the ideas and values of others, the same truth that is always available to us in silence. In the words of Ralph Waldo Trine, "There is no more important injunction in all the world, nor one with deeper interior meaning, than 'To thine own self be true.' " All paths back to the Godhead ultimately lead us here.

I feast on and caress the truth in whatever hand in which I find it and give myself over to it joyfully and yield to it from afar my conquered arms, whenever I see it approach.

— MICHEL EYQUEM DE MONTAIGNE

ANY PATH WILL BRING YOU HOME

Your world of illusion is too fond of drawing maps. When something calls you, follow it. Do not be afraid. The only path you are really on is your own. It is all illusion anyway. *In the Greater Reality you have never been on any path, because you have never left Home.*

— PAT RODEGAST AND JUDITH STANTON, *Emmanuel's Book II*

(Emmanuel speaking through Pat Rodegast)

All the hopes, desires, loves, and affections that people have for different things—fathers, mothers, friends, heavens, the earth, gardens, palaces, sciences, works, food, drink—the saint knows that these are desires for God and all those things are veils. When men leave this world and see the King without these veils, then they will know that all were veils and coverings, that the object of their desire was in reality that One Thing. . . . They will see all things face-to-face.   — JALAL AL-DIN RUMI

Many things continue to amaze me, even well into the sixth decade of my life. I'm startled or taken aback when people walk up to me and tell me they are Christians. My first response is the question "Already?" It seems to me a lifelong endeavor to try to live the life of a Christian. I believe that is also true for the Buddhist, for the Muslim, for the Jainist, for the Jew, and for the Taoist who try to live their beliefs. The idyllic condition cannot be arrived at and held on to eternally. It is in the search itself that one finds the ecstasy.   — MAYA ANGELOU, *Wouldn't Take Nothing for My Journey Now*

Religion is doing; a man does not merely *think* his religion or feel it, he "lives" his religion as much as he is able, otherwise it is not religion but fantasy or philosophy.

— GEORGE IVANOVICH GURDJIEFF

There is a road steep and thorny, and beset with perils of every kind, but yet a road, and it leads to the heart of the Universe. I can tell you how to find those who will show you the secret gateway that leads inward only, and closes fast behind the neophyte forevermore. . . . There is no danger that dauntless courage cannot conquer; there is no trial that spotless purity cannot pass through; there is no difficulty that strong intellect cannot surmount. For those who win onward, there is a reward past all telling: the power to bless and serve humanity. For those who fail, there are other lives in which success may come.

—HELENA PETROVNA BLAVATSKY

God speaks to all human beings and all human communities in various ways. All perceive the one God in their own way and take different paths to the service of the ultimate Godhead.

—RABBI HERBERT BRONSTEIN

Some would have us worship, uniformly, at the altar of oneness, using the *idea* of unity rather than an ongoing encounter with it to steamroller-like, flatten out all differences. But it is in the unique qualities of this and that, their particular individuality and properties—in their eachness and their suchness, if you will—that all poetry and art, science and life, wonder, grace, and richness reside.

All faces resemble each other, yet how easily we see in each uniqueness, individuality, an identity. How deeply we value these differences. The ocean is a whole, but it has countless waves, every one different from all the others; it has currents, each unique, ever-changing; the bottom is a landscape all its own, different everywhere; similarly the shoreline. The atmosphere is whole, but its currents have unique signatures, even though they are just wind. Life on earth is a whole, yet it expresses itself in unique time-bound bodies, microscopic or visible, plant or animal, extinct or living. So there can be no one practice, no one way to learn, no one way to love, no one way to grow or to heal, no one way to live, no one way to feel, no one thing to know or be known. The particulars count.

—JON KABAT-ZINN, *Wherever You Go, There You Are*

Just as a reservoir is of little use when the whole countryside is flooded, scriptures are of little use to the illumined man or woman, who sees the Lord everywhere. —THE BHAGAVAD GITA

As long as any people's spiritual force answers the basic questions of life, death, future, and how to live a good, just, and quality life, then it is doing its job. In that regard, all religions perform the same task; there are no inferior or superior religions. . . .

The true spirituality or religiousness of a person has nothing to do with a church, temple, mosque, shrine, or place. It has to do with an attitude, a point of consciousness that accepts the view that there is something greater than one's self at work in the universe. What guides me is my belief that there is a force greater than my physical body. Such a higher power is the source of unlimited energy and goodness and is not dependent upon any doctrine, dogma, or person outside of oneself.

—HAKI R. MADHUBUTI, *Claiming Earth*

I maintain that every major religion of the world—Buddhism, Christianity, Confucianism, Hinduism, Islam, Jainism, Judaism, Sikhism, Taoism, Zoroastrianism—has similar ideals of love, the same goal of benefiting humanity through spiritual practice, and the same effect of making their followers into better human beings. All religions teach moral precepts for perfecting the functions of mind, body, and speech. All teach us not to lie or steal or take others' lives, and so on. The common goal of all moral precepts laid down by the great teachers of humanity is unselfishness. The great teachers wanted to lead their followers away from the paths of negative deeds caused by ignorance and to introduce them to paths of goodness. —TENZIN GYATSO, THE XIVTH DALAI LAMA OF TIBET

ONE VOICE

In the next generation the question may not be which religion one belongs to, but whether religion itself is of value. Those who have had some experience of transcendence must find some way to communicate the fact that the experience of the Ultimate Mystery is open to every human person who chooses to pursue the search for truth and embark on the spiritual journey—a journey which is literally without end.   —THOMAS KEATING in *Speaking of Silence*, edited by Susan Walker

Believe nothing, O monks, merely because you have been told it . . . or because it is traditional, or because you yourselves have imagined it. Do not believe what your teacher tells you merely out of respect for the teacher. But whatsoever, after due examination and analysis, you find to be conducive to the good, the benefit, the welfare of all beings—that doctrine believe and cling to, and take it as your guide.   —THE BUDDHA

There are two ways of thinking about church and religion. One is that we go to church in order to be in the presence of the holy, to learn and to have our lives influenced by that presence. The other is that church teaches us directly and symbolically to see the sacred dimension of everyday life. In this latter sense, religion is an "art of memory," a way of sustaining mindfulness about the religion that is inherent in everything we do.   —THOMAS MOORE, *Care of the Soul*

Know that the Prophet built an external *kaaba*
Of clay and water,
And an inner *kaaba* in life and heart.
The outer *kaaba* was built by Abraham, the holy;
The inner is sanctified by the glory of God himself.

On the path of God
Two places of worship mark the stages,
The material temple

And the temple of the heart.
Make your best endeavor
To worship at the temple of the heart.

— ANSARI OF HERAT, Sufi mystic

There is something in every one of you that waits and listens for the sound of the genuine in yourself. It is the only true guide you will ever have. And if you cannot hear it, you will all of your life spend your days on the ends of strings that somebody else pulls.

— HOWARD THURMAN

And a man said, Speak to us of Self-Knowledge.
  And he answered, saying:
  Your hearts know in silence the secrets
of the days and the nights.
  But your ears thirst for the sound of your
heart's knowledge. . . .

Then said a teacher, Speak to us of Teaching.
  And he said:
  No man can reveal to you aught but that
which already lies half asleep in the dawning
of your knowledge.

— KAHLIL GIBRAN, *The Prophet*

Siddhartha wandered through the grove deep in thought.
  There he met Gotama, the Illustrious One, and as he greeted him respectfully and the Buddha's expression was so full of goodness and peace, the young man plucked up courage and asked the Illustrious One's permission to speak to him. Silently, the Illustrious One nodded his permission.

Siddhartha said: "Yesterday, O Illustrious One, I had the pleasure of hearing your wonderful teachings. I came from afar with my friend to hear you, and now my friend will remain with you; he has sworn allegiance to you. I, however, am continuing my pilgrimage anew."

"As you wish," said the Illustrious One politely. . . .

"I did not doubt you for one moment. Not for one moment did I doubt that you were the Buddha, that you have reached the highest goal which so many thousands of Brahmins and Brahmins' sons are striving to reach. You have done so by your own seeking, in your own way, through thought, through meditation, through knowledge, through enlightenment. You have learned nothing through teachings, and so I think, O Illustrious One, that nobody finds salvation through teachings. To nobody, O Illustrious One, can you communicate in words and teachings what happened to you in the hour of your enlightenment. The teachings of the enlightened Buddha embrace much, they teach much—how to live righteously, how to avoid evil. But there is one thing that this clear, worthy instruction does not contain; it does not contain the secret of what the Illustrious One himself experienced—he alone among hundreds of thousands. That is what I thought and realized when I heard your teachings. That is why I am going on my way—not to seek another and better doctrine, for I know there is none, but to leave all doctrines and all teachers and to reach my goal alone—or die." . . .

No, a true seeker could not accept any teachings, not if he sincerely wished to find something. But he who had found, could give his approval to every path, every goal; nothing separated him from all the other thousands who lived in eternity, who breathed the Divine.   —HERMANN HESSE, *Siddhartha*

There is no more important injunction in all the world, nor one with a deeper interior meaning, than "To thine own self be true." In other words, be true to your own soul, for it is through your own soul that the voice of God speaks to you. This is the interior guide. This is the light that lighteth every man that cometh into the world. This is conscience. This is intuition. This is the voice of the higher self, the voice of the soul, the voice of God.   —RALPH WALDO TRINE, *In Tune with the Infinite*

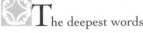Neither you nor I know the mysteries of eternity,

Neither you nor I read this enigma;

You and I only talk this side of the veil;

When the veil falls, neither you nor I will be here.

—OMAR KHAYYÁM, *The Rubá'iyát*

The deepest words

of the wise man teach us

the same as the whistle of the wind when it blows

or the sound of the water when it is flowing.

—ANTONIO MACHADO, Spanish poet

I believe that unarmed truth and unconditional love will have the final word.

—MARTIN LUTHER KING, JR.

My true religion is kindness.

—THE DALAI LAMA

A young man who had a bitter disappointment in life went to a remote monastery and said to the abbot: "I am disillusioned with life and wish to attain enlightenment to be freed from these sufferings. But I have no capacity for sticking long at anything. I could never do long years of meditation and study and austerity; I should relapse and be drawn back to the world again, painful though I know it to be. Is there any short way for people like me?"

"There is," said the abbot, "if you are really determined. Tell me, what have you studied? What have you concentrated on most in your life?"

"Why, nothing really. We were rich, and I did not have to work. I suppose the thing I was really interested in was chess. I spent most of my time at that."

The abbot thought for a moment, and then said to his attendant: "Call such and such a monk, and tell him to bring a chessboard and men." The monk came with the board and the abbot set up the men. He sent for a sword and showed it to the two. "Oh, monk," he said, "you have vowed obedience to me as your abbot, and now I require it of you. You will play a game of chess with this youth, and if you lose I shall cut off your head with this sword. But I promise that you will be reborn in paradise. If you win, I shall cut off the head of this man: Chess is the only thing he has ever tried hard at, and if he loses he deserves to lose his head also." They looked at the abbot's face and saw that he meant it: He would cut off the head of the loser.

They began to play. With the opening moves the youth felt the sweat trickling down to his heels as he played for his life. The chessboard became the whole world; he was entirely concentrated on it. At first he had somewhat the worst of it, but then the other made an inferior move and he seized his chance to launch a strong attack. As his opponent's position crumbled, he looked covertly at him. He saw a face of intelligence and sincerity, worn with years of austerity and effort. He thought of his own worthless life and a wave of compassion came over him. He deliberately made a blunder and then another blunder, ruining his position and leaving himself defenseless.

The abbot suddenly leant forward and upset the board. The two contestants sat stupefied. "There is no winner and no loser," said the abbot slowly, "there is no head to fall here. Only two things are required"—and he turned to the young man—"complete concentration, and compassion. You have today learnt them both. You were completely concentrated on the game, but then in that concentration you could feel compassion and sacrifice your life for it. Now stay here a few months and pursue our training in this spirit and your enlightenment is sure."

He did so and got it.

— TRADITIONAL ZEN TALE

The spiritual crisis that has happened, especially among the well-to-do Blacks, has taken the form of the quest for therapeutic release. So that you can get very thin, flat, and one-dimensional forms of spirituality that are simply an attempt to sustain the well-to-do Black folks as they engage in their consumerism and privatism. The kind of spirituality we're talking about is not the kind that serves as an opium to help you justify and rationalize your own cynicism vis-à-vis the disadvantaged folk in our community. We could talk about churches and their present role in the crisis of America, religious faith as the American way of life, the gospel of health and wealth, helping the bruised psyches of the Black middle class make it through America. That's not the form of spirituality that we're talking about. We're talking about something deeper—you used to call it conversion—so that notions of service and risk and sacrifice once again become fundamental. It's very important, for example, that those of you who remember the days in which Black colleges were hegemonic among the Black elite remember them critically but also acknowledge that there was something positive going on there. What was going on was that you were told every Sunday, in chapel, that you had to give service to the race. Now it may have been a petty bourgeois form, but it created a moment of accountability, and with the erosion of the service ethic the very possibility of putting the needs of others alongside of one's own diminishes. In this syndrome, me-ness, selfishness, and egocentricity become more and more prominent, creating a spiritual crisis where you need more psychic opium to get you over.

—CORNEL WEST, in dialogue with bell hooks, *Breaking Bread: Insurgent Black Intellectual Life*

Religion is often made into a comprehensive neurotic solution.　　　　—ALAN JONES

[P]erhaps God created nothing but merely is. And we spend our lives within him or her or it, wondering constantly where he or she or it can be found. . . .　　　　—PHILIP K. DICK

Man is an aspect of nature, and nature itself is a manifestation of primordial religion. Even the word "religion" makes an unnecessary separation, and there is no word for it in the Indian tongues. Nature is the "Great Mysterious," the "religion before religion," the profound intuitive apprehension of the true nature of existence attained by sages of all epochs, everywhere on Earth; the whole universe is sacred, man is the whole universe, and the religious ceremony is life itself, the common acts of every day.

—PETER MATTHIESSEN, quoted in *The Gaia Atlas of First Peoples: A Future for the Indigenous World*

The name of this infinite and inexhaustible depth and ground of all being is *God*. That depth is what the word *God* means. And if that word has not much meaning for you, translate it, and speak of the depths of your life, of the source of your being, of your ultimate concern, of what you take seriously without any reservation. . . . For if you know that God means depth, you know much about him. You cannot then call yourself an atheist or unbeliever. For you cannot think or say: Life has no depth! Life is shallow. Being itself is surface only. If you could say this in complete seriousness, you would be an atheist; but otherwise you are not. He who knows about depth knows about God.

— PAUL TILLICH, *The Shaking of the Foundations*

Like science, mysticism seems to be a universal enterprise. There is no parochialism in mysticism. Parochialism enters when religions simplify mystical teachings to make them more communicable to the masses of humankind.

— AMIT GOSWAMI, *The Self-Aware Universe*

"Why are we here?" may be the wrong question to ask because, as an organ with finite capabilities, the mind cannot consider the infinite possibilities the question implies. It would be like asking my four-and-a-half-year-old daughter to explain Einstein's theory of relativity. It requires a tremendous leap of faith to come up with a reason for being. And I don't think anybody can have an answer he believes in with rock-solid confidence.

In trying to concoct a reason for existence, we've created theologies. Through my travels as a tennis player, I have been exposed to Buddhism, Shintoism, Confucianism, Taoism, Islam, Christianity, Judaism, Santería, animism. And I have always been perplexed to find that most of the world's great organized religions tell you they have the only answer. Christ said, "No one cometh unto the Father but by me." In Islam, Allah is God and Muhammad is His one true prophet. I kept thinking, "Hey, somebody's got to be wrong!"

Despite my skepticism that any one religion can provide universal truths, I have synthesized many faiths and come up with some basic ideas. One is that all we see around us, living or inanimate, could not have come from nothing. There had to be an original cause. The second idea is that my life is part of a continuum that goes back as far as life itself has been around and that will be around after I'm gone.

— ARTHUR ASHE in *More Reflections on the Meaning of Life*

Though Nansi was sealed away from the outside world, many stories about the deeds of the colonials had slipped in. For example, in a nearby village missionaries had attempted to convert the people by using the symbol of Christ on the cross. One unfortunate man had taken the risk of objecting. "This man is not Black," he said. "He never came to any Black village. No one among his disciples was Black. So how could he have died for us, too? Are you trying to transfer the guilt of your ancestors upon us? Look—your ancestors killed somebody they should not have killed, then they found out that this man was a divine man. So they decided to share their regret with the rest of the world. Our ancestors never told us that you had committed such a crime against humanity. And if this man was a god, Mother Earth would have told us about it before you arrived here. Be clear about what you are saying."

— MALIDOMA SOMÉ, *Of Water and the Spirit*

Instead of clearing his own heart the zealot tries to clear the world. The laws of the City of God are applied only to his in-group (tribe, church, nation, class, or whatnot) while the fire of a perpetual holy war is hurled (with good conscience, and indeed a sense of pious service) against whatever uncircumcised, barbarian, heathen, "native," or alien people happens to occupy the position of neighbor. . . .

[But] once we have broken free of the prejudices of our own provincially limited ecclesiastical, tribal, or national rendition of the world archetypes, it becomes possible to understand that the supreme initiation is not that of the local motherly fathers, who then project aggression onto the neighbors for their own defense. The good news, which the World Redeemer brings and which so many have been glad to hear, zealous to preach, but reluctant, apparently, to demonstrate, is that God is love, that He can be, and is to be, loved, and that all without exception are his children.

— JOSEPH CAMPBELL, *The Hero with a Thousand Faces*

The spiritual journey is the search for the source. From where have I come? What is the source of this life? All the major religions of the world move toward this, the search for the source. But in the process people have gotten stuck in their positions.

Today the wars and the fights all over the world are in the name of religion. One takes his position—I am a Muslim or I am Christian, I am Hindu or I am Sikh, I am Buddhist—and those who are not that, they are not mine. They don't belong to me.

In divine creation the whole world is united, the earth is united. It is oneness. In the whole human race there is unity. The search for this unity, the unifying factor, is the real spiritual journey. Unfortunately, the so-called spiritual journey has divided human beings and torn apart the whole society.

The distinction between religion and spirituality should first become clear in our minds. I normally give this example of a banana and banana skin: religion is like the banana skin and spirituality is the banana. People have thrown away the banana and are holding on to the skin. Religion is outer ritual and habits, a way of life; spirituality is the quest for the source of life, going back to the source, knowing deep within us we are part of the divinity.

When this distinction becomes clear in the mind, it is then our journey towards the source begins. It is then we become human beings. It is then we become united to that principle which is beneath all existence, which is beneath every happening and has enormous intelligence and orderliness.

In this path everybody has to walk alone. There is no proxy walking. You cannot share someone else's walk and say, "Oh yes, I have walked." Someone else cannot eat for you or drink tea for you. "I have drunk tea for you, just relax." That doesn't happen. The quest is the need of the soul, of every growing soul. . . .

Success in life is attending to this source, inquiry of the source and living in that joy and unconditional love.

—SRI SRI RAVI SHANKAR, *Bang on the Door*

Any path is only a path, and there is no affront, to oneself or to others, in dropping it if that is what your heart tells you. . . . Look at every path closely and deliberately. Try it as many times as you think necessary. Then ask yourself, and yourself alone, one question. . . . Does this path have a heart? If it does, the path is good; if it doesn't it is of no use.

—CARLOS CASTANEDA, *The Teachings of Don Juan* (voice of Don Juan)

To step onto any path is to leave our source. Thus the world of charms, amulets, practices, and consultations, dissolves into the light of higher knowing. We can leave the raft on the river as we establish camp on the higher side of the mountain.

Eventually all who walk the road to higher knowing come to one realization: *I had it all the time.* Some arrive sooner, and some arrive later; some arrive by the path of pain, and others by way of joy; some come alone and some come together. In the end, the method is not as important as the goal.

—ALAN COHEN, *I Had It All the Time*

The process of enlightenment consists merely in becoming what we already are from the beginning. When the Zen master Po-chang was asked about seeking for the Buddha nature, he answered, "It's much like riding an ox in search of the ox."

—FRITJOF CAPRA, *The Tao of Physics*

Buddhists say religion is like a finger pointing at the moon: The person who is doing the pointing wants to show me something which, to him, is so obvious that one would think any fool could see it. He must feel as we all feel when trying to explain to a thick-headed child that two times zero is zero and not two, or some other perfectly simple little fact. And there is something even more exasperating than this. I am sure that many of you may, for a fleeting moment, have had one clear glimpse of what the finger was pointing at—a glimpse in which you shared the pointer's astonishment that you had never seen it before, in which you saw the whole thing so plainly that you knew you could never forget it . . . and then you lost it. After this, there may be a tormenting nostalgia that goes on for years. How to find the way back, back to the door in the wall that no longer seems to be there. . . .

One must take care not to mistake the finger for the moon. Too many of us, I fear, suck the pointing finger of religion for comfort, instead of looking where it points. —ALAN WATTS, *Become What You Are*

The purpose of a fish trap is to catch fish, and when the fish are caught the trap is forgotten. The purpose of a rabbit snare is to catch rabbits. When the rabbits are caught, the snare is forgotten. The purpose of words is to convey ideas. When the ideas are grasped, the words are forgotten. Where can I find a man who has forgotten words? He is the one I would like to talk to.

—CHUANG-TZU, Chinese Taoist philosopher and teacher

Why tell animals living in the water to drink? —WEST AFRICAN PROVERB

Nasrudin, when he was in India, passed near a strange-looking building, at the entrance of which a hermit was sitting. He had an air of abstraction and calm, and Nasrudin thought that he would make some sort of contact with him. *Surely*, he thought, *a devout philosopher like me must have something in common with this saintly individual.*

"I am a yogi," said the anchorite in answer to the Mulla's question, "and I am dedicated to the service of all living things, especially birds and fish."

"Pray allow me to join you," said the Mulla, "for, as I had expected, we have something in common. I am strongly attracted to your sentiments, because a fish once saved my life."

"How pleasurably remarkable!" said the yogi. "I shall be delighted to admit you to our company. For all my years of devotion to the cause of animals, I have never yet been privileged to attain such intimate communion with them as you. Saved your life! This amply substantiates our doctrine that all the animal kingdom is interlinked."

So Nasrudin sat with the yogi for some weeks, contemplating his navel and learning various curious gymnastics.

At length the yogi asked him: "If you feel able, now that we are better acquainted, to communicate to me your supreme experience with the life-saving fish, I would be more than honored."

"I am not sure about that," said the Mulla, "now that I have heard more of your ideas."

But the yogi pressed him, with tears in his eyes, calling him "Master" and rubbing his forehead in the dust before him.

"Very well, if you insist," said Nasrudin, "though I am not quite sure whether you are ready (to use your parlance) for the revelation I have to make. The fish certainly saved my life. I was on the verge of starvation when I caught it. It provided me with food for three days."　　—TRADITIONAL SUFI TALE

Don't be a searcher wrapped in the importance of his quest. Repent of your repenting!

—JALAL AL-DIN RUMI

The important thing is not to stop questioning. Curiosity has its own reason for existing. One cannot help but be in awe when he contemplates the mysteries of eternity, of life, of the marvelous structure of reality. It is enough if one tries merely to comprehend a little of this mystery every day. Never lose a holy curiosity.

—ALBERT EINSTEIN

CHAPTER TWELVE

Prayer and Communion

One evening while writing "In the Spirit," my monthly editorial in *Essence,* I was thinking about prayer. What is it? And what is its function? And the words of a Stevie Wonder song came to me: "They say that heaven is ten zillion light-years away. . . . Where is my God? He lives inside of me." Too often we pray to a god that is far away, believing that we can change God's mind or draw nearer to us things we're pleading for. But prayer, as Joseph Campbell reminds us, "is relating to and meditating on a mystery." We say that God is love, compassion and benevolence and life in abundance, and that prayer is the act of remembering that truth. But above all, God is a mystery, and prayer connects us to it.

We nodded our heads and said "Amen" when Dr. Martin Luther King, Jr., in his book *The Strength to Love,* made it clear that prayer is not synonymous with petition. Yet, more than thirty years later, even among the faithful of this "new age" of enlightenment and "new thought," there are those who view God as a kind of Ultimate ATM and devote the whole of their faith to trying to withdraw from it an earthly fortune.

The Hindu prayers included here, especially those taken from the sacred text of the Upanishads, have been offered daily since ancient times. They're universal, as Joel Beversluis notes in *A SourceBook for Earth's Community of Religions,* "offered for all and in the name of all, not for one group, religion, nation or collectivity; they show the interdependence of the welfare of one with the welfare of all, treating the whole world as a single family."

Our prayers take many forms, from public declarations of faith to private moments of quiet meditation. There are also surprising similarities in the forms that prayer takes in different traditions. In Hinduism and Buddhism, *japa* is the repetition of the holy name or some other sacred word or phrase called a *mantra.* Catholics recite the rosary, repeating the same prayer over and over again. The aim in each is to focus your mind until you have rid yourself of all distractions, all thought, and awareness of everything other than the single divine idea—to empty yourself in order to allow the inflooding of divine awareness.

The form of prayer that works well for some may not work at all for others. I've often told Susan that I find listening to Pharoah Sanders's recordings of "The Creator Has a Master Plan" or "Red, Black and Green," alone with eyes closed and headphones on, to be more effectively prayer than anything that can be said with words. For me, such music circumvents words and represents the experience of union with the divine more directly, recalling the experience more vividly: the rhythms mimicking the gently rocking arms of the Universal Mother; the tremulous voice of Pharoah's saxophone recalling the trembling of the heart overawed in the divine Presence; the screams of the saxophone recalling the cry of the soul overwhelmed with joy and love. I hear in John Coltrane's "Resolution" the call of the muezzin, and the compassion of Christ in his *Meditations* suite, "Love, Consequences, Serenity." Without ever uttering a word, these musicians communicate the transcendent experience of union with the divine, and I recognized instantly that they have been there and that they know what they're "talking" about.

A Muslim friend of ours, talking to us once about his pilgrimage to Mecca as a young man, said he asked a wise pilgrim there on the *hajj* what was the proper way to pray. "Make your life a prayer," he was told. Ultimately, prayer is a practice we must extend beyond our devout meditations and formal worship into the living of our lives. We must find communion with God in our relationships with others and the world. As with our prayers and mantras, we must find a rhythm in our way of being that is in harmony with the changing of the seasons and fortunes and the cycles of life and death and regeneration.

Rhythm shows us the way, as does the communal aspect of prayer. The Body of Christ is a metaphor for a church (not a building or particular religious denomination, but a spirit) in which every individual can come together as one body when individual identity fades and we feel ourselves to be one with our brothers and sisters. We experience it at times in group singing, group chanting, congregational worship, and when we forget ourselves in the rhythm of dancing the night away in a crowded space with people we don't even know. But we *do* know them; when we forget ourselves, we discover they are us.

This is also the point Shams of Tabriz makes so cleverly about Muslims who turn toward Mecca to worship—that they are in essence worshipping the divinity in one another.

The wine Omar Khayyám celebrates in *The Rubá'iyát* is also a metaphor for the spirit. Drink deeply of the spirit, he urges. An inscription found at the bottom of wine jars in ancient Egypt, *ankh ba,* similarly urged one to drink deeply "that the spirit may live."

Despite the admonitions of evangelists who warn us not to confuse the spirits, human beings have always looked for ways to step outside of ourselves, to weaken the tenacious hold of our egos and free ourselves of our sense of separateness.

Not until Khayyám has so saturated himself with the spirit that he is at last one with it will he be satisfied, and at that point he will have become the Wine Server. He imbibes God in the beauty and perfection of creation, noting that our physical selves will not be wasted but recycled to nourish the green grass for others to behold. The German romantic Novalis had a term for anyone so filled with the spirit: *ein gottbetrunkener Mensch,* "a God-intoxicated man."

As Yaya Diallo, a musician and healer from Mali, tells us in *The Healing Drum,* God communicates to us through nature. Streams have been a metaphor for meditation on the nature of God in cultures throughout the world. Our very lives are like streams, winding their way by various routes to the ocean. God is the stream as much as God is the ocean, which releases its moisture into the atmosphere to be carried by clouds to the tops of mountains to fall as snow to melt into streams in season after season eternally. This is the dynamic continuum that Ghanaian writer Ayi Kwei Armah describes.

Communion in Christianity implies the ritual of the communion service, which has its origins in ancient Egypt, Persia, and elsewhere. In Egyptian mythology, Osiris dies and is resurrected, just as the barley that makes the bread and the grapevine that produces the grapes that make the wine die in the fall and are resurrected in spring. In the ancient Egyptian coffin text (c. 2100–1750 B.C.E.), Osiris is saying eat and drink of these, his body and blood, and you, too, will be resurrected. Since bread and wine were staples of the ancient world, and everyone partook of them as a matter of course, what Osiris was offering was assurance that we are all resurrected, continually, naturally, because this is the nature of God in whom we all are.

Taking time to experience ourselves in solitude is one way that we can regain a sense of the divine that can feel the spirit moving in our lives. Solitude is essential to the spiritual for it is there that we cannot only commune with divine spirits but also listen to our inner voice. One way to transform the lonely feeling that overwhelms some of us is to enter that lonely place and find there a stillness that enables us to hear the soul speak . . .

Black women have not focused sufficiently on our need for contemplative spaces. We are often "too busy" to find time for solitude. And yet it is in the stillness that we also learn how to be with ourselves in a spirit of acceptance and peace. Then when we reenter community, we are able to extend this acceptance to others. Without knowing how to be alone, we cannot know how to be with others and sustain the necessary autonomy. Yet, many of us live in fear of being alone. To meditate, to go into solitude and silence, we find a way to be empowered by aloneness.

—BELL HOOKS, *Sisters of the Yam*

Be still, and know that I am God.

—PSALMS 46:10

How do we approach prayer? There's a world of difference, isn't there, between "Listen, Lord, your servant speaks" and "Speak, Lord, your servant listens"? Just as your child's request for an expensive toy is different from his request that you take him on your lap and sing to him. One is a bid for love and sharing; the other is more of a demand for a gift.

Receptivity is crucial to all relationships. We have to be quiet and listen if we want to set the stage for conscious contact. If we don't listen, we don't hear, and if we don't hear, we can't know who the other is and what the other is saying. Perhaps we're afraid to listen too closely to God, afraid that He will communicate disappointment and disapproval. Or perhaps we're afraid that God will remain silent.

Opening up is the only way to prove the matter. Making the connection is the only way to hear the new song.

—EARNIE LARSEN AND CAROL LARSEN HEGARTY, *Days of Healing, Days of Joy*

The purpose of this ritual prayer is not that you should stand and bow and prostrate yourself all day long. Its purpose is that you should possess continuously that spiritual state which appears to you in prayer: Whether asleep or awake, writing or reading, in all your states you should never be empty of the remembrance of God.

— JALAL AL-DIN RUMI

The idea that man expects God to do everything leads inevitably to a callous misuse of prayer. For if God does everything, man then asks him for anything, and God becomes little more than a "cosmic bellhop" who is summoned for every trivial need. Or God is considered so omnipotent and man so powerless that prayer is a substitute for work and intelligence.

— MARTIN LUTHER KING, JR.

Prayer does not deal with a capricious God. It is a technique for achieving unity with God and His limitless life, substance, and intelligence.

Prayer is not something we do to God but to ourselves.
　　It is not a position but a disposition.
　　　　It is not flattery but a sense of oneness.
　　　　　　It is not asking but knowing.
　　　　　　　　It is not words but feeling
　　　　　　　　　　It is not will but willingness.

— ERIC BUTTERWORTH

God — may He be exalted! — said, "When the Koran is recited" — whether it be by you yourself or by someone else who recites it for you — "listen to him and be silent . . ." *(Kor. 7:204)* for this Word is the very word of Allah and it is He alone who speaks it, and on the condition also that He who listens be Allah. For in every being, whether he knows it or not, Allah is He who speaks and He who listens.

When He who recites and He who listens are one, it is the same as when one speaks to oneself and when one listens to oneself.　　　　—AMIR 'ABD AL-KADER, *The Spiritual Writings of Amir 'Abd al-Kader*

Occupy yourself with *dhikr*, remembrance, until the Remembered manifests Himself to you and calling Him to memory is effaced in the actual recollection of Him.　　　—IBN 'ARABI, Sufi mystic

Affirmation of life is the spiritual act by which man ceases to live unreflectively and begins to devote himself to his life with reverence in order to raise it to its true value. To affirm life is to deepen, to make more inward, and to exalt the will to live.　　　　—ALBERT SCHWEITZER

Feel the transparency of the lines between aloneness and oneness.

Let your armor fall away. Your roles, your possessions, your identities—none of these are the truth of who you are. None of these can truly describe the vastness of your own being. None of these can describe the truth of your oneness and connectedness with all life. Let yourself just be, without any definition. Feel the fearlessness, the wonder of that being. Feel the oneness, the connectedness that emerges as you free yourself of the personal definitions that divide you from others, that compartmentalize the world into pieces. Feel the oneness that is the truth of your aloneness. Let yourself merge into a sense of being without definition, without separation.

Be present, be still. Allow the freedom of your aloneness to emerge. Allow the connectedness of aloneness to speak its own truth. Allow the love and compassion of oneness to fill your being.

　　　　—CHRISTINA FELDMAN, *Woman Awake*

Our prayer is a peace-be-still, a silent communion—even unto that storm at sea. The Master never prayed that it be dispelled: His only prayer was, "Be still." Was he addressing the water? No, he was addressing his consciousness and the consciousness of his disciples, "Peace, be still." If our consciousness is still, there are no stormy waters within or without. If our consciousness is still, everything about us takes on the complexion of that stillness.

Our need is for one thing alone—conscious communion with God. That is the highest form of prayer, and that form of prayer can only take place after we have learned, first of all, that God is, and, secondly, that all that exists in this universe is God "is-ing"—Is, Is, Is. That *Is,* is neither human good nor human ill; It is neither human health nor human sickness: It is just a spiritual Is.

When we have worked with these principles until we come to a point where we no longer put up even a mental defense against the problems besetting us, but like David walk out without armor in the name of God—when that time comes, our prayers and treatment will be performed without words and without thought.

—JOEL S. GOLDSMITH, *The Art of Spiritual Healing*

In meditation, as the mind settles down to dwell on a single focus, attention begins to flow in a smooth, unbroken stream, like oil poured from one container to another. As this happens, attention naturally retreats from other channels. The ears, for example, still function, but you do not hear; attention is no longer connected with the organs of hearing.

When concentration is profound, there are moments when you forget the body entirely. This experience quietly dissolves physical identification. The body becomes like a comfortable jacket: you wear it easily, and in meditation you can unbutton and loosen it until it scarcely weighs on you at all.

Eventually there comes a time when you get up from meditation and *know* that your body is not you. This is not an intellectual understanding. Even in the unconscious the nexus is cut, which means there are sure signs in health and behavior: no physical craving will be able to dictate to you, and any compulsion to fulfill emotional needs through physical activities will vanish. Most important, you lose your fear of death. You know with certitude that death is not the end, and that you will not die when the body dies. . . . [But] you realize you are not the mind, any more than you are the physical body.

When awareness has been consolidated even beyond the mind, little remains except the awareness of

"I." Concentration is so profound that the mind-process has almost come to a standstill. Space is gone, and time so attenuated that it scarcely seems real. This is a taste of *shanti,* "the peace that passeth understanding," invoked at the end of every Upanishad as a reminder of this sublime state. You rest in meditation in what the Taittiriya Upanishad calls the "body of joy," a silent, ethereal inner realm at the threshold of pure being.

For a long while it may seem that there is nothing stirring in this still world, so deep in consciousness that the phenomena of the surface seem as remote as a childhood dream. But gradually you become aware of the presence of something vast, intimately your own but not at all the finite, limited self you had been calling "I."

All that divides us from the sea of infinite consciousness at this point is a thin envelope of personal identity. That envelope cannot be removed by any amount of will; the "I" cannot erase itself. Yet, abruptly, it does vanish. In the climax of meditation the barrier of individuality disappears, dissolving in a sea of pure, undifferentiated awareness. . . . [T]his unitary awareness is also the ground of one's own being, the core of personality. This divine ground the Upanishads call simply *atman,* "the Self."

— EKNATH EASWARAN, Introduction to *The Upanishads*

And I cannot teach you the prayer of the seas and the forests and the mountains.

But you who are born of the mountains and the forests and the seas can find their prayer in your heart,

And if you but listen in the stillness of the night you shall hear them saying in silence,

"Our God, who art our winged self, it is thy will in us that willeth.

It is thy desire in us that desireth.

It is thy urge in us that would turn our nights, which are thine, into days which are thine also.

We cannot ask thee for aught, for thou knowest our needs before they are born in us."

— KAHLIL GIBRAN, *The Prophet*

Think of yourself as nothing, and totally forget yourself when you pray. Only have in mind that you are praying for the Divine Presence.

You can then enter the Universe of Thought, a state that is beyond time. Everything in this realm is the same, life and death, land and sea. . . . But in order to enter the Universe of Thought where all is the same, you must relinquish your ego, and forget all your troubles.

You cannot reach this level if you attach yourself to physical, worldly things. You are then attached to the division between good and evil. . . .

Furthermore, if you consider yourself as "something," and ask for your own needs, God cannot clothe Himself in you. God is infinite, and no vessel can hold Him at all, except when a person makes himself like Nothing.

—THE MAGGID OF MEZERITCH, Jewish mystic

It is in the watches of the night that impressions are strongest and words most eloquent; in the daytime you are hard pressed with the affairs of this world.

—THE KORAN 73:5

I LET GO OF MY ACCUMULATIONS

My ego is like a fortress.
I have built its walls stone by stone
To hold out the invasion of the love of God.

But I have stayed here long enough. There is light
Over the barriers. O my God—
The darkness of my house forgive
And overtake my soul.
I relax the barriers.
I abandon all that I think I am,
All that I hope to be,
All that I believe I possess.

I let go of the past,

I withdraw my grasping hand from the future,

And in the great silence of this moment,

I alertly rest my soul.

As the sea gull lays in the wind current,

So I lay myself into the spirit of God.

My dearest human relationships,

My most precious dreams,

I surrender to His care.

All that I have called my own

I give back. All my favorite things

Which I would withhold in my storehouse

From his fearful tyranny,

I let go.

I give myself

Unto Thee, O my God. Amen.

—HOWARD THURMAN, *Deep Is the Hunger: Meditations for Apostles of Sensitiveness*

The prayer of the monk is not perfect until he no longer recognizes himself or the fact that he is praying. —ST. ANTHONY

For what is prayer but the expansion of yourself into the living ether?

—KAHLIL GIBRAN, *The Prophet*

DEAR GOD, IF YOU PLEASE

Dear God, if you please, let me be paranoid.
I know this sounds like the strangest request.
But it's the only thing can fill this void.
And until it is fulfilled, I'll find no rest.

It seems today that the world is against me,
The only reason being that my skin is black.
I try to convince myself this just isn't true,
Yet all of the evidence shows it as fact.

I see poor education and unequal chances.
I see people mistreated—their skin like mine.
I am told these things don't really exist,
But I just don't think they're all in my mind.

Why then would I still not believe?
Because I'd lose all my hope, I'd lose all faith.
If I accepted my suspicions simply as truth,
Then wouldn't this world be an evil place?

So, God, you must see the need for me to be paranoid,
Then this world really wouldn't be so bad.
Then all that I see is not a true picture.
Lord, let me be paranoid so I know I'm not mad.

— MATTHEW L. WATLEY

A PRAYER FOR POWER

O Lawd, gib dy sarvint, dis Sunday mawnin', de eye of an eagle dat he may see sin f'om afar. Put his han's to de gospel pulpit; glue his ears to the gospel telefoam an' conneck him wid de Glory in de skies. 'Luminate his brow wid a holy light dat will make de fiahs of hell look like a tallah candle. Bow his head down in humility, in dat lonesome valley wheah de pearl of truth is much needed to be said. Grease his lips wid possum 'ile to make it easy fo' love to slip outen his mouth. . . .

Turpentine his 'magination; 'lectrify his brain wid de powah of the Word. Put 'petual motion in his arms. Fill him full of de dynamite of Dy awful powah; 'noint him all ovah wid de kerosene of Dy salvation, an' den, O Lawd, sot him on fiah wid de sperrit of de Holy Ghos'.   —ORRIN STONE, former slave

LOVING KINDNESS

May every creature abound in well-being and peace.
May every living being, weak or strong, the long and the small,
The short and the medium-sized, the mean and the great—
May every living being, seen or unseen, those dwelling far off,
Those near by, those already born, those waiting to be born—
May all attain inward peace.

Let no one deceive another. Let no one despise another in any situation.
Let no one, from antipathy or hatred, wish evil to anyone at all.
Just as a mother, with her own life, protects her only son from hurt,
So within yourself foster a limitless concern for every living creature.
Display a heart of boundless love for all the world
In all its height and depth and broad extent—
Love unrestrained, without hate or enmity.

Then as you stand or walk, sit or lie, until overcome by drowsiness,
Devote your mind entirely to this, it is known as living here the life divine.   — BUDDHIST PRAYER

A CALL TO PRAYER (NATIVE AMERICAN)

O Great Spirit,
Whose breath gives life to the world
   and whose voice is heard in the soft breeze,
We need your strength and wisdom —
May we walk in beauty.
May our eyes
   ever behold the red and purple sunset;
Make us wise so that we may understand
   what you have taught us.
Help us learn the lessons you have hidden
   in every leaf and rock;
Make us always ready to come to you
   with clean hands and straight eyes,
So when life fades, as the fading sunset,
   our spirits may come to you without shame.

       — THE UNITED NATIONS ENVIRONMENT PROGRAM, *Only One Earth*

A PRAYER OF AWARENESS

Now, Talking God,
With your feet I walk,

I walk with your limbs.
I carry forth your body,
For me your mind thinks,
Your voice speaks for me.
Beauty is before me,
Above and below me hovers the beautiful—
I am surrounded by it,
I am immersed in it.
In my youth I am aware of it,
And in old age I shall walk quietly
The beautiful trail.

—Hindu prayer

You are the breath that inspires me. The food
That nourishes and gratifies. Yours is
The mind with which I pray, and Yours the life
By which I live. Your peace leads me to heal.
Yours are the thoughts I offer all in love.
You open wide my eyes and guide my feet.
You still my anxious heart. You are my love,
My Father, and my Self. I recognize
All others in Your Face. You are the Friend
In all my friends, my one relationship.
You are my rest and my Identity.
You are but all there is. I am complete in You.

—HUGH PRATHER, *The Quiet Answer*

It is not easy to overcome the thought of God as the Supreme Being "out there" who can help us in our times of need if we ask Him and if He is in the right mood. When we thus endow God with human qualities, our "asking" implies the possibility of a "yes" or "no" answer. We may very well receive an answer of "no." However, the "no" has come out of our own consciousness, the effect of our own inertia in negative thinking.

God doesn't have what you want or need. God *is* the substance of that need. You don't have to ask God for life, for God *is* life. You are the projection of that life into visibility. . . . You don't have to ask God for wisdom, for God *is* wisdom. Your mind is an activity in the Infinite Mind of God. If there is any break in the flow of the inspiration of the Almighty in you, that break is in you—not in God. Your need is to reestablish yourself in the consciousness of the all-knowing Mind of God in you.

How do you ask the sun for sunlight? By getting out into the sun. How do you ask electricity for light for your lamp? By turning on the switch. How do you "ask" God for what you want? By getting into the Spirit. It is not something that God must do for you. It is what you must do for yourself to enable God to do for you that which it is His ceaseless longing to do.

— ERIC BUTTERWORTH, *Discover the Power Within You*

Kle is the Supreme Being, God, the creator of all. This word is always singular, never plural. Kle was not and cannot be created, but gave rise to everything else. Kle is undefined, infinite, unknowable, the master of both the visible and the invisible. To enter into contact with Kle, one goes by way of an intermediary such as a stream. Outsiders may mistakenly think the Minianka worship the stream itself.

— YAYA DIALLO, *The Healing Drum*

If you want to tell anything to God, tell it to the wind.

— AFRICAN PROVERB

The spirit of man communes with Heaven; the omnipotence of Heaven resides in man. Is the distance between Heaven and man very great?

— EPIGRAM FROM THE MING DYNASTY

The most beautiful and most profound emotion we can experience is the sensation of the mystical. It is the dower of all true science. He to whom this emotion is a stranger, who can no longer wonder and stand rapt in awe, is as good as dead. To know what is impenetrable to us really exists, manifesting itself as the highest wisdom and the most radiant beauty which our dull faculties can comprehend only in their most primitive forms—this knowledge, this feeling is at the center of true religiousness.

—ALBERT EINSTEIN

If the doors of perception were cleansed every thing would appear to man as it is, infinite.

—WILLIAM BLAKE

Before the revelations of the soul, Time and Space and Nature shrink away.

—RALPH WALDO EMERSON

The silence of the stars is the silence of creation and re-creation. . . . The physical silence of the universe is matched by its moral silence. A child flies through the air toward injury, and the galaxies continue to whirl on well-oiled axes. But why should I expect anything else? There are no Elysian Fields up there beyond the seventh sphere where gods pause in their revels to glance down aghast at our petty tragedies. What's up there is just one galaxy after another, magnificent in their silent turning, sublime in their huge indifference. The number of galaxies may be infinite. Our indignation is finite. Divide any finite number by infinity and you get zero.

As a student, I came across a book by Max Picard called *The World of Silence*. The book offered an insight that seems more valuable to me now than it did then. Silence, said Picard, is the source from which language springs, and to silence language must constantly return to be re-created. Only in relation to silence does sound have significance. It is for this silence, so treasured by Picard that I turn to the marsh near Queset Brook in November. It is for this silence that I turn to the stars, to the ponderous inaudible turning of galaxies, to the clanging of God's great bell in the vacuum. The silence of the stars is the silence of creation and re-creation. It is the silence to be explored alone.

—CHET RAYMO, American astronomer

But when you finally discover me, the one naked Truth arisen from within, Absolute Awareness permeates the Universe.

— PADMASAMBHAVA, Indian mystic

To be with God is really to be involved with some enormous, overwhelming desire, and joy, and power which you cannot control, which controls you. God is a means of liberation and not a means to control others.

— JAMES BALDWIN, *Nobody Knows My Name*

The servant is a "Lord" manifested in the form of a "Servant" and, in the appearance of a worshipper, it is Himself who adores Himself.

— AMIR 'ABD AL-KADER

The *kaaba* is in the middle of the world. All faces turn toward it. But if you take it away, you'll see that each is worshipping the soul of each.

— SHAMS OF TABRIZ, Sufi mystic

The linking of those gone, ourselves here, those coming; our continuation, our flowing, not along any meretricious channel, but along our living way, the way: it is that remembrance that calls us. The eyes of seers should range far into purposes. The ears of hearers should listen far towards origins. The utterer's voices should make knowledge of the way of heard sounds and visions seen, the voices of the utterers should make this knowledge inevitable, impossible to lose.

— AYI KWEI ARMAH, *Two Thousand Seasons*

Drink wine since for our destruction
The firmament has got its eye on our precious souls;
Sit where it is green and enjoy the sparkling liquor,
Because this grass will grow nicely from your dust and mine.

— OMAR KHAYYÁM, *The Rubá'iyát*

Whether I live or die I am Osiris,
I enter in and reappear through you,
I decay in you, I grow in you . . .
Whether I live or die I am Barley,
I am not destroyed.

—ANCIENT EGYPTIAN COFFIN TEXT (C. 2100–1750 B.C.E.)

Unless you eat the flesh of the Son of Man, and drink his blood, you do not have life in yourselves. The eater of my flesh and the drinker of my blood has eternal life. . . . —JESUS OF NAZARETH

In Mediterranean cultures at the time of Jesus, bread and wine were the staple food and drink . . . [and] constituted the material life of mankind, the physical body and blood, in that "man is what he eats."

[But] one of the prohibitions of Jewish law was the drinking of blood. Blood was felt to be the life-essence of men and animals, and thus the property of God alone. . . . [T]he implication is that if only God may drink blood, to drink blood—and especially the blood of the Son of Man—is to have equality with God, and for that reason eternal life. . . .

Jesus is saying, in the symbolism of the Last Supper, that all flesh which is eaten is his flesh, and all blood which is shed is his blood. Do not, therefore, feel guilt for it any more. It is "shed for many for the remission of sins," remitted in the realization that all the wheat ground and the grapes crushed for us, all the steaks broiled and the fish grilled for us, are—along with the human corpses offered for worms and vultures—the innumerable disguises in which the Lord gives himself away.

—ALAN WATTS, *Beyond Theology*

If we have listening ears, God speaks to us in our own language, whatever that language is.

—MOHANDAS GANDHI

CHAPTER THIRTEEN

Death, Rebirth, and Change, Change, Change

We don't deal very well with death. In fact, we think of it as the enemy. But death is as natural as birth and as inseparably linked to it as left is to right, as day is to night, as exits are to entrances, as breathing out is to breathing in. It signals a cycle completed. Being able to embrace death as an essential part of living is fundamental to the embrace of life itself. Our awareness that our time on earth is measured drives us to find meaning and purpose in life. Without that deadline, we would feel no need to strive, no urgency to complete any task, and life itself would stagnate or explode. Death ensures that the stream of life is not dammed up, but is allowed to flow. And the inevitability of death actually infuses our existence with life—knowing we have only a finite amount of time here keeps us lively.

But we simply cannot conceive of an end to ourselves or our loved ones. And this is a natural and appropriate response. Intuitively, we know we endure. We sense deeply that we are immortal, and we view death as the archadversary of life, as something sinister, something maliciously imposed on us by an evil external force. And it's been that way for as long as people have lived and died.

Noted physician and psychiatrist Elisabeth Kübler-Ross, whose groundbreaking work has brought insight to how we view death and dying, says the ancient Hebrews regarded the body of a dead person as unclean and not to be touched. Native Americans, she writes, would shoot arrows into the air after someone died to drive away evil spirits. According to Dr. Kübler-Ross, many "cultures have rituals to take care of the 'bad' dead person, and they all originate in this feeling of anger which still exists in all of us, though we dislike admitting it. The tradition of the tombstone may originate in this wish to keep the bad spirits deep down in the ground. . . ."

As sophisticated as we've become, we still view death as an evil, too morbid to be discussed around children and even the dying themselves. But our fear seems to be a learned fear. Child psychologists have observed that children often don't see death as permanent; that's something they have to be taught. Children tend to see life much as the wise and enlightened do—in the eternal present. For them, the kingdom of heaven is at hand. It is always at hand. To enter it, as Jesus wisely counseled, we must become like little children. We must trust the impulses of our heart and spirit.

Our anxiety about death comes from our confusion about who we really are and the fact that we mistakenly identify our true self with our physical self, our opinions, associations, memories, and illusions about ourselves. But within this lifetime we have already died and been reborn many times. We are not who we were at two or ten or twenty-one. We have forgotten many of the experiences that defined the person each of us refers to as "I." What we do remember is partly fiction, since we seldom remember things strictly as they happened, but rather in the ways we most need to remember them. Pieces of us are dying all the time, and new experiences are always giving birth to a new consciousness and identity.

Birth is not the beginning of life, nor is death the end. Both are part of the continuous flow of life, deconstructing and reconstructing itself endlessly. And where there is life there is change, the all-encompassing theme of existence. Without change, there would be no growth, no life, no death—nothing. But change is the one constant in all the universe. As science fiction author Octavia Butler reminds us, God is change. To become one with God, the mystics have long counseled, go with the flow, become one with change. This is easier said than done. At our very core, we long for a return to that changeless bliss at the center of the Godhead, out of which everything manifests and around which everything revolves. And so we welcome any change in our emotional or material circumstances we think will approximate (no matter how feebly) that ultimate pleasure and peace. We think, *If I could only fall in love . . . If I only had a fabulous home, a new car, more money . . . then everything would be all right.* But any change that puts us a step farther away from having such things is seen as the enemy of our happiness, something to be resisted at all costs. We talk about "going through changes." We don't have a large enough perspective (God's perspective) to be able to see that, perhaps, the expensive car we didn't get was the one in which we would have lost our life. God manifests in infinite variety, and it is God's good pleasure to give us the kingdom—the whole kingdom. We make judgments about that boundless gift and accept or reject portions of it according to how broad or narrow our vision. We try to hang on to the pleasure and dodge the pain, both of which are ultimately no more substantial than images that form briefly in the clouds and then disperse.

Our lives are characterized by necessary losses. Birth, puberty, menstruation, marriage, menopause, balding—all are little deaths with subsequent rebirths, heralding change and opportunities for growth. Malidoma Somé refers to birth as an event in which one dies into being human. In order to become an adult, we must say goodbye to our adolescence. To be married, the freewheeling bachelor in us must die. Just as we cannot listen to music by stopping it and holding on to a particular note, we cannot live except as an ongoing succession of births, deaths, and rebirths. To have life you must lose it, like the grain of wheat that falls to the ground to produce a rich harvest. Perhaps we don't bury our dead as much as we plant them in the faith that their spirit is raised up into new life.

We've included Jain and Buddhist thoughts on the Creation here because they speak to the cycle of birth, death, and resurrection on a cosmic scale. Both views coincide with the "closed model" of the universe held by many scientists. That model says that everything in creation was born in the Big Bang, which sent all matter in the universe expanding outward into space, evolving into galaxies, suns, and worlds. Given several billion years, the combined gravity of all the matter in the universe will slow that expansion down and eventually stop it. Then, like a rubber band that has been stretched to its limit, the universe will begin to contract; slowly at first, but with increasing speed, galaxies, suns, and worlds will all rush toward the center of the universe to collide in another Big Bang of creation. This cycle of birth, death, and rebirth repeats itself eternally. And as above so below, on earth as it is in heaven. In the image and likeness of God, we, too, are life eternal.

How most of us dread change, fight against it, or refuse to acknowledge it, even unto the last look in the coffin. We stand there, forcing ourselves to "see" that everything is as it was, that "he" really still looks the same, looks "just as he did in life." Of course "he" does not. What we [know] is gone forever. And did we ever know it. For even in the moment, moments, of our knowing, it was changing: was never the same from moment to moment, from second to second: was always leaving.

— GWENDOLYN BROOKS, *Report from Part One*

Multitudes of people are continually keeping away from them higher and better things because they are forever clinging to the old. If they would use and pass on the old, room would be made for new things to come. Hoarding always brings loss in one form or another. Using, wisely using, brings an ever-renewing gain.

If the tree should as ignorantly and as greedily hold on to this year's leaves when they have served their purpose, where would be the full and beautiful new life that will be put forth in the spring? Gradual decay and finally death would be the result. If the tree is already dead, then it may perhaps be well enough for it to cling to the old, for no new leaves will come. But as long as the life in the tree is active, it is necessary that it rid itself of the old ones, that room may be made for the new.

—RALPH WALDO TRINE, *In Tune with the Infinite*

The sign of being a dried-up branch,
unconnected to root-water in the deep ground,
is that you have no inclination to sway.

—JALAL AL-DIN RUMI

The phrase "letting go" has to be high in the running for New Age cliché of the century. It is overused, abused daily. Yet it is such a powerful inward maneuver that it merits looking into, cliché or no. There is something vitally important to be learned from the practice of letting go.

Letting go means just what it says. It's an invitation to cease clinging to anything—whether it be an idea, a thing, an event, a particular time, or view, or desire. It is a conscious decision to release with full acceptance into the stream of present moments as they are unfolding. To let go means to give up coercing, resisting, or struggling, in exchange for something more powerful and wholesome which comes out of allowing things to be as they are without getting caught up in your attraction to or rejection of them, in the intrinsic stickiness of wanting, of liking and disliking. It's akin to letting your palm open to unhand something you have been holding on to.

Stillness, insight, and wisdom arise only when we can settle into being complete in this moment, without having to seek or hold on to or reject anything. This is a testable proposition. Try it out just for fun. See for yourself whether letting go when a part of you really wants to hold on doesn't bring a deeper satisfaction than clinging.

—JON KABAT-ZINN, *Wherever You Go, There You Are*

Some women wait for something
to change   and nothing
does change
so they change
themselves.

—AUDRE LORDE

The moment you are willing to change, it is remarkable how the Universe begins to help you. It brings you what you need. It could be a book, a tape, a teacher or even a friend making a passing remark that suddenly has deep meaning to you.

—LOUISE L. HAY, *The Power Is Within You*

THE GUEST-HOUSE

This being human is a guest-house.
Every morning a new arrival.

A joy, a depression, a meanness,
some momentary awareness comes
as an unexpected visitor.

Welcome and entertain them all!
Even if they're a crowd of sorrows,
who violently sweep your house
empty of its furniture,

still, treat each guest honorably.
He may be clearing you out
for some new delight.

The dark thought, the shame, the malice,
meet them at the door laughing,
and invite them in.

Be grateful for whoever comes,
because each has been sent
as a guide from beyond.

—JALAL AL-DIN RUMI

One day, my mother and I were working together in the garden. We were transplanting some plants for the third time. Grown from seed in a small container, the plants had been transferred to a larger container; then transplanted into the garden. Now, because I was moving, we were transplanting them again.

Inexperienced as a gardener, I turned to my green-thumbed mother. "Isn't this bad for them?" I asked, as we dug them up and shook the dirt from their roots. "Won't it hurt these plants, being uprooted and transplanted so many times?"

"Oh, no," my mother replied. "Transplanting doesn't hurt them. In fact, it's good for the ones that survive. That's how their roots grow strong. Their roots will grow deep, and they'll make strong plants."

Often, I've felt like those small plants—uprooted and turned upside down. Sometimes, I've endured the change willingly, sometimes reluctantly, but usually my reaction has been a combination.

Won't this be hard on me? I ask. Wouldn't it be better if things remained the same? That's when I remember my mother's words: That's how the roots grow deep and strong.

God, help me remember that during times of transition, my faith and my self are being strengthened.

—MELODY BEATTIE, *The Language of Letting Go*

All that there is, is change. Our body has undergone so many changes! If you look at your own childhood photographs, many times you will have to say, "This is me." Your friends will not recognize you as the same person. You looked very different when you were young. Your appearance has changed.

The body has changed in size and shape. Your thoughts have undergone many, many changes. The way you feel has changed, hasn't it? About a particular thing you felt good some days ago and then you didn't feel so good and then again you felt good. Your opinions and your ideas, your feelings, your emotions all have changed. You identify yourself by things that change. . . .

Yet you can hold on to that one thing which does not change in you. Be with that. That is you. The body has changed; you have not changed. Some centered point in you has not changed. It is the same principle that is beneath the whole existence, that is beneath the orderliness of this flower. That same principle is responsible for the colors in this flower, the shape of these leaves. The same intelligence is in the entire creation.

When we realize this, a grand unification happens in the consciousness. Our perception changes. Anything we look at, we look at sharply. When we hear, we hear sharply. We merge with what we see and hear. . . .

—SRI SRI RAVI SHANKAR, *Bang on the Door*

Music shows us how to maintain pleasure and ecstasy. Normally we tend to think of a moment of euphoric realization as unbearable and impossible to continue. It slips away and then we pursue it again. It does so because we are unwilling to let it go, we are unwilling to conceive of being away from it. But if we take the example of music, letting go of one note to hear the next, then our pleasure can be constant though the vibrations change.   —THADDEUS GOLAS, *The Lazy Man's Guide to Enlightenment*

[P]atterns weave, unweave, reweave: light becomes leaf becomes coal becomes light.

—HUGH KENNER, *The Pound Era*

The Chinese . . . not only believed that flow and change were the essential features of nature, but also that there are constant patterns in these changes, to be observed by man. The sage recognizes these patterns and directs his actions according to them. In this way he becomes "one with the Tao," living in harmony with nature and succeeding in everything he undertakes.   —FRITJOF CAPRA, *The Tao of Physics*

Create no images of God.
Accept the images
that God has provided.
They are everywhere,
in everything.
God is Change —
Seed to tree,
tree to forest;
Rain to river,
river to sea;
Grubs to bees,
bees to swarm.
From one, many;
from many, one;
Forever uniting, growing, dissolving —
forever Changing.
The universe
is God's self-portrait.

—OCTAVIA E. BUTLER, *Parable of the Sower*

God is much more a verb than a noun. Verbs are action words. They name an energy, a movement, a happening. Nouns are solid and static, they don't move. God is more a force than a monument. To think of God as a verb is to discover a meaningful dimension of that relationship. "Up there" or "in here" doesn't by any means tell the whole story of what goes on between us and our Higher Power. . . .

Our lives are always in process, moving, changing. To begin to see our Higher Power in that way is to recognize the Power behind our power and the Thought behind our thoughts. God is the juice, the energy, that moves us from death to life.

—EARNIE LARSEN AND CAROL LARSEN HEGARTY, *Days of Healing, Days of Joy*

From time to time we hear about people making sudden and drastic changes in their lives in response to major trauma. A heart attack, for example, precipitates long-delayed soul-searching, which leads to a career change or new life-style. Similarly, an unexpected divorce or the loss of a loved one leads to a complete reordering of priorities.

When such crisis-triggered metamorphoses work out for our friends or relatives, we're happy for them. But what about ourselves? Must we also be hit over the head with a sledgehammer before we're able to break out of rigid molds or stultifying patterns? Why does it have to take a catastrophe to spur us to action?

The point is that we can make these decisions anytime. God expects us to change. That's why we seek His guidance; that's why He has given us the power of choice and free will.

Once we become willing to make major changes, it can be frightening to take those first steps. But that's where our partnership with God comes into play again. He will always be there to guide and protect us. He will always provide us with the courage and strength we need to carry out His will in our own best interest.

— ANONYMOUS, *A New Day: 365 Meditations for Personal and Spiritual Growth*

Four words I will train myself to say until they become a habit so strong that immediately they will appear in my mind whenever good humor threatens to depart from me. These words, passed down from the ancients, will carry me through every adversity and maintain my life in balance. These four words are: *This too shall pass....*

For all worldly things shall indeed pass. When I am heavy with heartache I shall console myself that this too shall pass; when I am puffed with success I shall warn myself that this too shall pass. When I am strangled in poverty I shall tell myself that this too shall pass; when I am burdened with wealth I shall tell myself that this too shall pass. Yea, verily, where is he who built the pyramid? Is he not buried within its stone? And will the pyramid, one day, not also be buried under sand?

— OG MANDINO, *The Greatest Salesman in the World*

It is the everlasting and unchanging rule of this world that everything is created by a series of causes and conditions and everything disappears by the same rule; everything changes, nothing remains constant.

—THE BUDDHA

Nasrudin was now an old man looking back on his life. He sat with his friends in the tea shop telling his story. "When I was young I was fiery—I wanted to awaken everyone. I prayed to Allah to give me the strength to change the world.

"In mid-life I awoke one day and realized my life was half over and I had changed no one. So I prayed to Allah to give me the strength to change those close around me who so much needed it.

"Alas, now I am old and my prayer is simpler. 'Allah,' I ask, 'please give me the strength to at least change myself.'"

—TRADITIONAL SUFI TALE

All that you touch
You Change.

All that you Change
Changes you.

The only lasting truth
Is Change.

God
Is Change.

—OCTAVIA E. BUTLER, *Parable of the Sower*

Only a little while, and Nature, the universal disposer, will change everything you see, and out of their substance will make fresh things, and yet again others from theirs, to the perpetual renewing of the world's youthfulness.
—MARCUS AURELIUS, *Meditations*

Life lives by eating itself, casting off death and being reborn.
—JOSEPH CAMPBELL

Every now and then someone comes along saying, "It is I."
He arrives with favors, silver and gold, saying, "It is I."
When his little affair is sorted out for a day,
Death suddenly jumps out of ambush saying, "It is I."
—OMAR KHAYYÁM, *The Rubá'iyát*

The Master-Maker in His making had made Old Death. Made him with big, soft feet and square toes. Made him with a face that reflects the face of all things, but neither changes itself, nor is mirrored anywhere. Made the body of death out of infinite hunger. Made a weapon of his hand to satisfy his needs. This was the morning of the day of the beginning of things.
—ZORA NEALE HURSTON, *Dust Tracks on a Road*

THE DISPUTE BETWEEN A MAN AND HIS BA

Death is in my eyes today
like the unveiling of the heaven
as when a man attains to that which he knew not.

Death is in my eyes today
like the desire of a man to see his home
when he has passed many years in captivity.

Death is before me today
like a well trodden way
like a man coming home from warfare.   —ANCIENT EGYPTIAN POEM (c. 1990–1785 B.C.E.)

We may be about to rediscover that dying is not such a bad thing to do after all. Sir William Osler took this view: he disapproved of people who spoke of the agony of death, maintaining that there was no such thing.

In a nineteenth-century memoir on an expedition in Africa, there is a story by David Livingstone about his own experience of near-death. He was caught by a lion, crushed across the chest in the animal's great jaws, and saved in the instant by a lucky shot from a friend. Later, he remembered the episode in clear detail. He was so amazed by the extraordinary sense of peace, calm, and total painlessness associated with being killed that he constructed a theory that all creatures are provided with a protective physiologic mechanism, switched on at the verge of death, carrying them through in a haze of tranquillity. . . .

We will be having new opportunities to learn more about the physiology of death at first hand, from the increasing numbers of cardiac patients who have been through the whole process and then back again. Judging from what has been found out thus far, from the first generation of people resuscitated from cardiac standstill (already termed the Lazarus syndrome), Osler seems to have been right. Those who remember parts or all of their episodes do not recall any fear, or anguish. Several people who remained conscious throughout, while appearing to have been quite dead, could only describe a remarkable sensation of detachment. One man underwent coronary occlusion with cessation of the heart and dropped for all practical purposes dead, in front of a hospital; within a few minutes his heart had been restarted by electrodes and he breathed his way back into life. According to his account, the strangest thing was that there were so many people around him, moving so urgently, handling his body with such excitement, while all his awareness was of quietude. . . .

I find myself surprised by the thought that dying is an all-right thing to do, but perhaps it should not surprise. It is, after all, the most ancient and fundamental of biologic functions, with its mechanisms worked out with the same attention to detail, the same provision for the advantage of the organism, the same abundance of genetic information for guidance through the stages, that we have long since become accustomed to finding in all the crucial acts of living. —LEWIS THOMAS, *The Lives of a Cell*

I imagine death to be like sleep. When death comes to you, you just pass out, just the way you passed out last night. —RAY CHARLES

I am besieged with painful awe at the vacuum left by the dead. Where did she go? Where is she now? Are they, as the poet James Weldon Johnson said, "resting in the bosom of Jesus"? If so, what about my Jewish loves, my Japanese dears, and my Muslim darlings. Into whose bosom are they cuddled? There is always, lurking quietly, the question of what certainty is there that I, even, I will be gathered into the gentle arms of the Lord. I start to suspect that only with such blessed assurance will I be able to allow death its duties. —MAYA ANGELOU, *Wouldn't Take Nothing for My Journey Now*

Those who have the strength and love to sit with a dying patient in the *silence that goes beyond words* will know that this moment is neither frightening nor painful, but a peaceful cessation of the functioning of the body. Watching a peaceful death of a human being reminds us of a falling star; one of a million lights in a vast sky that flares up for a brief moment only to disappear into the endless night forever. To be a therapist to a dying patient makes us aware of the uniqueness of each individual in this vast sea of humanity. It makes us aware of our finiteness, our limited life span. Few of us live beyond our three-score and ten years, and yet in that brief time most of us create and live a unique biography and weave ourselves into the fabric of human history.   —ELISABETH KÜBLER-ROSS, *On Death and Dying*

Natural death is to man the greatest of the sacraments, of which all the others are but symbols; for it is the final and absolute union with the Creator, and it is also the pylon of the temple of life, even in the material world, for Death is Love.   —ALEISTER CROWLEY

[I]t may seem to many that the ultimate requirement—to give up one's self and one's life—represents a kind of cruelty on the part of God or fate, which makes our existence a sort of bad joke and which can never be completely accepted. This attitude is particularly true in present-day Western culture, in which the self is held sacred and death is considered an unspeakable insult. Yet the exact opposite is the reality. It is in the giving up of self that human beings can find the most ecstatic and lasting, solid, durable joy of life. And it is death that provides life with all its meaning. This "secret" is the central wisdom of religion.

The process of giving up the self (which is related to the phenomenon of love) is for most of us a gradual process which we get into by a series of fits and starts . . . for all that is given up even more is gained. Self-discipline is a self-enlarging process. The pain of giving up is the pain of death, but death of the old is birth of the new. The pain of death is the pain of birth, and the pain of birth is the pain of death. For us to develop a new and better idea, concept, theory or understanding means that an old idea, concept, theory or understanding must die.

Since birth and death seem to be but different sides of the same coin, it is really not at all unreasonable to pay closer heed than we usually do in the West to the concept of reincarnation. But whether or not we are willing to entertain seriously the possibility of some kind of rebirth occurring simultaneously with our physical death, it is abundantly clear that *this* lifetime is a series of simultaneous deaths and births. "Throughout the whole of life one must continue to learn to live," said Seneca two millennia ago, "and what will amaze you even more, throughout life one must learn to die."

— M. SCOTT PECK, *The Road Less Traveled*

Your fear of death is but the trembling of the shepherd when he stands before the king whose hand is to be laid upon him in honor.

— KAHLIL GIBRAN, *The Prophet*

The light we encounter on the road of death is our being in the act of coming home to itself.

— MALIDOMA SOMÉ

And after death? Am I quite sure that I could be reconciled to the ultimate disappearance of this precious Alan Watts game in which I have invested so much time and energy? This is always a hard question for a young person, for he is not at that point in the rhythm of mortal time where he is ready to give up. He is set to continue as a matter of biological necessity, for the action of living requires "follow-through" like the blow of the hand upon a drum: it aims beyond the skin. Willingness to vanish is incompatible with that spirit of "follow-through," except in an individual who has vividly realized the eternal identity beneath the temporal. Furthermore, even an old man whose mind remains alert is always possessed by curiosity to know what will happen in the future, what new discoveries and creations the genius of man will bring forth, what course history will take, and what we shall find out about the inner secrets of the world.

Yet it seems to me that after several hundred years of this sort of thing, I might have altogether too much of that haven't-we-been-here-before feeling. Surely, those who insist on the supreme value of individual personality continuing forever have not fully thought through their desire. Such a wish is comparable to the increasing confusion of Manhattan—a city trying to grow by making its individual buildings higher and higher. But this reaches a point of diminishing returns, for, after a certain height, the gain in living space ceases, because more and more of the lower floor areas have to be taken up by elevators. In other words, the indefinite prolongation of the individual is bad design—architecturally, bio-logically, and psychologically. The entity that is supposed to be prolonged is not the individual but some greater organism in which he belongs, as our cells belong in our bodies. The tragedy of mortality lies in not being aware of this belonging, and, above all, in not having found one's true identity in the inmost Self. And if that is found, then the disappearance of the ego-mask beyond death is not, as it is sometimes called, absorption of the soul into the Godhead. Nothing is absorbed; there is simply clear recollection of that which one is.

—ALAN WATTS, *Beyond Theology*

What is soundless, touchless, formless, imperishable,
Likewise tasteless, constant, odorless,
Without beginning, without end, higher than the great, stable—
By discerning That, one is liberated from the mouth of death.

—THE KATHA UPANISHAD

Your entire life should be a preparation to die happily, for only when you have learned to be willing to face death happily can you live life happily. Because then you will realize that death, like life, is also a truth. You will realize that death is not complete annihilation, but complete freedom from the grip of ego.

Children, learn to accept death, welcome death, and say hello to death. Be friendly with death and death will become your friend. Once you learn to receive death, fears of all kinds disappear, and you will begin to live in real peace.

The next moment is not ours. Only the present belongs to us. Living in the present, dropping the past, and forgetting the future is real life. We do not know whether we will be here in this body in the next moment. We do not know whether we will need the things and objects we use now in the next moment. We may breathe out and may never breathe in again. Who knows whether we will wake up tomorrow? The great saints and sages always lived moment-to-moment. . . .

Only a person who leads a moment-to-moment life can be completely free from fear. He alone can embrace death peacefully. . . . For those who live moment-to-moment, death is not a fearful experience; on the contrary, it becomes a peaceful and loving experience.

—SRI SRI MATA AMRITANANDAMAYI, *Awaken, Children!*

Death is always close by. And what's important is not to know if you can avoid it, but to know that you have done the most possible to realize your ideas.

—FRANTZ FANON

I am not going to die, I'm going home like a shooting star.

—SOJOURNER TRUTH

SPIRITS

Listen to Things
More often than Beings,
Hear the voice of fire,
Hear the voice of water.
Listen in the wind,
To the sighs of the bush;
This is the ancestors breathing.
Those who are dead are not ever gone.

—BIRAGO DIOP

From the realm where the ancestors dwell this fire can be seen in each and every one of us, shining like the stars that you see above your heads. . . . The fire is the rope that links us with our real home that we abandoned when we died into being human. We leave our real homes to come into this life, but there is nothing wrong with this. You will understand why long before the end of your learning here.

—MALIDOMA SOMÉ, *Of Water and the Spirit*

I personally find it impossible to regard Handel's *Largo*, Keats's "Ode to a Grecian Urn," and the higher ethics as mere by-products of the chemical interaction of a collection of hydrocarbon molecules. With energy, matter, space, and time continuous, with nothing lost or wasted, are we ourselves the only manifestation that comes to an end, ceases, is annihilated at threescore years and ten?

What we crudely call the spirit of man makes new compounds, plays with the laws of chemical action, guides the forces of the atom, changes the face of the earth, gives life to new forms, and takes it away from millions of animals and plants. Here is a flame that controls its own flaming, a creative spirit which cannot reasonably be less than the continuity it controls. This thing, soul, mind, or spirit, cannot well be an exception. In some way, as yet impossible to define, it, too, must possess continuity.

—HEBER D. CURTIS, American astrophysicist

For half a century I have been writing my thought in prose and verse and history and philosophy. . . . But I feel I have not said the thousandth part of what is in me. When I go down to the grave I can say . . . "I have finished my day's work," but I cannot say, "I have finished my life." My day's work will begin again the next morning. The tomb is not a blind alley; it is a thoroughfare. It closes on the twilight, it opens on the dawn.

—VICTOR HUGO, French poet

LIFE SEEMS UNAWARE

Once again the smell of death rides on the winds
　And fear lurks within the shadows of the mind.
One by one the moments tick away.
　Days and nights are interludes
Between despairing hope and groping faith.
　Of this bleak desolation, Life seems unaware:
Seeds still die and live again in answer to their kind;
　Fledgling birds awake to life from prison house of shell;

Flowers bloom and blossoms fall as harbingers of fruit to come;
    The newborn child comes even on the wings of death;
The thoughts of men are blanketed by dreams
    Of tranquil days and peaceful years,
When love unfettered will keep the heart and mind
    In ways of life that crown our days with light.

    — HOWARD THURMAN, *Meditations of the Heart*

WHEN I HAVE SACRIFICED MY ANGEL SOUL

I died a mineral and became a plant.
I died a plant and rose an animal.
I died an animal and I was a man.
Why should I fear? When was I less by dying?
Yet once more I shall die as man, to soar
With the blessed angels; but even from angelhood
I must pass on. All except God perishes.
When I have sacrificed my angel soul,
I shall become that which no mind ever conceived.
O, let me not exist! for Non-Existence proclaims,
"To Him we shall return."

    — JALAL AL-DIN RUMI

As a man abandons worn-out clothes and
acquires new ones, so when the body is
worn out a new one is acquired by the Self,
who lives within.

    — THE BHAGAVAD GITA

To grow as a person will cost you your life—and then will give it back again.

— Swami Chetanananda, *The Breath of God*

A grain of wheat remains a solitary grain unless it falls into the ground and dies; but if it dies, it bears a rich harvest.

— Jesus of Nazareth

I consist of a formal element and a material. Neither of these can ever pass away into nothing, any more than either of them came into being from nothing. Consequently every part of me will one day be refashioned, by a process of transition, into some other portion of the universe; which in its turn will again be changed into yet another part, and so onward to infinity. It is the same process by which I myself was brought into existence, and my parents before me, and so backward once more to infinity.

— Marcus Aurelius, Roman emperor and philosopher

This pot a workman drinks from
Is made from the eyes of a king, the heart of a vazir;
This wine-bowl in a drunkard's palm
Is made from a cheek flushed with wine and a lady's lip.

— Omar Khayyám, *The Rubá'iyát*

Buddhism, like some current cosmological theories in science, insists that the universe expands and contracts, dissolves into nonbeing and reevolves into being in an eternal rhythm.

— Barbara C. Sproul, *Primal Myths*

THERE NEVER WAS A CREATION

Know that the world is uncreated, as time itself is, without beginning and end. And it is based on the principles, life and the rest. Uncreated and indestructible, it endures under the compulsion of its own nature.

—JINASENA, Jain teacher

According to the Stoic doctrine of the cyclic conflagration, all souls are resolved into the world soul or primal fire. When this universal dissolution is concluded, the formation of a new universe begins, and all things repeat themselves.

—JOSEPH CAMPBELL

CHAPTER FOURTEEN

In the Eye of the Beholder, In the Image of God

How assuredly, how easily we would move through life if we knew that we are life itself. Our physical aspect is a miracle made of dust—dust that has been recycled and re-formed countless times over billions of years. There are more than five billion people in the world today, and no two of us are exactly alike. That each of us is a divine original is testimony to the awesome beauty of creation. That this miracle of dust, for all its glory, is here today and gone tomorrow makes it almost unbearably beautiful; and we ache to drink as deeply of it as we can while we may, or we spend this brief time fretting the inevitable end and miss the beauty altogether.

But we are so much more than the body, more even than our intelligence, wit, and personality. We are human *and* divine. We are the incarnation of spirit, the reflection of a divine light. And this greater dimension of our being—Love, the life force, the energy we call God—is changeless and eternal. The great challenge for each of us is to let go of our limited view of ourselves and trust the intimations of our soul, which whispers to us, *Rejoice, you are a child of God.*

Too many of us live and die without ever realizing how truly beautiful we are as expressions of God. We feel alienated from ourselves because, like sponges, we absorb the messages all around us that we are weak, incomplete, and in need of something outside ourselves to fix us and make us whole. We focus outward on the material when the beauty we long for and often try to paste on is already within us.

In the biblical story of Genesis, God says, "Let us make man in our image, after our likeness," and, ever since, we have mistaken those words, recreating God in man's image and likeness. Not only have we anthropomorphized the Infinite and Eternal, but we have often imbued "Him" with the worst traits of humankind (vengefulness, cruelty, jealousy, jingoism). In our churches and in the popular imagination, we are stuck with Renaissance images of God as a very old and omnipotent White man with a long white beard—an image which slave traders, colonialists, and missionaries found empowering, but which has been psychologically damaging to women and people of color.

But it was not "man," as in the male of our species, that the God of Genesis created in his image and likeness: Adam, from the Hebrew word *adamah*, simply meant "red clay," an undifferentiated earth creature. Only subsequently does Genesis say, "male and female he created them."

Bishop Desmond Tutu has said, "[W]e refer to the Fatherhood of God, which is as it should be. But we have missed out on the fullness that is God when we have ignored that which corresponds to our femaleness."

We are made in the image and likeness of God in that, through love, we can create; through love we can be fruitful and multiply; and through love we can bind ourselves in unity as a first step on the road of return to that divine Unity which was in the beginning. The oneness of God, out of love, gave itself away—divided itself into duality (light and darkness, heaven and earth, male and female) and infinite variety, and in God's image and likeness, this pattern is repeated throughout all creation. It is reflected in the procreation of life from a single cell (the fertilized egg), which divides into two, and from two into the billions of cells that make up each of us and every living thing.

In the image and likeness of God, man is the source of the seed, and woman's womb echoes the oceans and the dark expanses of space — the incubator of stars, worlds, and the seeds of life. The power that gave birth to the universe is your birthright. Just as the world had its genesis in the Word of God, and every newborn child is created out of the cryptic syntax of our DNA, everything that human beings have ever created began with a word — a thought or idea; an intangible seed of creative energy conceived in the mind, brought into the world by an utterance and nurtured by hands. The power is yours. Speak and know that the world you want is yours to create.

Once our eyes are opened, we begin to see evidence of the Divine Presence everywhere: in the vast expanse of the universe, in the sweep of geologic time, in the radiant sun, in expanding circles on the surface of still water. It is there in the unique features of every face and in the generosity of spirit displayed by those who give because giving is their nature.

Poets tell us that beauty is a reflection of the face of God, which we only glimpse as if in a fogged mirror so as not to be blinded by its brilliance. And though it manifests itself in infinite variety, too often our appreciation of beauty does not penetrate beyond physical attractiveness and sexual appeal. Malidoma Somé, a shaman from Burkina Faso, suggests that our relentless pursuit of beauty, even at this superficial level, is driven by a vague memory we have of true Beauty, lodged somewhere in the deepest recesses of our soul. And it may be that we are so obsessed with youth because we equate the physical beauty of youth with immortality, and what we experience as attraction is really a desire for union with the divine.

That beauty is in fact ubiquitous has led mythographer Joseph Campbell to muse that all of Creation is merely the fulfillment of Eternity's desire to gaze at Her own glory in the mirror. When we, the reflection, gaze back at Her, we find ourselves in awe and at one with Her. This is the experience of transcendence that seizes us when we cease to discriminate between what is beautiful and what is not. Beauty is infinite because God is One.

Because "each eye sees from its own angle," as Zora Neale Hurston reminds us, Jalal al-Din Rumi advises us to borrow a thousand eyes. For if beauty is in the eye of the beholder, then seeing God is reserved for those who are capable of seeing the beauty in all and from every angle. Once we tap into the beauty that is God in us, a veil is lifted, and the radiance of our own true beauty shines forth like a beacon, illuminating everything in our world.

God created man in his own image, in the image of God he created him; male and female he created them.

—GENESIS 1:27

There is something in the nature of God that corresponds to our maleness and our femaleness. We have tended to speak much more of the maleness, so we refer to the Fatherhood of God, which is as it should be. But we have missed out on the fullness that is God when we have ignored that which corresponds to our femaleness. We have hardly spoken about the Motherhood of God, and consequently we have been the poorer for this. —DESMOND TUTU, quoted in *The Words of Desmond Tutu* by Naomi Tutu

This assumption that beauty is an accessory, and dispensable, shows that we don't understand the importance of giving the soul what it needs. The soul is nurtured by beauty. . . .

Beauty assists the soul in its own peculiar ways of being. For example, beauty is arresting. For the soul, it is important to be taken out of the rush of practical life for the contemplation of timeless and eternal realities. Tradition named this need of the soul *vacatio*—a vacation from ordinary activity in favor of a moment of reflection and wonder. You may find yourself driving along a highway when you suddenly pass a vista that catches your breath. You stop the car, get out for just a few minutes, and behold the grandeur of nature. This is the arresting power of beauty, and giving in to that sudden longing of the soul is a way of giving it what it needs. . . .

Sōetsu Yanagi, founder of Japan's modern craft movement, defines beauty as that which gives unlimited scope to the imagination; beauty is a source of imagination, he says, that never dries up. A thing so attractive and absorbing may not be pretty or pleasant. It could be ugly, in fact, and yet seize the soul as beautiful in this special sense. James Hillman defines beauty for the soul as things displaying themselves in their individuality. Yanagi's and Hillman's point is that beauty doesn't require prettiness. Some pieces of art are not pleasing to look at, and yet their content and form are arresting and lure the heart into profound imagination.

If we are going to care for the soul, and if we know that the soul is nurtured by beauty, then we will have to understand beauty more deeply and give it a more prominent place in life. Religion has always understood the value of beauty, as we can see in churches and temples, which are never built for purely practical considerations, but always for the imagination. A tall steeple or a rose window are not designed to allow additional seating or better light for reading. They speak to the soul's need for beauty, for love of the building itself as well as its use, for a special opportunity for sacred imagination.

—THOMAS MOORE, *Care of the Soul*

[B]eauty is life when life unveils her holy face.

But you are life and you are the veil.

Beauty is eternity gazing at itself in a mirror.

But you are eternity and you are the mirror.

—KAHLIL GIBRAN, *The Prophet*

The mirror, reflecting the goddess and drawing her forth from the august repose of her divine nonmanifestation, is symbolic of the world, the field of the reflected image. Therein divinity is pleased to regard its own glory, and this pleasure is itself inducement to the act of manifestation or "creation."

—JOSEPH CAMPBELL

O Lord, how manifold are Thy works.
The whole land is in joy and holiday because of Thee.
They shout to the height of heaven.
All that Thou hast made leaps before Thee.
Thou makest the beauty of form through Thyself alone.

— PHARAOH AKHENATON

THROUGH THE VARIED PATTERNED LACE

As I look into each different face,
I am exalted.
I am exalted to recognize His Grace
shimmering through the varied patterned lace.

— MARGARET DANNER

[M]y parents decide to buy my brothers guns. These are not "real" guns. They shoot "BBs," copper pellets my brothers say will kill birds. Because I am a girl, I do not get a gun. Instantly I am relegated to the position of Indian. Now there appears a great distance between us. They shoot and shoot at everything with their new guns. I try to keep up with my bow and arrows.

One day while I am standing on top of our makeshift "garage"—pieces of tin nailed across some poles—holding my bow and arrow and looking out toward the fields, I feel an incredible blow in my right eye. I look down just in time to see my brother lower his gun. . . .

I am twenty-seven, and my baby daughter is almost three. Since her birth I have worried about her discovery that her mother's eyes are different from other people's. Will she be embarrassed? I think. What will she say? Every day she watches a television program called "Big Blue Marble." It begins with a picture of the earth as it appears from the moon. It is bluish, a little battered-looking, but full of light, with whitish clouds swirling around it. Every time I see it I weep with love, as if it is a picture of Grandma's house. One day when I am putting Rebecca down for her nap, she suddenly focuses on my eye. Something inside me cringes, gets ready to try to protect myself. All children are cruel about phys-ical differences, I know from experience, and that they don't always mean to be is another matter. I as-sume Rebecca will be the same.

But no-o-o-o. She studies my face intently as we stand, her inside and me outside her crib. She even holds my face maternally between her dimpled little hands. Then, looking every bit as serious and lawyerlike as her father, she says, as if it may just possibly have slipped my attention: "Mommy, there's a *world* in your eye." (As in, "Don't be alarmed, or do anything crazy.") And then, gently, but with great interest: "Mommy, where did you *get* that world in your eye?"

For the most part, the pain left then. (So what, if my brothers grew up to buy even more powerful pellet guns for their sons and to carry real guns themselves. So what, if a young "Morehouse man" once nearly fell off the steps of Trevor Arnett Library because he thought my eyes were blue.) Crying and laughing I ran to the bathroom, while Rebecca mumbled and sang herself off to sleep. Yes indeed, I re-alized, looking into the mirror. There *was* a world in my eye. And I saw that it was possible to love it: that in fact, for all it had taught me of shame and anger and inner vision, I *did* love it. Even to see it drift-ing out of orbit in boredom, or rolling up out of fatigue, not to mention floating back at attention in ex-citement (bearing witness, a friend has called it), deeply suitable to my personality, and even character-istic of me.

That night I dream I am dancing to Stevie Wonder's song "Always" (the name of the song is really "As," but I hear it as "Always"). As I dance, whirling and joyous, happier than I've ever been in my life, another bright-faced dancer joins me. We dance and kiss each other and hold each other through the night. The other dancer has obviously come through all right, as I have done. She is beautiful, whole and free. And she is also me.

— ALICE WALKER, *In Search of Our Mothers' Gardens*

I am black, *and* comely, O ye daughters of Jerusalem, as the tents of Kedar, as the curtains of Solomon.

— SONG OF SONGS 1:5

EDITORS' NOTE: In the earlier Septuagint version of the Bible, the verse reads "and," not "but" as in the later Vulgate translation. "I am black," says the Bride of the Song of Songs, "because the sun has looked upon me."

Theorizing about self-worth is ineffective. So is pretending. Women can die in agony who have lived with blank and beautiful faces. I can afford to look at myself directly, risk the pain of experiencing who I am not, and learn to savor the sweetness of who I am. I can make friends with all the different pieces of me, liked and disliked. Admit that I am kinder to my neighbor's silly husband most days than I am to myself. I can look into the mirror and learn to love the stormy little Black girl who once longed to be white or anything other than who she was, since all she was ever allowed to be was the sum of the color of her skin and the textures of her hair, the shade of her knees and elbows, and those things were clearly not acceptable as human.

Learning to love ourselves as Black women goes beyond a simplistic insistence that "Black is beautiful." It goes beyond and deeper than a surface appreciation of Black beauty, although that is certainly a good beginning. But if the quest to reclaim ourselves and each other remains there, then we risk another superficial measurement of self, one superimposed upon the old one and almost as damaging, since it pauses at the superficial. Certainly it is no more empowering. And it is empowerment—our strengthening in the service of ourselves and each other, in the service of our work and future—that will be the result of this pursuit.

—AUDRE LORDE, *Sister Outsider*

God, in fact, does not consider your exterior form but only your heart—which is the "divine face" proper to each of you, and it is this "divine face" which, in you, "contains" God even though His sky and His earth cannot contain Him.

—AMIR 'ABD AL-KADER

Be under no illusion, you shall gather to yourself the images you love. As you go, the shapes, the lights, the shadows of the things you have preferred will come to you, yes, inveterately, inevitably as bees to their hive. And there in your mind and spirit they will leave with you their distilled essence, sweet as honey or bitter as gall, and you will grow unto their likeness because their nature will be in you.

As men see the color in the wave, so shall men see in you the thing you have loved most. Out of your eyes will look the spirit you have chosen. In your smile and in your frown the years will speak.

You will not walk nor stand nor sit, nor will your hand move, but you will confess the one you serve, and upon your forehead will be written his name as by a revealing pen.

Cleverness may select skillful words to cast a veil about you, and circumspection may never sleep, yet will you not be hid. No.

As year adds to year, that face of yours, which once like an unwritten page, lay smooth in your baby crib, will take to itself lines, and still more lines, as the parchment of an old historian who jealously sets down all the story. And there, more deep than acids etch the steel, will grow the inspired narrative of your mental habits, the emotions of your heart, your sense of conscience, your response to duty, what you think of your god and of your fellow men and of yourself. It will all be there. For men become like that which they love, and the name thereof is written on their brow.

— OSWALD W. S. McCALL, *The Hand of God*

The immanence of God is the infinite expressing itself in the finite. It is God becoming concrete in finite human existence. We are able to speak of the divine because the divine is revealed in the concreteness of this world.

— JAMES H. CONE, *A Black Theology of Liberation*

Nothing that God ever made is the same thing to more than one person. That is natural. There is no single face in nature, because every eye that looks upon it, sees it from its own angle. So every man's spice-box seasons his own food.

— ZORA NEALE HURSTON

This is the right way of approaching or being initiated into the mysteries of love, to begin with examples of beauty in this world, and using them as steps to ascend continually with that absolute beauty as one's aim, from one instance of physical beauty to two and from two to all, then from physical beauty to moral beauty, and from moral beauty to the beauty of knowledge, until from knowledge of various kinds one arrives at the supreme knowledge whose sole object is that absolute beauty, and knows at last what absolute beauty is.

— PLATO, *Symposium*

At different stages, different things appear to be beautiful, but beauty is not that object or that thing. It is a sensation, a wave that comes in you that is your very nature. Whatever beauty you see here and there is only a projection of your Being. Whenever you have felt a sense of great beauty, that is when you have reached your home, that is when you have been in touch with yourself. Because you are so, so beautiful. That's why something else in the world also looks beautiful to you.

You get a glimpse of Self; a little shower from this glimpse comes to you. When waves of beauty come to you unceasingly, that is called Enlightenment.

You have this depth; it's not that you don't. Take off all the silt and you'll see that you are so deep, you are so beautiful.

—SRI SRI RAVI SHANKAR, *The Way of Grace*

To any vision must be brought an eye adapted to what is to be seen, and having some likeness to it. Never did eye see the sun unless it had first become sunlike, and never can the Soul have vision of the First Beauty unless itself be beautiful.

—PLOTINUS, *The Enneads*

Since His Image is so, behold how His Beauty must be! His Beauty displays itself in the Image, which cannot display Him.

His Image is sunlight shining upon the spirits, His Beauty the sun burning in the fourth heaven.

—JALAL AL-DIN RUMI

Beauty is unbearable, drives us to despair, offering us for a minute the glimpse of an eternity that we should like to stretch out over the whole of time.

—ALBERT CAMUS

Sublimity seizes us, almost unbearably,
But our fear turns to wonder
As it loftily disdains
To dissolve us utterly.

— RAINER MARIA RILKE

The spirit cannot bear to see Thy Face unveiled, and Thy Beauty is greater than whatever I say.

— JALAL AL-DIN RUMI

Our shallow appreciation of outward beauty might be more a confused reaction to the memory of true beauty than an actual encounter with it. In that case the beauty that exists on the outside of a person would serve only as a reminder to us of the real beauty of the spirit behind it. [The] elders had long ago understood this and chose to focus their energies where they really count — on matters of the soul.

— MALIDOMA SOMÉ, *Of Water and the Spirit*

The beauty of the Unseen Form is beyond description — borrow a thousand illuminated eyes, borrow!

— JALAL AL-DIN RUMI

In the pursuit of happiness many people are too busy to find that which they seek. Frequently the happiness we so passionately desire is found in little events that are but whispered. If we don't pay attention, we miss them.

There can be happiness in the way light falls through the trees or in the way autumn leaves flutter to the ground. There can be happiness in the way our children call for us by name or in the familiar sight of our home as we round the corner two blocks away. Happiness weaves its way through precious memories and valueless keepsakes that are priceless to us. Many take enormous delight in the presence of a beloved pet, just the way they look at us or the unconditional love they pour out upon us. For some, there is genuine delight in the taste of a specially loved food.

We are surrounded by that which can be meaningful and full of delight. The question is, will we be still and quiet long enough to enjoy?

—EARNIE LARSEN AND CAROL LARSEN HEGARTY, *Days of Healing, Days of Joy*

I was born in Nature's wide domain! The trees were all that sheltered my infant limbs, the blue heavens all that covered me. I am one of Nature's children. I have always admired her. She shall be my glory: her features, her robes, and the wreath about her brow, the seasons, her stately oaks, and the ever-green—her hair, ringlets over the earth—all contribute to my enduring love of her.

And wherever I see her, emotions of pleasure roll in my breast, and swell and burst like waves on the shores of the ocean, in prayer and praise to Him who has placed me in her hand. It is thought great to be born in palaces, surrounded with wealth—but to be born in Nature's wide domain is greater still!

I would much more glory in this birthplace, with the broad canopy of heaven above me, and the giant arms of the forest trees for my shelter, than to be born in palaces of marble, studded with pillars of gold! Nature will be Nature still, while palaces shall decay and fall in ruins.

Yes, Niagara will be Niagara a thousand years hence! The rainbow, a wreath over her brow, shall continue as long as the sun, and the flowing of the river—while the work of art, however carefully protected and preserved, shall fade and crumble into dust!

—GEORGE COPWAY (KAHGEGAGAHBOWH), chief of the Chippewa

Siddhartha learned something new on every step of his path, for the world was transformed and he was enthralled. He saw the sun rise over forest and mountains and set over the distant palm shore. At night he saw the stars in the heavens and the sickle-shaped moon floating like a boat in the blue. He saw trees, stars, animals, clouds, rainbows, rocks, weeds, flowers, brook and river, the sparkle of dew on bushes in the morning, distant high mountains blue and pale; birds sang, bees hummed, the wind blew gently across the rice fields. All this, colored and in a thousand different forms, had always been there. The sun and moon had always shone; the rivers had always flowed and the bees had hummed, but in previous times all this had been nothing to Siddhartha but a fleeting and illusive veil before his eyes, regarded with distrust, condemned to be disregarded and ostracized from the thoughts, because it was not reality, because reality lay on the other side of the visible. But now his eyes lingered on this side; he saw and recognized the visible and he sought his place in this world. He did not seek reality; his goal was not on any other side. The world was beautiful when looked at in this way—without any seeking, so simple, so childlike. The moon and the stars were beautiful, the brook, the shore, the forest and rock, the goat and the golden beetle, the flower and butterfly were beautiful. It was beautiful and pleasant to go through the world like that, so childlike, so awakened, so concerned with the immediate, without any distrust.

—HERMANN HESSE, *Siddhartha*

Additional Biographical Notes

We've included here a few brief notes on some of the less well known of the wide-ranging authors we've mined for the writings in this book, as well as any sources that have not been attributed elsewhere in *Confirmation.*

'Abd al-Kader. Nineteenth-century Sufi mystic.

Abdu'l-Baha. Thirteenth-century Sufi mystic.

Ahbez, Eden. American songwriter. From the song "Nature Boy."

Akhenaton. Fourteenth-century B.C.E. Egyptian Pharaoh who first introduced the idea of monotheism.

Alighieri, Dante (1265–1321). Italian poet.

Allen, Geri. Contemporary jazz musician.

Amritanandamayi, Sri Sri Mata. Indian mystic.

Ansari of Herat. Eleventh-century Sufi mystic and poet.

Armah, Ayi Kwei. Ghanaian writer.

Baba Metzia. Title of a tract from the Talmud.

Baha'u'llah. Tablets of Baha'u'llah.

Bailey, Alice A. Established the Arcane School in 1923. From *The Externalization of the Hierarchy.*

Bailey, Pearl. African American singer, writer, and diplomat.

Bambara, Toni Cade. African American writer.

Bambi Baaba. Ugandan mystic and teacher.

Banks, C. Tillery. African American poet. From *Hello to Me with Love.*

Benn, Tony. British Labour politician.

Besant, Annie (1847–1933). English theosophist.

Besserman, Perle. *The Way of the Jewish Mystics.* Excerpts include Levi Yitzchak of Berdichev, the Maggid of Mezeritch.

Beversluis, Joel D. *A SourceBook for Earth's Community of Religions.* Excerpts include "Until one is committed" by Goethe; "So live your life" by Tecumseh; "The Golden Rule"; Abdu'l-Baha; Rabbi Chanina; Lizo Doda Jafta; Rabbi Herbert Bronstein; Ansari of Herat; "A Call to Prayer" (Native American); "A Prayer of Awareness" (Hindu).

Bhagavad Gita. Hindu sacred text dating from around 500 B.C.E.

Black Elk. A holy man of the Oglala Sioux. From *Black Elk Speaks* by John G. Neihardt.

Blake, William. Eighteenth-century English poet. From *William Blake: A Selection of Poems and Letters* by J. Bronowski.

Blavatsky, Helena Petrovna. Russian-born theosophist and founder of the Theosophical Society. From "Misconceptions," *Collected Writings*, 1887, and *The Voice of the Silence*, 1889.

Bronowski, Jacob. Scientist and philosopher. From *A Sense of the Future: Essays in Natural Philosophy*.

Bronstein, Herbert. Council member of the Parliament of the World's Religions.

Brooks, Gwendolyn. African American poet and Pulitzer Prize winner.

Buddha, Gautama (563?–483? B.C.E.). Indian mystic. From *The Teaching of Buddha* by Bukkyo Dendo Kyokai (Buddhist Promoting Foundation).

Budge, E. A. Wallis. From *The Book of the Dead: The Papyrus of Ani*.

Burger, Julian. From *The Gaia Atlas of First Peoples: A Future for the Indigenous World*.

Butler, Octavia. African American writer.

Camus, Albert. French existentialist philosopher and writer.

Catherine Adorna of Genoa. Fifteenth-century Christian mystic from Italy. From *Purgation and Purgatory*.

Rabbi Chanina. Third-century B.C.E. rabbinical scholar.

Chao Tze-chiang. From *A Chinese Garden of Serenity: Epigrams from the Ming Dynasty*.

Charles, Ray. African American musician and singer. From *Brother Ray*.

Chesterton, G. K. (1874–1936). British writer.

Chuang-tzu. Fourth-century B.C.E. Chinese philosopher. From *Chuang-tzu*.

Cleary, Thomas. From *The Wisdom of the Prophet: Sayings of Muhammad*.

Clifton, Lucille. African American poet. From *The Book of Light*.

Coltrane, John. African American musician and mystic. From the album *A Love Supreme*.

Cone, James H. African American Christian theologian. From *A Black Theology of Liberation*.

Confucius (551–479 B.C.E.). Chinese philosopher.

Copway, George (1818–1863). Chippewa chief and author.

Cousineau, Phil. From *Soul: An Archaeology*.

Crowley, Aleister (1875–1947). British occultist.

Dadistan-i-dinik. Zoroastrian sacred text.

Dame Julian of Norwich (1343–c. 1419). From *Meditations with Julian of Norwich*.

Danner, Margaret. African American poet. From *To Flower*.

Dick, Philip K. From *The Shifting Realities of Philip K. Dick: Selected Literary and Philosophical Writings*.

Diop, Birago. Senegalese writer. From *Gleams and Glimmers*.

"The Dispute Between a Man and His Ba." This is a fragment from a poem embedded in a prose dispute between a man and his soul (*ba*) over the issue of suicide. From *Technicians of the Sacred: A Range of Poetries from Africa, America, Asia, & Oceania*, edited with commentaries by Jerome Rothenberg.

Dōgen (1200–1253). Zen master.

Du Bois, W. E. B. African American writer, scholar, social activist, and a founder of the NAACP.

Einstein, Albert (1879–1955). Scientist and humanitarian.

Ellington, Edward Kennedy. African American composer and bandleader.

Emerson, Ralph Waldo. Nineteenth-century American poet. From *The Best of Ralph Waldo Emerson*.

Empedocles. Fifth-century B.C.E. Greek philosopher.

Epictetus (A.D. c. 50–c. 138). Greek Stoic philosopher.

Evans, Mari. African American poet. From *Nightstar*.

Fanon, Frantz. Martiniquan psychiatrist, philosopher, and political activist.

Feldman, Christina, and Kornfield, Jack. *Stories of the Spirit, Stories of the Heart: Parables of the Spiritual Path from Around the World*. Excerpts include Sufi tales of Nasrudin, Zen tale of the chess match.

Fillmore, Charles. Christian philosopher and cofounder with his wife, Myrtle Fillmore, of Unity. From *Prosperity*.

Friend, David. *More Reflections on the Meaning of Life*. Including quotes from Mario Cuomo, Oprah Winfrey, Mustapha Mahmoud, Bernie Siegel, Maharishi Mahesh Yogi, Arthur Ashe.

Ghālib (1797–1869). Indian poet.

Gibran, Kahlil. Syrian-born American mystic poet and painter.

von Goethe, Johann Wolfgang (1749–1832). German poet, dramatist, novelist, and scientist.

Gurdjieff, George Ivanovich (1877–1949). Greek-Armenian mystic. Quoted in *In Search of the Miraculous, Fragments of an Unknown Teaching* by P. D. Ouspensky.

Guru Granth Sahib. The Sikh scriptures dating from the early seventeenth century.

Ha-Babli (c. 30 B.C.E.). The Babylonian Talmud (see Talmud).

Hanh, Thích Nhât. Vietnamese monk, Zen master, and poet. Nominated by Dr. Martin Luther King, Jr., for the Nobel Peace Prize in 1967.

Hildegard of Bingen (1098–1179). German nun and mystic. From *Meditations with Hildegard of Bingen*.

Hillman, James. From *We've Had a Hundred Years of Psychotherapy—And the World's Getting Worse*.

Victor Hugo (1802–1885). French writer.

Hui-Neng. An illiterate peasant from sixth-century China, whose sudden illumination resulted in the founding of Zen Buddhism.

Hurston, Zora Neale. African American anthropologist, folklorist, and writer. From *Dust Tracks on a Road*.

Ibn 'Arabi, Muhyiddin (1165–1240). Sufi mystic.

I Ching. Chinese book of ancient origin embodying Taoist philosophy.

James, William (1842–1910), American psychologist and philosopher.

Jinasena (c. A.D. 900). Jain teacher.

Jones, Alan. American author and dean of Grace Cathedral in San Francisco. From *Soul Making: The Desert Way of Spirituality*.

Jordan, June. African American poet. From *I Was Looking at the Ceiling and Then I Saw the Sky* and from *Revolutionary Petunias* by Alice Walker.

Jung, Carl Gustav (1875–1961). Swiss psychiatrist and founder of analytical psychology.

Keating, Thomas. From *Speaking of Silence* by Susan Walker.

Kenner, Hugh. From *The Pound Era*.

Khayyám, Omar. Eleventh-century Persian poet.

Krishnamurti, Jiddu (1895–1986). Indian mystic.

Lao-tzu. Sixth-century B.C.E. founder of Taoism. From the Tao-te Ching.

Lincoln, Abbey. African American singer, songwriter. From the album *A Turtle's Dream*.

Li Po (701–762). Chinese poet.

Lizo Doda Jafta. From "The One, the Other, the Divine, the Many in Zulu Traditional Religion of Southern Africa."

Lomax, Alan. African American folklorist and musicologist. From *3000 Years of Black Poetry*.

Lorde, Audre. African American poet. From *Sister Outsider* and *Our Dead Behind Us*.

Machado, Antonio (1875–1939). Spanish poet.

Madhubuti, Haki R. African American poet, writer, publisher, and founder of Third World Press.

Maggid of Mezeritch. Sixteenth-century Jewish mystic.

Mahābhārata. Ancient Hindu epic poem.

Maharishi Mahesh Yogi. Indian teacher and popularizer of Transcendental Meditation in the West.

Mahmoud, Mustapha. Egyptian physician, Islamic scholar, and author of *God and Man*.

Marcus Aurelius (121–180). Roman emperor, philosopher.

Matthiessen, Peter. Native American writer.

Mays, Benjamin. African American educator and dean of the School of Religion, Howard University.

Mitchell, Stephen. *The Enlightened Heart: An Anthology of Sacred Poetry*. Excerpts include "Cutting up an ox" by Chuang-tzu; "The Mind of Absolute Trust"; Antonio Machado; "The purpose of a fish trap" by Chuang-tzu.

Montaigne, Michel Eyquem de (1533–1592). French essayist.

Moses de León. Thirteenth-century Kabbalist believed to be the author of the Zohar. From *Major Trends in Jewish Mysticism* by G. G. Scholem.

Needleman, Jacob. From *Lost Christianity*.

Nietzsche, Friedrich Wilhelm (1844–1900). German philosopher.

Padmasambhava. Eighteenth-century Indian mystic credited with bringing Tantric Buddhism to Tibet. From *Sky Dancer: The Secret Life and Songs of Lady Yeshe Tsogyel* by K. Dowman.

Paine, Thomas (1737–1809). A leader of the American Revolution.

Plato (427?–347? B.C.E.). Greek philosopher.

Plotinus (A.D. 205–270). Hellenistic philosopher.

Pushkin, Alexander (1799–1837). Afro-Russian father of Russian poetry. From *The Bronze Horseman and Other Poems*.

Raymo, Chet. American astronomer. From *The Soul of the Night*.

Rich, Adrienne. American poet and feminist.

Rilke, Rainer Maria (1875–1926). German poet.

Rumi, Jalal al-Din (also Jalal-Uddin, Jelaluddin) (1207–1275). Sufi mystic poet. From *The Perennial Philosophy* by Aldous Huxley; *Love Is a Stranger* by Kabir Edmund Helminski; *The Sufi Path of Love: The Spiritual Teachings of Rumi* by William C. Chittick; and *Say I Am You* by Coleman Barks.

Sai Baba, Sathya. Southern Indian mystic and teacher.

Sanchez, Sonia. African American poet. From *Love Poems* and *Three Hundred and Sixty Degrees of Blackness Comin' At You*.

Saraswati, Sunyata. Interdisciplinary teacher of the healing arts of India, Napal, China, Peru, and Egypt.

Schiller, David. *The Little Zen Companion*. Excerpts include quotes from Empedocles, Chuan-tzu, West African proverb, Goethe, Teilhard de Chardin, Nietzsche, St. Anthony.

Schweitzer, Albert (1875–1965). Physician, organist, philosopher.

Seattle (1784–1866). Chief of the Duwamish and Suquamish Native American tribes.

Seng-Ts'an (?–606). Zen master.

Shams of Tabriz. Thirteenth-century Sufi mystic.

Shange, Ntozake. African American poet and playwright.

Shankar, Sri Sri Ravi. Contemporary Indian mystic and teacher.

Shankara. Eighth-century Hindu mystic. From *Crest Jewel of Discrimination*.

Siegel, Bernie. Surgeon and author of *Love, Medicine, and Miracles*.

Silesius, Angelus (1624–1677). German poet and priest.

Silver, Horace. Jazz pianist and composer.

Simpkins, Cuthbert Ormond, M.D. African American biographer. From *Coltrane: A Biography*.

Sojourner Truth (1797–1883). African American abolitionist and feminist.

Somé, Malidoma Patrice. African mystic and shaman from Burkina Faso.

Spinoza, Benedict (Baruch) (1632–1677). Dutch philosopher.

Sproul, Barbara C. *Primal Myths: Creation Myths Around the World*.

St. Anthony (251?–c. 350). Egyptian hermit and Christian founder of monasticism.

St. Augustine of Hippo (A.D. 354–430). African doctor of early Christian theology.

St. Bernard of Clairvaux (1091–1153). Christian monk. *On the Love of God*.

St. Teresa of Ávila (1515–1582). Spanish nun and mystic.

Sunnah. The prescribed way of life, based on the teachings and practices of Mohammad.

Sun Ra. Musician, composer, philosopher.

Tagore, Rabindranath (1861–1941). Bengali poet. From *Unending Love*.

Ta'anit. Title of a tract from the Talmud.

T'ai Shang Kan Ying P'ien. Taoist sacred text.

Talmud. A compilation of Jewish oral law.

Tecumseh (1768?–1813). Chief of the Shawnee.

Teilhard de Chardin, Pierre. French philosopher and priest.

Thomas, Lewis. American biologist, physician, and writer.

Thurman, Howard. African American Christian mystic.

Tillich, Paul (1886–1965). Christian theologian and philosopher.

Toomer, Jean. A major figure of the Harlem Renaissance. From *Essential*.

Traherne, Thomas (1636?–1674). English metaphysical poet. From *Man or Matter* by Ernst Lehrs.

Tutu, Desmond. South African prelate and Nobel Peace Prize recipient. From *The African Prayer Book* and from *The Words of Desmond Tutu* by Naomi Tutu.

Udana-Varga. Buddhist sacred text.

Upanishads. Hindu mystical scriptures beginning c. 900 B.C.E.

Vanzant, Iyanla. African American writer and Yoruba priestess.

Voltaire (1694–1778). French philosopher whose works epitomize the Age of Enlightenment.

Wallace, Robert Keith. From *The Psychology of Consciousness*.

Washington, James Melvin, Ph.D., editor. *Conversations with God: Two Centuries of Prayer by African Americans*. Excerpts include "Dear God, If You Please" by Matthew L. Watley and "A Pryer for Power" by Orrin Stone, a former slave.

Watts, Alan. British-born American philosopher.

West, Cornel. African American philosopher.

Whitman, Walt (1819–1892). American poet.

Wonder, Stevie. African American composer and musician. From the album *Songs in the Key of Life.*

Zahan, Dominique. From *The Religion, Spirituality, and Thought of Traditional Africa.*

Zohar ("The Book of Splendor" or "Illumination"). Thirteenth-century mystical writings by Moses de León.

About the Authors

KHEPHRA BURNS is a professional television and magazine writer who has written for several award-winning series. SUSAN L. TAYLOR has been the editor in chief of *Essence* magazine (circulation 5.2 million) since 1981. Through her column, "In the Spirit," her extensive travels, and her numerous public appearances, she has become an example and inspiration to millions of readers. The two live in New York City.